FAROE: THE EMERGENCE OF A NATION

FAROE
THE EMERGENCE OF
A NATION

BY

JOHN F. WEST

LONDON
C. HURST & COMPANY

NEW YORK
PAUL S. ERIKSSON, INC.

First published in the United Kingdom by
C. Hurst & Co. (Publishers) Ltd.,
40a Royal Hill, Greenwich, London S. E. 10
and in the United States of America and Canada
by Paul S. Eriksson, Inc.,
119 West 57th Street, New York, N.Y. 10019

ISBN 0-8397-2063-7
LC 77-151438

PRINTED IN CZECHOSLOVAKIA BY STÁTNÍ TISKÁRNA, PRAGUE

PREFACE

The Faroe Islands, Britain's nearest neighbour to the north-west, have not hitherto been the subject of any historical treatment in the English language, and the present work is designed in some measure to remedy this lack. But because people read history for many different reasons, I have tried to write a book of service to the general reader, yet which I hope the scholar will not despise.

This double aim is my reason for not providing an apparatus of detailed reference. Instead, I have drawn up two biblio-graphies. The first gives some of the main printed sources I have used, which are for obvious reasons mostly in Danish or Faroese. The second is an English language bibliography, listing all the books and articles of which I am aware, regard-less of their quality, provided only that they have a bearing on the history, sociology or culture of Faroe.

My principal theme is the development of Faroe from a remote and insignificant Danish province into a nation with a constitutional and cultural life of its own. The earlier chapters, therefore, are introductory in character, without the statistical illustration provided for the events of the last century and a half.

I am not a protagonist of any particular historical theory, and have tried to let the material speak for itself. It will, however, be interesting to see whether the historical evolution of so small a community may be interpreted according to theories derived from the course of events in the larger countries of the world.

A nation with a population of less than 40,000 is highly exceptional. Special conditions are needed for so small a group to develop and retain a sense of national identity and a willingness to support a national culture. The Faroe Islands, indeed, constitute a sociological laboratory of peculiar interest in a world where national feeling plays so prominent a part in human affairs. The effects and influences connected with national feeling may well be more plainly seen in a tiny nation than in a large one.

For instance, in Faroese history we see with special clarity the influence of the writer, the artist and the thinker on the national consciousness and on the course of political and social life. In great nations, these effects, if in the long run profound, are usually slow-moving and indirect. Although currents of thought have usually been slow to reach the isolated Faroe Islands, their subsequent spread through the community has often been surprisingly rapid.

In a world of ever larger human agglomerations, the politically interested have much to learn from the recent history of Faroe. The 1948 home rule ordinance, for example, suggests a way of establishing a flexible relationship between a metropolitan power and a small dependency, and might also be applied to relations between a central government and a variety of provincial administrations. It will be instructive to see how stable the 1948 settlement proves to be. But in a general way, the experiences of so tiny a national group may point the way towards methods of preserving in the individual citizen a feeling of personal involvement with the fate of his community, a feeling that tends to become eroded as the economic units of mankind become ever bigger and more complex.

It is my hope, too, that here and there a reader may become sufficiently interested in this miniature nation in the north Atlantic to take an interest in its literature and its scholarship. Its larger neighbour, Iceland, has long had its devotees. I trust that the day is not far distant when Faroese studies, undertaken both by the amateur and the professional, will take a tiny, but respected place in the academic life of our country.

CONTENTS

MAP

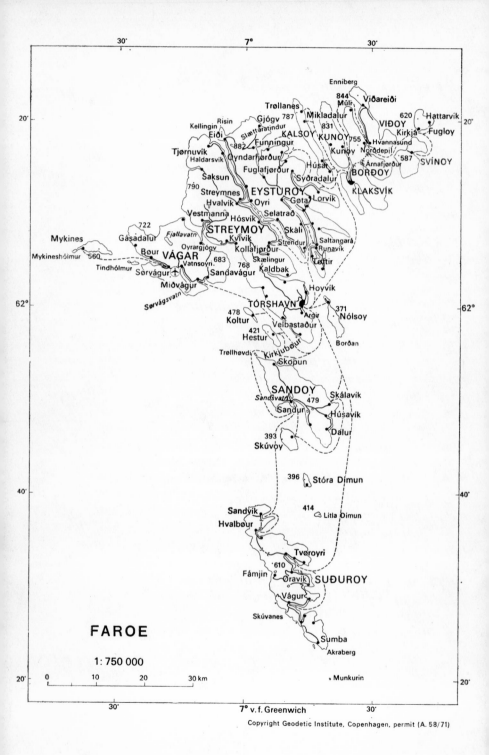

FAROE

1 : 750 000

0   10   20   30 km

CHAPTER I

THE LAND AND ITS PEOPLE

THE LAND

The Faroe Islands lie roughly half-way between Shetland and Iceland. The capital of Faroe, Tórshavn, is almost exactly in 62°N latitude and 6°45′W longitude. The archipelago, which forms part of the Wyville-Thompson submarine ridge through the north Atlantic, has the shape of an inverted triangle with its 50-mile-long base aligned W.S.W. to E.N.E., its apex being 70 miles south of its northern extremity — a geographical spread comparable with that of Lincolnshire. The total land area, however, is rather less than 550 square miles.

Geologically, the Faroe Islands form part of the great volcanic region of the north Atlantic, which takes in Antrim, the Hebrides, Jan Mayen, Iceland, a large portion of central Greenland, and all the area between. Faroe consists of layer upon layer of basalt, laid down by submarine volcanic action during the tertiary period. These basalt layers are generally separated by layers of tuff, a friable stone formed from volcanic ash. In Faroe, the tuff often resembles a red sandstone, at times contrasting markedly in colour with the dark grey-green of the basalt. The alternation between the hard basalt and the more easily eroded tuff has given a peculiar "layer-cake" appearance to the hills of the islands, especially since in the main, the strata hardly vary from the horizontal. Apart from basalt and tuff, a few thin seams of coal are to be found, but only on Suðuroy, the southernmost island of the group, in any significant quantity.

Erosion by glacier, ocean and climate has worn down what was originally a great plateau into a group of some twenty islands, separated by channels all aligned N.N.W. to S.S.E. Some of the more northerly channels are very narrow indeed, but towards the south they tend to be wider. The coasts are generally precipitous, the most northerly ones dramatically so. Here, vertical cliffs of 1500 feet are not at all uncommon, and there are also tremendous rock pinnacles hundreds of feet high where patches of harder material have resisted the onslaught of the winter storms of the north Atlantic.

Inland, there is a good deal of wet moorland, with many barren stony patches, especially on the tops of hills. Naturally there are no large rivers, but there are many streams. The limited areas suitable for cultivation are either valley bottoms, isthmuses, or in a few places, tiny coastal plains formed out of material eroded from the hillsides above. These last have sometimes been overwhelmed by landslides.

The climate is remarkably mild. This is at first sight surprising, since the islands lie in a sub-arctic latitude which they share with such cold spots as Yakutsk in eastern Siberia, Frederikshaab in south Greenland, and the Ungava peninsula, the northernmost tip of Labrador. The mild climate is due to the position of the islands in the middle of the north Atlantic, for an oceanic situation makes summers cooler and winters warmer, because of the high specific heat of water compared with that of earth. Faroe also lies in the main track of the Gulf Stream, which raises the air temperature round the islands considerably, especially in winter. From December to March, the average temperature is about 4.5 °C (40 °F), while in July and August it is about 11 °C (52 °F) — an annual range of only 7.5°, compared with 17° in Denmark. The lowest temperature ever recorded was —11.6 °C (11.1 °F), and the highest 21.2 °C (70.1 °F). Prolonged frosty weather is most uncommon; indeed, two-thirds of the winter nights in Faroe are free of frost.

Temperatures, then, are moderate; but the islands have plenty of rain — some will fall on more than two-thirds of the days in every year. Overcast skies are the rule, even more in summer than in winter, and there is a great deal of mist. The winter storms, too, can be tremendous and last for days on end. It is a common thing during these storms for squalls to blast the water out of the streams and scatter it as spray far across the hillsides.

Since Faroe lies south of the Arctic Circle, the midnight sun cannot be observed there, but around midsummer the sun is never far below the horizon, and one may easily read at midnight without artificial light. The lighthouses are turned off from 1 June to 15 July every year. In winter, of course, the days are correspondingly short, but the sky is then often brilliantly aflame with the aurora borealis.

The natural vegetation of the islands is what one might expect from such a climate, soil and latitude. Trees are unknown and bushes are rare. Apart from the seaweeds along the shoreline, Faroese vegetation consists principally of grasses where the land is drained and marsh plants where it is not. There are few or no plant species peculiar to the islands, because, geologically speaking, Faroese vegetation is quite recent. When, during the last glacial ages, the islands were covered by an ice-cap, all traces of ancient vegetation were scoured away; and the present species are in consequence closely related to those of northern Scotland, from which, botanically speaking, Faroe was recolonised.

The animal life of Faroe is also restricted. Apart from domestic species, land mammals are represented only by rats, mice, and arctic hares, all introduced by man, the first two accidentally, the last deliberately (in 1855). Frogs, toads, snakes, and non-migratory freshwater fish are completely absent, though there are good trout and salmon, as well as eels, in the Faroese lakes. Insects are represented chiefly by the smaller species.

If the land is poor, the sea and the air are rich. Faroese waters are visited by about 150 species of fish, of which the most important commercially are cod, herring, haddock, coalfish, ling, cusk, Norway haddock, halibut, and lemon sole. The grey seal breeds in caverns round the islands; and dolphins and the north Atlantic species of whale are also to be found. Of the latter, the small caaing-whale or blackfish is the most important to the Faroeman. Formerly, it was hunted as a serious economic undertaking. Today, the arrival of a school provides the Faroemen with a day's holiday and a supply of free meat — a welcome break from the everyday routine (see pages 21-2).

The immense sea-cliffs of the Faroe Islands are the home of millions of sea-birds, which were formerly an important source of food for the inhabitants, and which are still killed and eaten in great numbers. The species most relished are puffins, guillemots, Manx shearwaters, gannets, and, since they first came to Faroe 130 years ago, fulmars.

Thus the possible economic bases for human settlement on the Faroe Islands are rather limited. The climate is somewhat unfavourable. Driftwood is the only timber supply in the country. There are pockets of highly fertile soil, but they form only seven per cent of the land area. The remaining 93 per cent is mostly rough pasture. Mineral resources are scanty, and the hydro-electric potential, unlike that of Iceland, is insufficient to support heavy manufactures based on imported raw materials. It is not surprising that through most of its history, the population of the Faroe Islands has stood at under 5,000. The sea is the one resource of the Faroemen that is open to expans   Th development of the islands hitherto, and th progressive increase in population up to the present 38,000, have been the direct results of the more efficient exploitation of the sea.

SETTLEMENT AND EARLY HISTORY

The Faroe Islands were among the last territories in the world to be discovered and peopled; and it is one of the curiosities of history that the credit for their eventual discovery should belong to an unknown Irish priest of the eighth century, sailing across the north Atlantic in a skin boat. For a century the islands were the resort of only a few hermits in search of solitude. Then, starting about A.D. 800, Norse settlers began to arrive, probably from western Norway, and some, at least, from the Norse settlements in the Hebrides.

It is not difficult to see why the Faroe Islands should have remained undiscovered for so long — they lie two days' sail in a direction in which no reasonable early sailor would want to go. They are, moreover, so constantly shrouded in mist that even if an early navigator had chanced to be blown off course, he would quite easily not have seen their steep cliffs and grey hills. Orkney and Shetland, plainly visible to anyone rounding the north of Scotland, have a rich prehistory; Faroe has no stone-age or bronze-age remains. The clue to the eventual discovery of the islands may have been the annual migration of birds north-westwards, suggesting to an Irish priest in Shetland that in that direction there might be a land with inhabitants to be converted to Christianity.

The first Norsemen reached Faroe during the Viking Age, and the hermits thereupon abandoned the country. Yet although the Irish geographer Dicuil called these new settlers "Norse pirates", all the archaeological evidence points to their having constituted a peaceful pastoral community, uninvolved in the warlike expeditions of the period. Not a single weapon has been found on Viking-age sites in the Faroe Islands. True, a hoard of ninety-eight coins found on Sandoy in 1863 was perhaps a warrior's treasure, but since the latest coin was dated about 1070, the money was hidden long after the first settlement of the islands.

The name Faroe (Faroese *Føroyar*, pronounced *førja*) means *Sheep Islands*. When the Norsemen arrived, they found the islands stocked with a breed of small wild sheep not unlike the Soay breed that still survives on St. Kilda. This breed, perhaps introduced by the hermits, was still common enough in the thirteenth century for special regulations to be made concerning it; but it was progressively replaced by bigger and better domesticated strains. The last survivors of the wild breed were exterminated on the island of Lítla Dímun in 1866. Wool from Faroese sheep, either in raw or knitted form, was the chief article of export until the nineteenth century, and early settlers doubtless used it to pay for the timber, corn and iron which their own land could not provide.

Excavations of a Viking-age dwelling at Kvívík, on the west side of Streymoy, carried out in 1942, revealed a more or less self-sufficient homestead. The byre, next to the farmhouse itself, contained eight to twelve cows. Pigs, sheep and horses lived in the outfield. The settlers wove their own clothes on the old-style upright loom. Stone sinkers for fishing-lines showed that the resources of the sea, too, were not neglected.

The course of Faroese history from the Norse settlement right through the mediaeval period is quickly told, because the sources of information are so scanty. The islands are briefly mentioned in several of the Icelandic sagas, and it is clear that Christianity came to Faroe about the same time as it was received in Iceland. According to the *Færeyinga Saga*, a historical romance written down in Iceland in the thirteenth century, Christianity became the religion of Faroe about 1000, and the right of the Norwegian kings to collect tribute was finally conceded about 1035. The saga cannot in general be considered a reliable historical source, but there is nothing improbable about these details.

About 1100, a bishopric was set up in Faroe, the see being at Kirkjubøur, a settlement near the southern tip of Streymoy, the largest of the islands. The names of thirty-three bishops of Faroe, from the twelfth century until the abolition of the see soon after the Reformation, are known, though little is known of their lives. Some of them certainly never came to the islands. However, in the modern village of Kirkjubøur may still be seen remains of a mediaeval episcopal palace, and the walls of an unfinished cathedral of the late thirteenth century. As in every other part of Europe, the Church accumulated immense landed wealth, and by the time of the Reformation, was in possession of about 40 per cent of the land in the islands.

The most illustrious of the Faroese bishops was Erlendur, who held the see from 1268 until his death in 1308. Of him it

is recorded that "more than all his predecessors, he enriched
the Faroese church with privileges, lands, and worldly goods.
In his time the episcopal church and palace were destroyed
by a treacherously raised fire." Legend has a few more details
to add about this tycoon amongst the Faroese bishops, and
speaks of two battles fought between Faroese supporters and
opponents of the bishop. Unfortunately, the records of the see
have been lost, and it can only be surmised that these broils
were the reason why Kirkjubøur cathedral was never roofed
over after the walls had been completed.

During Faroe's period of independence, before 1035, the
legislative body and high court, as in Iceland, was an *althing,*
or assembly of freemen. This met in Tórshavn, on the peninsula
still called Tinganes (Assembly Headland). Until the thirt-
teenth century, this assembly may have retained much of its
original authority, but when its continuous written records
began, in 1615, it had long been one of the king's courts, and
known as the Løgting (in Danish *Lagting*), like the provincial
courts of Norway. The code of law used in Faroe was the Gulath-
ing code which operated in the western provinces of Norway.

However, the Faroe Islands also had a code of their own,
the so-called *Seyðabrævið,* or Sheep Letter, regulating the use
of land, especially the joint use of the outfield pastures. This
code was first drawn up in 1298, and was repromulgated in
1637. Apart from very minor amendments, its provisions were
not superseded until the new outfield laws were passed in 1866
— and even then a good deal from the old code passed into
the new legislation, which forms the basis of the present-day
code for the management of the common pastures. Some of
the provisions of the Sheep Letter protected the small farmer
from oppression by the large landowner; others safeguarded
the labour supply of the better-off farmers by forbidding
the harbouring of runaway servants, and by prohibiting any
poor man from setting up an independent household without
certain minimum resources.

Faroese commerce during the middle ages is very badly
documented. The policy of the Norwegian kings was to channel

all Faroese trade through Bergen, where customs dues could be collected. By the fourteenth century, the Hanseatic League had begun to dominate Norwegian trade, but a series of ordinances forbade the Germans to visit Iceland, the Faroe Islands, or any Norwegian ports north of Bergen. In 1361, however, the Hanseatic traders were given the same privileges of trading to Faroe as native Norwegians — a concession reflecting the commercial and political subservience of Norway to the German trading towns at that time. There is some evidence that the Norwegians were not, however, driven completely out of the Faroe trade.

The weakness of Norway in late mediaeval times was in part due to the Black Death, which probably also visited Faroe with great severity. According to tradition, some villages were completely wiped out. The population was subsequently slow to recover. An estimate based on the assessment by the Vatican for "Peter's Pence" suggests that in 1327 the population stood at about 4,000.[1] A count taken in 1769 shows that it was then 4,773. If we assume a figure following the epidemic of 2,500, this would mean that the Faroese population had the extraordinarily slow average growth rate during this period of 1.5 per cent per decade. The explanation may lie partly in severe epidemics arriving periodically from abroad and causing a vast mortality amongst a population with no natural immunity. There was, for instance, a smallpox epidemic that took a severe toll in Tórshavn in 1709.

The crown of Norway was united with that of Denmark in 1380, and from that time, Iceland and the Faroe Islands came to be governed more and more not as Norwegian, but as Danish provinces. The memory of the connection between Norway and the north Atlantic dependencies never died out, but in 1814 when Denmark lost Norway to the Swedes, it was

---

[1] The estimate is based on a count of 270 households, reckoned to be equivalent to fifteen persons each. (Anton Degn's article, *Vardin*, Vol. 12, pp. 127—133). The author does not, however, say why he fixes on the figure of fifteen persons per household, which might be considered on the high side.

not thought unnatural that she should retain Faroe, Iceland and Greenland.

The Reformation came to the Faroe Islands at the same period as it came to Norway, during the years 1535 to 1540. The extensive church lands passed into royal ownership, and henceforth the king's bailiff in the Faroe Islands exercised an immense power of patronage, later to be curtailed by making leases hereditary (see page 16). The one and only Lutheran bishop appointed to the Kirkjubøur see, an elderly man, abandoned his post after being plundered by pirates three times, and no successor was appointed. The highest authority in the Faroese church from this time onwards was the provost, who was at first subject to the bishopric of Bergen in Norway, later to that of Sjælland in Denmark. The language used in the churches was no longer Latin but Danish — almost equally foreign to the islanders, whose native tongue was a form of old Norse.

It was about this period that the Faroese trade monopoly, for three centuries one of the characteristic institutions of the islands, came to be established. The first known monopoly grant was made by Christian III, when in 1535 he gave a Hamburg merchant, Thomas Koppen, the entire royal income of the Faroe Islands, and the sole right to trade with the inhabitants. King Christian's motives were probably threefold. He wanted to exclude the Lübeck merchants from Faroe, since Lübeck had supported his rival, ex-king Christian II, in the civil war that had been raging in Denmark since 1533. On at least one occasion, Lübeck merchants did indeed try to intrigue in Christian II's interests in the islands. In the second place, he wanted to favour a faithful servant without cost to his exchequer. Probably, too, he wanted to build up good will in Hamburg. The monopoly went through a succession of private hands until 1709, when the government itself took over its management, an arrangement which lasted until 1856.

From the time of the Reformation, enough documentation exists to give a clear picture of Faroese society in each age.

In particular, the records of the Løgting, which are preserved from the year 1615 onwards, reveal much of the islanders' public and domestic life. Changes did take place during the seventeenth and eighteenth centuries, but on the whole, society was remarkably stable, and important features of the old Faroese village life have survived into our own century. The characteristics of Faroese peasant society in these centuries will be the subject of the next chapter.

CHAPTER II

A STABLE PEASANT SOCIETY

From the time of the Reformation until well into the nineteenth century, social changes in the Faroe Islands were few and slow.[1] Examination of the stable peasant society of the seventeenth and eighteenth centuries reveals the magnitude of the social revolution during which the Faroe Islanders entered the world fish market, and at the same time developed a national consciousness. It also shows how the national and cultural life of the modern Faroese have some deep roots in distinctive features of the old life.

This old life was lived almost entirely in small villages. Until the islands were opened to international commerce in 1856, even Tórshavn had hardly any pretensions to be called a town. It was no more than a fortified trading post near which lived a few score of landless labourers, carrying out the unskilled work for a handful of commercial agents and government officials. The peasant population was scattered through about eighty-five small villages, each containing an average of ten or a dozen families. Every village was by the sea, so that the scanty produce of the soil could be eked out by the abundance of the ocean.

Looking down on a Faroese village from a neighbouring hill, one can easily pick out the three main divisions of land usage, which have remained unchanged to this day. There is the actual village area, consisting of houses, byres, barns, boat-houses, and the narrow lanes between — much more heavily built up today, of course, than two centuries ago. Next comes the cultivated infield, nowadays mostly under hay, drained by deep ditches which split the land up into tiny

---

[1] A chronological table illustrating this chapter will be found on pages 14-15.

pieces of different levels. The outer limit of the infield is marked by a stout dry-stone wall. Finally, beyond the wall, lies the outfield, by far the largest portion of the village territory. As in the old times, this is devoted principally to the pasturage of sheep.

Infield is individually owned and worked. The boundary marks, though invisible to a stranger, will be perfectly well known to all the villagers. The outfield, collectively owned, is worked on joint-stock principles. It is not permitted to own outfield without at the same time owning infield. The converse was formerly true, but when the population increased during the nineteenth century, an allotment system came into being, so that today it is possible to have tenure of cultivated land without having any share of outfield. In general, however, the two types of land complement each other, both being necessary for making a living by the traditional subsistence economy.

FAROESE LAND TENURE

The unit of Faroese land measurement is the *mark*, which is subdivided into 16 *gylden*, each gylden dividing further into 20 *skind*.[1] Whether the mark ever had any standardised significance is not known, but today it is a highly variable unit. The infield of a mark of land in one village may be six or seven times the area of a mark of infield in another village — and indeed, marks may vary a good deal within a single village commonwealth. However, this strange unit formed, until 1899, the basis for the assessment of land tax, and it still forms the measure by which jointly-produced outfield wealth

---

[1] The above are the Danish terms. In Faroese the units are called *mørk* (pl. *merkur*), *gyllin*, and *skinn*. It is my practice to use the Danish form of technical terms when dealing with the period before the revival of Faroese as a written language, except for terms such as *Løgting*, which are destined to much later use in their Faroese spelling. It is impossible, however, to be completely consistent without anachronism, pedantry, or confusion to the reader. For a glossary see Appendix A.

is divided. The largest villages, according to the mark scale, are Hvalbøur on Suðuroy (98¼ marks) and Sandur on Sandoy (97 marks). The smallest villages are Norðskáli on Eysturoy, and Norðtoftir on Borðoy, each with only 4 marks. Most villages have between 10 and 50 marks.

Occupation of a mark of land gives absolute control over a definite plot of infield, subject only to rights of winter common, by which the gates in the infield wall are thrown open from 25 October to 14 May each year, when the flocks are brought down from the higher outfields, and graze over the lower outfield and the infield. The mark of land also gives proportional rights over the produce of the outfield, subject to the customs of the village and the obligation to provide a proportional labour force for the joint outfield tasks. The products of the outfield, besides the wool and carcasses of the flocks, include peat from the turbaries and sea-birds from the cliffs, as well as a range of products valued more in former times than today, such as driftwood, shellfish and seaweed.

During the seventeenth and eighteenth centuries, land in the Faroe Islands might be occupied by ownership or by lease. It could be owned by recent purchase or allodially. Leases were in nearly every case held from the Danish crown, which from the time of the Reformation owned more than half the land in Faroe.

Allodial land was land possessed by a family for a certain period. Under Christian IV's Norwegian Law, this was thirty winters; but the actual time was later varied, until in 1771 it finally became twenty winters. Allodial rights also pertained to land received in exchange for allodial land, or land given by the king. Allodial land was attached to a family. If a man wished to sell his allodial land, he had first to offer it to his kinsmen at a price fixed by neutral valuation. If it were sold to anyone else, a member of the family with the allodial rights could redeem it within fifteen years. Land owned by recent purchase, on the other hand, could be disposed of without reference to the family, and could not be redeemed.

CHRONOLOGICAL TABLE ILLUSTRATING CHAPTER II

	DENMARK	DEFENCE	LAW	RELIGIOUS ESTABLISHMENT	MONOPOLY
1535				1535—1540 Reformation	THOMAS KOPPEN (Hamburg) 1535—1553
				— 1557 Kirkjubøur bishopric abolished	Monopoly in various hands 1554—1597 (Magnus Heinason 1580—1583)
	1563—1570 War with Sweden	— 1580 Magnus Heinason builds first fort	— 1591 Office of Sorenskriver established		
1600			— 1604 Christian IV's Norwegian Law comes into force		BERGEN PARTNERSHIPS 1597—1619
	1611—1612 War with Sweden	— 1615—1616 Pirate Attacks			THE ICELANDIC COMPANY (Copenhagen) 1620—1662
	1624—1628 Involvement in 30 Years' War	— 1629 Barbary pirates attack Suðuroy			

Wars	Events	Laws & administration	Church / farms	Feudal Lords	Monopoly
1643—1645 War with Sweden	1630—1653 Fort built on Tinganes		1632 Additional farms granted to priests	FEUDAL LORDS	
1657—1660 War with Sweden	— 1666 Defence Rate doubled until 1691			Christoffer von Gabel 1655—1673	GABEL MONOPOLY 1662—1709
1675—1679 War with Sweden and France	— 1677 French destroy fortifications of Tórshavn	— 1672—3 Royal Commission on Faroese affairs	— 1673 Dower farms for priests' widows	Frederik von Gabel 1673—1708	
		— 1688 Christian V's Norwegian law comes into force			
		— 1691 Land and Monopoly Law			
		— 1698 Individual ownership of sheep forbidden			
1700					
1709—1720 Involvement in Great Northern War against Sweden					DANISH CROWN MONOPOLY 1709—1856

Apart from a small quantity of land owned by two families of nobility until the latter part of the seventeenth century, all leased land was held from the crown, usually against the payment of an annual rent, but in certain cases as a stipend for the performance of administrative or ecclesiastical duties. The crown tenants (Danish *kongsbønder,* Faroese *kongsbøndur*) were the richest and most influential section of the peasantry, frequently intermarrying with the families of the priests and officials. They often owned considerable allodial land in addition to their tenancies.

The reason for this prosperity is to be sought in the inheritance system. On the death of a peasant, his allodial estate was divided between all his children, sons taking twice the share of daughters. The consequent fragmentation of allodial holdings was already considerable in the eighteenth century, and today has proceeded to such an extent that only crown tenants may really be said to be farmers at all. For crown tenancies were not subject to division.

By a law of 1559, Faroese crown tenants were granted lifelong security of their leases, provided that they maintained their farms in good order and paid their rents regularly. By a further law of 1673, crown leases were made heritable by the deceased tenant's eldest son or other heir. These laws were originally passed to prevent royal bailiffs from extorting bribes from the peasantry for the renewal of leases, for the rents were fairly low, and the tenancies in consequence valuable; the patronage in the hands of the bailiff was therefore immense. However, the effect was also to create a privileged class. The children of priests were given preference when a crown tenant died without an heir, or when in some other way a tenancy became vacant. This practice, first embodied in law in 1673, arose because the priests were usually Danes who came to the islands as young men, and settled permanently — often raising large families. During the seventeenth and eighteenth centuries, there were about 300 substantial farmers, mostly crown tenants, who farmed 2 to 8 marks, but occasionally as much as 30 or even 50 marks.

The village hill pasture was usually divided into two or more outfield sections, an arrangement which still holds good. Nólsoy, for instance, has at the present time two outfield sections in a village of 48 marks; Mykines has four outfield sections in a village of 40 marks. From 1698 onwards, it was illegal for peasants to keep individually marked sheep; in each outfield section, the flocks had henceforth to be held in common. As already explained (page 13), the produce of the flocks, and the work involved in their maintenance, were divided among the part-owners in proportion to their land-holding in marks, gylden and skind. The arithmetic of division could, at times, be complicated but it was often made easier by genealogical mnemonics.

THE YEAR'S WORK

As soon as winter was over, work began in the infield. Towards the end of March, the men would begin digging over and manuring that portion of their cultivated land (usually a seventh of the whole) on which they intended to raise corn. The plough was not used, although many attempts were made to introduce it into the islands. These attempts failed chiefly because of the steep, rocky and fragmented nature of the average Faroese infield, as well as the difficulty of feeding horses to the degree necessary for good results with the plough.

The best manure available was cow-dung, but there was never enough of it. It had to be supplemented with seaweed, patiently gathered from the shore and left in shallow middens to rot for a few weeks. (It used to be said that a boatful of seaweed in spring was as valuable as a boatload of cod.) In some places fish-offal also was put on the land.

Sowing took place in the latter part of April. Barley was the only grain sown. People tried oats and rye from time to time, but never with any real success. The barley was usually of the hardy local strain, less well flavoured than Danish barley, but less likely to be lost when conditions were bad.

Early in May, the cattle, kept on starvation rations all

through the winter, were brought out to graze the nearer
stretches of the outfield, where the women would go to milk
them morning and evening. (Each peasant was entitled to
keep cows in the outfield in proportion to the marks of land he
held. The stock for a village was usually slightly more than
one per mark.) In the middle of May, the sheep were driven
out of the infield into the high outfield pastures, and the
infield gates were shut.

Two other tasks took place in May. The first fowling of the
year was undertaken. Young puffins were pulled out of their
holes either by hand or with a special hook. The other, more
important work was peat-cutting in the outfield. Peat was the
only fuel available for heating the house and for cooking; and
a great deal was also needed for the kiln-house at harvest-
time. It was stacked in the turbaries and left there all summer
to dry.

June was another busy month. The women would now
have to weed the growing corn, while the men rounded up
the sheep to take their wool and mark the new season's lambs.
This meant that most of the men and boys would make a
systematic drive of the whole outfield. The wool was not
sheared from the animals, but plucked off, a practice which
was still common in the nineteenth century, and which used
to horrify visitors to the islands who witnessed it. The lambs
were marked by a cut on one ear to indicate which outfield
section they belonged to, and on the other to show the particular stretch of pasture they grazed.

After a lull of a week or two at the beginning of July, a
further busy period began with the summer fowling. Puffins
and guillemots were caught on the cliffs with the *fleygistong*,
a V-shaped net on the end of a ten-foot pole. This occupation,
though a favourite one amongst most Faroemen, was often
extremely hazardous, the fowlers either clambering from
their boats up the vertical cliffs to ledges hundreds of feet
above the sea, or being lowered by their companions from the
cliff-top on stout ropes. The latter method of reaching the
fowling-places was quite as dangerous as the former, because

of the risk from loose stones dislodged by the rope. The birds caught were either eaten fresh or salted away for the winter.

Hunting the grey seal was a task for late July and early August. The seals breed in caverns, which used to be visited by the villagers' boats in pairs. One boat, containing at least three men, would enter the cavern. Between this boat and the other was stretched an eighty-fathom rope, so that if the boat in the cave became waterlogged, the other would be able to drag it out. The men entering the cavern were provided with a kind of candle, or rather flare, made of old linen dipped in tallow. These lights would be concealed until the men had arrived at the breeding-ground itself at the inner end of the cavern. Two of the men would then spring from the boat with their clubs, while the third would hold up a flare in each hand. The art was to kill the old seals as quickly as possible with well-aimed blows to the head or snout, after which the young ones could be dispatched at leisure. The seal-oil was used in the house-lamps, the skins were used for making shoes and bags, and the flesh was eaten.

August was also the month for haymaking. Hay was a vital crop, for if it was short, cows might have to be killed which would otherwise give milk during the winter. The grass was cut with a short-bladed scythe by the menfolk, after which everyone would join in the job of turning it, building tramp-cocks, and finally fetching it home to barn or to haystack. After the hay, it was the turn of the barley. This was cut with a kind of sheath-knife, and the ears were stripped off and brought in for drying.

About harvest-time, the peat was fetched home from the turbary where it had been drying; it was now needed for the kiln-house. This was a small stone out-house in which the newly-reaped barley was dried out over a peat fire, and later threshed. (Faroese barley will not ripen on the stalk). The barley would be stored in a dry loft, and the straw saved for various purposes such as the repair of roofs.

The harvest gathered would not be a great one. An eight-fold return on the seed-corn was common, a few favoured places securing a harvest of ten- or twelve-fold. In some years the barley harvest would be completely lost in early autumn storms, or through an early frost after prolonged August rains. No dependence could be placed on a Faroese barley harvest until it was gathered. Wise peasants reckoned to keep a year's barley in hand as an insurance against a bad year. Even with the most careful management, however, Faroe was never self-sufficient in grain. On an average, three-quarters of the annual consumption would have to be imported by the Monopoly — something between 10,000 and 20,000 bushels.

As the harvest was dried and stored, the autumn fishing would begin. This was conducted from small boats, on fishing-grounds often several miles from land. Great skill was needed to find the tiny banks where past experience had shown the fishing to be particularly rich — they might be only a few yards across, and had to be identified by bearings and landmarks which would be carefully taught from father to son.

Apart from fishing, which was carried on as and when the weather permitted, the last outdoor task of the year was the sheep slaughter. In October, the sheep were fetched off the outfield, and all except the winter stock were slaughtered. The carcasses were hung up in special outhouses built so that the winter wind could pass through and dry the meat out thoroughly, making the prized *skerpikjøt,* the islanders' favourite food. This wind-dried mutton, which is still made, is eaten raw in thin slices. It has a fine, rich flavour, but most visitors to the islands find it rather stringy, and that it needs a lot of chewing.

The winter period was occupied with indoor tasks. Working up the wool was the most important of these. The men did the carding and spinning, while the women did the knitting. The Faroese used five different vegetable dyes to colour their woollen yarn; and Faroe, like Shetland, has a range of characteristic knitting patterns of both complexity and beauty. The spinning was formerly done with the hand-spindle — still used occasionally for making short lengths of woollen yarn for darning or other casual purposes. The Scottish pattern of spinning-wheel was introduced into the Faroe Islands late in the seventeenth century, when a Shetlander and his wife were brought over to instruct the inhabitants in its use. Besides knitting their own garments, or weaving a coarse cloth on the old-fashioned upright loom, the Faroese used to make great quantities of knitted hose for sale to the Monopoly. These long stockings were, indeed, almost a currency.

Other winter tasks were the making of fishing-lines and ropes from imported hemp, the tanning of skins for shoes and fishermen's garments, the making of spoons from slices of horn, or carving vessels of all kinds from whatever pieces of drift-wood were available. There was manufacture of baskets in some villages and, in two places, of a crude kind of pottery.

On fine days in early spring was the best fishing of the year. All, however, were not free to take part in it or not as they wished, as in the autumn fishing. Some of the larger farmers had the obligation of keeping specially large boats in order to ferry the priests or the officials from place to place on business. In return, they had the right to call on the local cottagers to man the boats during the spring fishing, though of course, in return for a share of the catch.

At any time of the year, all other work might be suddenly interrupted by a call to a whale-drive. Whale-driving is still carried on in the Faroe Islands, and is one of the most exciting spectacles a visitor can witness. The whale in question is the small caaing-whale or blackfish *(globicephala melaena)*, from 12 to 25 feet long, which moves about in schools of from fifty to 1000. Any boat which sights a school signals the land by raising a garment to the masthead. The alarm is given (in former times by beacon and runner; today by a priority telephone call), and every available boat puts out to drive the whales into a suitable bay and kill them, as many as possible by being beached, the rest by spearing. The flesh is today divided among all the households in the district. Nowadays the blubber is also eaten, but formerly it was used as a source of train-oil for sale to the Monopoly. In former times the bulk of the catch was divided equally between the owners of the land where the whales had been stranded and the hunters, but local custom was variable, and many details may have been forgotten during the fifty years 1745 to 1795, when practically no schools were killed.

The modern visitor to Faroe is profoundly impressed by the efficiency with which several hundred whales may be divided among perhaps a thousand persons within three or four hours, with no sign of wrangling. It was during the period when whale-driving once again rose to importance during the early decades of the nineteenth century that methods were devised for making the division both swift and fair. In the old days, there was always much acrimony and not infrequently open violence on the beach when the men were sharing the kill. Indeed, except when attempts were made to apprehend sheep-stealers, the sharing of whale-meat seems to have been almost the only cause of serious outbreaks of violence amongst the people of Faroe in former times.

Peasant life in Faroe in the seventeenth and eighteenth centuries was hard, and often dangerous; but it had plenty of variety and interest, and many of its features are part of the Faroe scene to this day, even though some of the more picturesque can hardly be justified in strictly economic terms.

THE LAW

The government of Faroe was concerned, broadly speaking, with three main matters: law, revenue, and defence. Law was administered through local courts of first instance, and an annual provincial assize in Tórshavn. The revenue was collected, and the country's expenses paid out, by the king's bailiff. The defence establishment was merely a small garrison in Tórshavn for the defence of the Monopoly warehouses.

Although from the time of the Reformation, in administrative, ecclesiastical, and commercial affairs, Faroe found its ancient connections with Norway loosened in favour of new links with Denmark, Norwegian law remained the code by which the islands were governed. From 1604, this was the Norwegian Law of Christian IV, which broadly speaking was nothing more than a Danish translation of the existing thirteenth-century code of King Magnus the Lawmender. But a translation was badly needed, for old Norse had become obscure and some of the laws difficult to interpret, while the language of the law-courts had long been Danish. Even with Christian IV's Law, many old-fashioned terms remained, but to help courts and people to understand them, a Norwegian chancellor, Jens Bjelke of Østraat, published in 1657 a summary of the code — in verse.

Besides these Norwegian codes, Faroe had also its own *Seyðabrævið*, regulating the management of the outfields, and a code of ecclesiastical law devised primarily for Iceland, the chief application of which was in certain types of sexual offence. In 1687, however, there was a fresh codification of the law, known as Christian V's Norwegian Law, which from 1688 superseded all old codes in Faroe except the *Seyðabrævið*, which continued in force until 1866.

The country was divided into six *sysler*, or law-districts: Streymoy, Sandoy, Eysturoy, Vágar, Suðuroy and the Northern Islands. Each of these districts had six law-right-men or jurymen, who with the *sysselmand* or district sheriff as prosecutor, acted as a court of first instance. Both the jurymen and the district sheriff were appointed by the king's bailiff from among the substantial farmers of each law-district. The local sessions normally took place in spring.

Appeals, and the more difficult cases, were referred to the *Løgting*, or provincial assize. This consisted of the lawman, who was the chief judge of the islands appointed by the king, and all the jurymen, though only twelve were employed on any individual case. From the decisions of the Løgting, the only appeal was to the king's court in Copenhagen.

Christian V's Norwegian Law eroded the influence of the jurymen, although their number was increased from six to ten per law-district. It was no longer permitted for farmers to be appointed year after year; all had to take their turn. Hence

few men built up any great legal experience. In the end, the
Løgting became a mere shadow of its former self, and few
opposed its abolition in 1816. Even by 1591, the law had
become complex for unlettered farmers to manage — in
mainland Norway as well as in Faroe. Christian IV, therefore,
in that year had instituted the office of judicial clerk, or
sorenskriver, a lawyer paid to advise the jurymen, just as a
magistrates' clerk advises justices of the peace in England.
The *sorenskriver*, at first little more than a clerk, by virtue of
his knowledge rapidly became a judge. Each spring, he would
travel round the different law-districts to hear cases with the
jurymen; in summer, he would act as clerk of the court for
the Løgting, when one of his duties was to maintain the court
record book.

The local sessions was summoned when the *sorenskriver*
arrived at the traditional place for holding the court, usually
one of the large crown farms. The summons was sent out by
means of a bidding-stick, the *tingakrossur*, which passed from
village to village over a fixed route. The sessions would
normally last three or four days, but could take up to a week.
During the seventeenth century, the jurymen at these local
sessions were reduced progressively to the role of mere
spectators, until the *sorenskriver* was carrying out the real
administration of justice. By 1688, indeed, we find him
explicitly recognised as in his own person constituting the
court of first instance, save in cases affecting a man's life or
honour, or in land ownership cases, when he was required
to sit with a jury.

The first meeting of the Løgting took place in Tórshavn
on St. Olaf's Day (29 July). The officials, the priests, and a
great many of the peasants would have arrived in the immediately preceding days. The king's bailiff, if he was not
resident in the islands through the winter (in the earlier part
of the seventeenth century he usually was not), would have
arrived by the first trading ship of the year. The law sessions
would normally last a week, each day's business lasting from
6 a.m. to 3 p.m.

On the first day, the proceedings began with a church service, after which the court members walked in procession to the sessions-house on Tinganes. All officials and priests, and any officers of Danish naval vessels lying off the islands would be present for the first session, and a great crowd of the public would be standing outside to listen. The lawman would read the official formula for opening the court, and business would begin.

The first thing to come before the court each year was the supply position, especially regarding corn, the most important food import, and boat timber, the most important raw material. The jurymen inside, and the public outside, were asked whether were any complaints against the Monopoly, either over supply, or the weights and measures used. After this any official intending to leave the islands that summer would take his public testimonial. Jurymen and people would be asked to declare whether anyone had any injustice to complain of against him, or whether he had conducted himself as befitted his office. The third item of public business was bringing in the beak tax. In the course of the year, every Faroese male between fifteen and fifty had to take the district sheriff either one raven's beak or two crows' beaks; this was in order to keep these birds under control. The six district sheriffs brought the beaks into court. and they were burnt on a flat rock near the end of Tinganes Peninsula, the immediate vicinity of which still bears the name Krákusteinur, or Crow's Rock. At the close of the first day's court session, the provost and priests would hold their annual meeting.

The following days were taken up with civil and criminal cases. The court consisted of the lawman, the *sorenskriver,* and twelve jurymen, while the prosecutor in criminal proceedings was the king's bailiff. When all cases were concluded, the lawman ceremonially closed the Løgting for that year.

Serious crime was rare. Violent crime was then, and remains to this day, highly exceptional — almost unknown. From 1615 to 1665 only one murder is recorded: in 1662 one Ole Joensen beat his wife to death, and was sentenced to be beheaded. During the same period, there were two or three homicide cases, but all were judged to be accidents. Two cases of unlawful wounding occurred, in 1621 and 1623.

Offences against property were usually limited to the lifting of sheep from the outfield or dried mutton from the wind-houses. Gold and silver were never stolen — their ownership was too well known for any thief to hope to dispose of them. A fourth conviction for theft could be punished with a death sentence: thieves were hanged in 1626, 1638 and 1657. Vagrancy was sometimes punished severely. In 1642, fourteen persistent and hardened vagrants were sent to Denmark to work in chains in the royal dockyards.

Witchcraft was alleged on three occasions between 1615 and 1665, but in no case did a death penalty follow. Minor crimes included sabbath-breaking, slander, petty assault and unlawful journeying into the outfield.

The bulk of the cases each year were sexual offences. Extra-marital intercourse was an offence punishable by a fine. Even the anticipation of the marriage ceremony was punished, although nominally. Incest was comparatively common, and between close relatives was a capital offence: executions for incest took place in 1615, 1664, 1679 and 1706. Before 1688, the man was beheaded and the woman drowned in a sack. In the 1706 case (the last occasion when capital punishment was carried out in the islands) both the man and the woman were beheaded. The population was, generally, law-abiding and the law-courts, by the standards of the time, were humane.

The lawman was usually, though not always, a Faroeman. As payment, he had the 24-mark farm Steigargarður on the island of Vágar, and 1 skind in goods annually from every male between fifteen and fifty. The *sorenskrivers* of the seventeenth century and early eighteenth century were often appointed from among the better-educated Faroemen, but after about 1770 the office was filled by Danes or Norwegians. The *sorenskriver's* income was 55 gylden a year from the public revenue.

PUBLIC REVENUE

The chief revenue official in Faroe was the king's bailiff. This was a crown appointment, paid out of the royal revenue in kind. During the eighteenth century, the bailiff was normally a resident official, but in the earlier part of the seventeenth, he commonly came to Faroe only for the summer months, leaving a deputy to do his work through the winter.

The royal rents and taxes were paid in kind, according to a standard tariff also used by the Monopoly, and the king's bailiff had warehouses in Tórshavn for storing the goods in which he was paid. The accounting unit was the gylden in money (a distinct unit from the gylden in land), originally representing the value of the mediaeval Rhineland guilder. This was divisible into 20 skind, which originally represented the value of so many sheepskins. No coins were ever minted to the value of the Faroese gylden and skind, which were merely a reckoning device. The king's bailiff, making his reckoning in the same units, forwarded the revenue of the islands, less expenses, to some merchant with whom the king stood in account.

The chief sources of revenue were crown rents, the land taxes and tithe. The income was not large. Between 1600 and 1650, it stood at a little under 3,000 gylden, the expenses within the islands being only 300 gylden, but the king's bailiff met only a few of the country's expenses, the priests and most of the officials being paid by means of beneficed farms, and the garrison being paid by the king. By 1790, the revenue had risen only to 3,800 gylden.

Crown rents were assessed according to the quality and quantity of the infield of that particular farm. Valuations of 10 to 20 skind per mark of land was common. Sometimes there were additional rents for inventory or stock. Every third year, crown tenants had to pay an extra 10 skind per mark of land; the other occasional payment was that made on entry into a crown tenancy, standardised in 1673 at one rigsdaler per lease, equivalent to 1 gylden 10 skind. These payments were the only obligations. The Faroese peasant was never compelled, as was his Danish counterpart at this period, to work on his landlord's estate without payment. The rents, too, were moderate. The six crown tenants on Nólsoy, for instance, paid altogether about 1½ gylden per mark annually for their farms. 1½ gylden was the purchase price of 2½ bushels of barley at the Monopoly, or the selling price of 40 lb. of smelted tallow, 7 gallons of train-oil, or 10 lbs. of white washed wool. A mark of outfield on Nólsoy will carry a winter stock of sixteen to twenty sheep, each yielding 2¼ lb. of wool yearly, so that a crown tenant paying his rent in the most thriftless manner, in raw wool, would have to give up only about a quarter of his wool crop; the remaining produce of the farm would be his own.

The land tax consisted of two imposts, known as *kongsskat* and *matrikelskat*. The *kongsskat* (the king's tax) was a small customary payment intended for the maintenance of the royal household. It may originally have been a tax levied not on the land, but on the houses in each village, but because, as a matter of convenience, it was collected by the more substantial farmers for payment in bulk to the king's bailiff, it came in time to be a small tax of arbitrary size levied on each crown tenancy. The *matrikelskat* (defence rate) was applied to the maintenance of the Tórshavn forts. This was paid at the annual rate of 2 skind per mark of leased land, and 3 skind per mark of privately-owned land until 1666 when these rates were doubled, but in 1691 they were reduced to 3 skind per mark for leased land and 5 for privately-owned land.

Tithe was collected in Faroe on barley, butter, fish, whales, seals, sea-fowl and wool. Of these, the wool and fish tithes were the most important. Tithe was an ancient tax in Faroe, and was originally divided into four: a quarter each for the bishop, the church, the priest and the poor. After the Reformation, the crown continued to collect the bishop's share as a secular tax. By the Norwegian Law of Christian V, the tithe was divided into three parts only, for king, church and priest, though many Faroeman resented the introduction of this new method of division, having been accustomed to distribute the quarter share of the tithe to the poor of their own village.

A minor source of income for the crown was wreckage cast up on the islands. Legally, driftwood, so valuable in the treeless country, might be of two kinds. A whole tree cast ashore was called peasants' wood, and belonged to the owners or tenants of the land on which it was washed up. If, however, any mark of man's hand was visible on the timber, it was the king's wood, and had to be auctioned by the district sheriff. In either case, however, the finder was entitled to one-third of the value.

The district sheriffs were normally substantial farmers, appointed to their posts by the king's bailiff. They collected the royal portion of the tithes, and in general acted as the local representatives of the king's bailiff in each law-district. They could receive crown rents and land taxes, but most peasants preferred to pay these direct to the king's bailiff at the time of the July sessions of the Løgting. The district sheriffs received their payment simply by retaining certain of the tithes they collected. Their emoluments were not large for the amount of work they were expected to do.

From time to time the Faroe Islands were granted as a fief, and the bailiff would then send the income not to the king but to the feudal lord, who in turn paid a fixed annual sum into the royal treasury. The best-remembered of the feudal lords of Faroe were Christoffer von Gabel, who held the fief from 1655 until his death in 1673, and his son Frederik, who succeeded his father and governed the islands until his death in 1708. From 1662, the Gabels held not only the royal income of the islands, but also the Monopoly. The two were heartily detested in Faroe, especially the father, principally because of the rapacity of their subordinates in the islands. During this period Denmark was constantly involved in foreign wars, which did not help matters. From 1709, however, Faroe came directly under the Danish Treasury, and thereafter there were few complaints about the administration of the public revenue.

DEFENCE

The first fortification in the Faroe Islands, on the easterly headland overlooking Tórshavn harbour, is said to have been built about 1580 after a pirate raid on the warehouses there. The builder was a Faroese adventurer called Magnus Heinason[1] (1545-89). Magnus Heinason was born on Eysturoy, the son of the first Lutheran provost of Faroe. As a young man he took naval service with the Dutch, and acquitted himself with distinction. In 1579, he was granted the monopoly of the Faroe trade by King Frederik II.

That very summer, however, he suffered substantial loss at the hands of an English pirate. The king thereupon gave Magnus Heinason a licence to fit out his vessel as a warship and to pursue all pirates in northern waters and bring them to justice. He was also empowered to arrest Dutch ships attempting to sail round north Norway to trade with the northern ports of Russia. His captures were to be brought to Bergen, and the proceeds would be shared equally with the king. It was probably in pursuance of his privateering that Magnus Heinason built his fort, which stood close to the present Tórshavn lighthouse.

Legend tells much of Magnus Heinason's valour in combat with the pirates, but he was a most unsatisfactory monopolist for the Faroe Islands. Complaints were raised against him of false measure, adulterated provisions and over-charging. To curry favour with the king, he undertook an expedition to Greenland in the summer of 1581, and stretched the terms of his commission to provision his ship at the expense of his countrymen. In 1583 his malpractices lost him his monopoly privileges, and the following year he went into exile following charges of rape and incest. He re-entered Dutch service for two years, until he was allowed to return to Denmark in 1587. However, he had committed a piracy against an English ship

---

[1] In Danish his name is usually given as Mogens Heinesøn, and in English and Scottish documents as Mons or Mauns Hennison.

in the spring of 1585, and after this had been proved against him, he was beheaded in Copenhagen in January 1589. The Faroese of modern times have tended to regard Magnus Heinason as a national hero, claiming that his death was due to the machinations of an implacable enemy at court, Christoffer Valkendorff. It is true that in the proceedings against Heinason there were technical illegalities; and these eventually led to Valkendorff's disgrace and Magnus Heinason's posthumous rehabilitation. But few historians outside the islands can be convinced that he was innocent of the piracy for which he suffered death.

Magnus Heinason's well-placed fort was later supplemented by a second one near the tip of Tinganes, not far from the Monopoly warehouses. The Tinganes fort took from 1630 to 1653 to build, and was paid for by the defence rate (see page 28). The garrison of Tórshavn usually consisted of a commandant, three corporals, and thirty soldiers. The soldiers, however, were not Danish army regulars, but a badly-paid and ill-trained local militia.

There was no hope of defending the islands as a whole, which in the unsettled days of the sixteenth and seventeenth centuries were constantly exposed to plunder. When pirates or hostile naval vessels approached, the Faroemen resorted to specially-prepared refuges in the hills. Fear of hostile ships was very real as late as 1821, when panic was created by a Shetland boat's crew rowing ashore from their whaler by mistake, believing they were off Lerwick.

The Løgting records show that the worst attacks in the early seventeenth century were in the years 1615, 1616 and 1629. The most serious was that made in 1629, when three Algerian ships decended on Hvalbøur in Suðuroy, and took away thirty of the inhabitants to be sold as slaves. They never returned, for the Danish exchequer had been emptied by Christian IV's participation in the Thirty Years' War, and the Faroese themselves were too poor to raise the ransoms. Not only pirates but foreign fishermen often attacked the more exposed villages and removed stock or personal property, and there was little that either the garrison or the scattered population could do about it.

After 1629, the Faroe Islands had peace for several decades, although whenever Denmark was at war, extreme nervousness prevailed throughout the islands about the possible visit of warships. Two hostile inroads of little importance occurred in 1667, but the islands suffered most during 1675—9, when Denmark, in alliance with Holland, was at war with France. Dutch East Indiamen would make for Faroe on their return voyages, in order to be convoyed home by ships of the Dutch Navy. But French cruisers would also sometimes lie in wait. In 1677, a French landing party destroyed the fortifications in Tórshavn and thoroughly plundered the town. The fear of hostile attack was so great that a royal commission in 1709 considered it out of the question for the Monopoly to re-establish a former out-station on Suðuroy, where it could so easily be visited by pirates.

In 1780, Tórshavn was completely re-fortified. By then the Tinganes blockhouse had long been demolished, but the fort on the eastern headland was strengthened by a skilful artillery captain. The quality of the militia, however, remained inadequate to hold the fort against a determined attack. During the Napoleonic War, when it might have been put to the test, the commandant surrendered without a shot being fired.

THE RELIGIOUS ESTABLISHMENT

There were seven priests' livings in the Faroe Islands, corresponding with the law districts, except that Streymoy had two priests, for its northern and southern portions respectively. These seven priests served a total of thirty-nine churches. When the priest was not present for the Sunday service, it would be conducted by the deacon, who would be a local farmer; instead of preaching a sermon, he would read from a book of Danish homilies.

The financial position of the Faroese clergy was poor until

1632 when, in response to a petition, Christian IV granted them extra glebe farms of about six marks each. With tithes and other income, they were now among the wealthiest of their little community, Indeed, one Sandoy priest of the mid-seventeenth century improved his means to the extent that he eventually controlled 47 marks of land in his own and perhaps in other islands. This was the equivalent of half the land in his home village, which was anyway the second largest in Faroe.

A law of 1673 made provision for priests' widows. They were allotted small farms on condition that they did not remarry, and remained chaste. When there was no widow, the dower farm was added to the priest's glebe. There were occasions when two widows had to share the dower farm; the normal practice, however, was for the widow to marry the new incumbent.

As has been mentioned earlier, the priests serving in Faroe often had very large families. The Sandoy priest who did so well for himself in land fathered no fewer than twenty-three children. This was in contrast to the families of Faroese peasants, which were usually small. The sons of priests were often provided for by the grant of crown tenancies that fell vacant, while their daughters tended to marry into the wealthier peasantry.

The provost, the chief ecclesiastical authority in the islands, was chosen from among the seven priests. His farm of $11\frac{1}{2}$ marks on Eysturoy was cultivated by a tenant. The provost was, of course, subject to his bishop (during the seventeenth and eighteenth centuries the bishop of Sjælland), but the physical remoteness of his superior gave him considerable autonomy.

A Latin school was maintained in Tórshavn, and one master and the South Streymoy priest would give instruction in reading, writing, catechism and Latin. It was the custom for any student wishing to enter Copenhagen University first to spend one or two years in a Danish school. Former pupils often returned to the islands as priests, while a small number more were presented to livings in Denmark.

The principal endowment of the school was 100 gylden a year, paid out of the public revenue. 70 gylden constituted the schoolmaster's salary, and the remainder was spent on writing materials and maintaining two poor pupils. The school never taught many pupils, but it flourished modestly during the seventeenth century, slowly declined during the eighteenth, and finally passed out of existence in 1804.

There was a single institution in Faroe for the sick and poor: the hospital at Argir, a little to the south of Tórshavn, with twelve places for lepers and the destitute. Like the school, it received an annual allowance of 100 gylden, from the public revenue, and owned 4 marks of infield. Most of the poor and sick, however, were maintained by their families and fellow-villagers.

THE MONOPOLY

The Faroese trade monopoly, from its inception in 1535 until 1709, was granted to various individuals or companies, usually against a fixed annual payment into the royal treasury. From 1709 until 1856, the Danish government itself conducted the trade. The Monopoly was not generally oppressive; indeed, it acted as a valuable cushion against hard times. It only did damage in that it encouraged commercial and intellectual stagnation.

The rules by which the Monopoly was to be conducted were strictly defined. The conditions laid down for the Bergen consortium which took over the trade in 1597 were typical:

(i) the monopolists had to keep the country well supplied;

(ii) they must buy and sell only at the customary prices;

(iii) they were not to bring any adulterated goods into the islands;

(iv) both in purchase and sale, they were to use the ancient Faroese weights and measures;

(v) they must carry any prosecution, whether for debt or any other cause, before the lawman and the Løgting;

(vi) they must conduct themselves in a friendly manner towards all inhabitants of the islands;

(vii) they must treat the king's bailiff with honour and respect, and give him free passage to and from Bergen, though at the king's expense for provisions;

(viii) they must give a cheap passage to any islander who wished to leave the islands in order to petition the king.

The tariff in force until the beginning of the Gabel period in the 1660s was as follows:

EXPORTS

1 vog (40 lbs) of wool, train-oil, raw tallow, feathers or fish	1 gylden
1 bundle of 40 sheepskins	2 gylden
1 vog of butter or smelted tallow	1½ gylden
1 tun (26 gallons) of butter or smelted tallow	10 gylden
1 tun of train-oil	6 gylden
1 pair of red stockings	5 skind
1 pair of white stockings	4 skind
40 fresh or 30 salt fish	1 gylden
1 lamb	5 skind
1 pack (about 200 sq. feet) of homespun cloth	6 gylden

IMPORTS

Barley, per barrel (about 4 bushels)	2 gylden
Malt, per barrel	3 gylden
Barley flour, per barrel	3 gylden
Coarse salt, per barrel	2 gylden
Beer, per tun	3 gylden
Spirits, per kande (about 26 pints)	1 gylden
Vinegar, per tun	3 gylden
Rhine Wine, per kande	10 skind
French Wine, per kande	6 skind
Mead, per tun	6 gylden
Oatmeal, per barrel	4 gylden

Ryebread, per barrel	2 gylden
Biscuit, per barrel	3 gylden
Fine salt, per barrel	4 gylden

The goods exported from Faroe were often sold in Holland, which at this period was in the forefront of European trade. Until 1619 the Monopoly was conducted by various Bergen merchants, usually in partnership. They were succeeded by the Icelandic Company, a Copenhagen venture that also held the monopoly of trade to Iceland. From 1662 until 1709, the Gabel family conducted the trade. The Løgting records show that the Icelandic Company served the islands best. The Bergen merchants were probably under-capitalised, while the Gabels held their concession during difficult war years, when corn was dear. By that time, moreover, the old tariff had become unrealistic in relation to European market prices.

The Monopoly trading station stood on Tinganes, the headland jutting into Tórshavn harbour, and most of its buildings survive today. In 1709, when they were transferred from Gabel's heirs to the Danish crown at a valuation, they consisted of five warehouses, a brewery, two dwelling-houses, four boat-houses and a tiny lock-up. The buildings were all of timber, either planks or round logs. The brewery was small, its brewing-copper having a capacity of 80 gallons. For unloading cargoes there were four boats, one a sailing-boat.

Apart from a short period when an out-station was maintained on Suðuroy, Tinganes was the only place where trade could legally be conducted. The Faroemen had to resort to the Monopoly for everything that they could not grow or make for themselves. In good sailing weather, a great crowd of boats might press in from every part of the islands. At those times the men of Mykines had the right to be served first, since their remote island had the most difficult landing-place in the whole of Faroe, and it was often impossible to get on or off for weeks at a time. The men of Suðuroy used to keep specially large boats for their trading journeys to Tórshavn, since theirs was a journey of thirty miles, nearly all across open sea. Much good farming or fishing weather was lost every year through the necessity of journeying to Tórshavn to fetch trade goods.

The islands suffered their period of greatest hardship from 1658 to 1673. Denmark's war with Sweden from 1657 to 1660 came near to extinguishing the kingdom, and it raised prices so high that the Icelandic Company was driven out of business. For long periods, the Tinganes warehouses were empty. A temporary tariff allowed the prices of corn, flour and malt to be raised, and the higher prices remained in force until late in 1669. The position was made worse by the inexperience and corruption of Gabel's agents in the islands. A royal commission in Copenhagen investigated the affairs of the islands from 16 December, 1672, to 16 April, 1673, and rectified a number of abuses in both the trade and the administration.

In the same period, and for some time afterwards, there was another difficulty, for both the Faroese and the Gabels, resulting from a shift in the terms of trade. After 1620, because of a decline in the fishing around Faroe, the poorer people had taken to knitting great quantities of woollen stockings, which by the terms of the monopoly grant, the trading company was bound to accept. Before long, 60,000 pairs were being exported every year. But from 1657, the price of stockings in Holland, the chief market, began to decline. By 1689, Frederik von Gabel was complaining that more hose was being sent out of Faroe in one year than could be sold in Holland in three. But the Faroese stubbornly resisted all attempts to have the buying price of stockings reduced or output restricted.

The hose dispute led to a second royal commission sitting over Faroese affairs. The commission's report led to a royal ordinance dated 30 May, 1691, laying down a new tariff, which was to last in the main for the next hundred years. The following were the principal items:

EXPORTS

1 bundle of 40 sheepskins	2 gylden 10 skind
1 vog (40 lbs) of feathers or raw tallow	1 gylden
1 vog of smelted tallow	1 gylden 10 skind
1 vog of belly-feathers	1 gylden 10 skind
1 tun (26 gallons) of butter	10 gylden
1 tun of train-oil	5 gylden 14 skind
1 vog of white washed wool	6 gylden
1 vog of dried fish	16 skind
1 pair of stockings, old pattern	3 skind
1 pair of stockings, new pattern	5 skind
1 pack (200 sq. feet) of homespun cloth	6 gylden

The chief modifications here were in the direction of better quality goods. Sheepskins and wool rose in price, while train-oil and dried fish went down. Butter, feathers, cloth and tallow remained at their old prices. But a new category — belly-feathers — was introduced, and the wool, paid for at the high price of 6 gylden per vog, had to be white and washed. The old-pattern hose would not be accepted except when accompanied by half the number of pairs of new-pattern hose, and a quantity of unworked wool.

IMPORTS

Barley, per barrel (about 4 bushels)	2 gylden 8 skind
Malt, per barrel	3 gylden 4 skind
French salt, per barrel	2 gylden 10 skind
Beer (Faroe brewed) per tun	4 gylden
French spirits, per kande (about 26 pints)	1 gylden 10 skind
Danish spirits, per kande	17 skind
French wine, per kande	10 skind
Mead, per tun	8 gylden 12 skind
Lüneburg salt, per tun	4 gylden 10 skind

The prices of nearly all these commodities show an increase
over the old rates. Barley, the most important food import,
was 20 per cent dearer than in the old tariff, but the new price
was lower than the temporary wartime price. Besides the
selection given above, the ordinance laid down prices for
several other foodstuffs (including a special section for spices)
and about sixty types of general wares. The tariff seems to
have satisfied everyone: during the following century few
modifications were made. The chief alteration was the
lowering of the wool price to 3 gylden, a more realistic figure,
in 1723.

For the concession-holders the Faroese Monopoly was not
a particularly profitable trade. Unfortunately, few figures
have survived for the profit and loss of the different seventeenth-
century companies, but nobody made a fortune out of the
islands. The Danish government made losses on the trade from
1709 until 1722, the high price of washed wool being the
principal factor; and in no year between 1722 and 1777 were
more than 13,000 rigsdaler paid into the Treasury. (This sum
corresponds to 19,500 Faroese gylden, or £2,925 at contem-
porary rates of exchange.) The average trading surplus during
this period was less than 7,000 rigsdaler. From 1777 to the
end of the century the Monopoly normally ran at a loss.

There was a good deal of smuggling, either in a small way
with passing fishing-boats, or on a more considerable scale
with professional Dutch or English smugglers. Repeated
ordinances against trade with foreigners indicate the persistence of this practice. Each year the district sheriffs were
expected to submit to the Løgting a list of foreign ships and
the people with whom they had traded. But the Løgting was
composed of Faroemen, who knew the inconvenience of
coming to Tórshavn to supply every want. The reports for
1620 showed that in the previous summer, the lawman, some
of the priests, and most of the Løgting, as well as many of the
general populace, had traded with smugglers.

The penalties for trading with smugglers were, for a priest
or official, the loss of his post, and for a peasant the loss of his

farm, and that the smuggled goods should be forfeit; however, the court had ways of getting round the law. An accused person who could show that there had been no corn in the Monopoly at the material time would almost certainly not be punished for buying it from a smuggler. The priests and officials often evaded the law by sending their wives on board the boats to do the trading, especially choosing times when they themselves were away from home on business. The inhabitants of Suðuroy were especially noted for their propensity to trade with smugglers, so great was the distance from Tórshavn. Its most celebrated smuggling case was in 1687, when most of the islanders, including the wives of both the priest and the district sheriff, bought corn from a Dutch smuggler, who was subsequently arrested. Several of the Suðuroy peasants lost their land as a result of this case, although it was restored to them in 1691.

Monopoly is not a popular institution in modern times. However, the Faroese Monopoly was to some degree justified by the need to concentrate a store of vital imports in a place that could be defended. The total volume of trade was not large; and more than a single defended trading post was impractical, at least in the seventeenth century. The system had its drawbacks — the chief being the waste of travelling time, the tendency to deliver the lowest possible quality of goods when the price is a fixed one, and the tardiness of the importer in bringing in new and improved products. Yet the islanders were reasonably well served by the system, at least when it was operated by the Danish government.

INTELLECTUAL AND CULTURAL LIFE

Although Iceland had a rich literary life during the middle ages, the Faroe Islands had none. At least, no written Faroese literature surived to the seventeenth century. No ancient manuscripts have ever come to light in the islands, though from certain references in old stories and ballads, and from some of their themes, it is possible that Icelandic parchment codices were not unknown. Yet they must have been of extreme rarity, and without influence on the development of the Faroese vernacular, which is rich in the dialects a written literature would have tended to blur.

Yet there was a rich oral literature. When, during the winter evenings, the household was at work spinning, knitting and weaving, it was the custom for someone to entertain the company in the smoky living-room by telling stories. These might be historical in purport *(sagnir)* or fictitious *(ævintýr)*. Many of these were collected in the nineteenth century, and although the *sagnir* often contain fictitious accretions, they supplement our knowledge of the islands during and after the middle ages.

In the Faroese ballad, too, was to be found an art form combining poetry, music and movement. The Faroese ring-dance has preserved into modern times a mediaeval ballad tradition of great interest, centuries after it has perished everywhere else. It is believed to be related to the line-dance which originated in French courtly circles in the thirteenth century, and over the next 200 years spread all over Europe. In it the dancers provided their own music by singing ballads, to which the steps of the dance were a choreographic complement.

Faroese dancing used to take place at weddings, at whale-killings, and other festivals such as St. Olaf's day, and regularly during the period between Christmas and Shrovetide. To the simple steps of the ring-dance were sung the old ballads *(kvæði)*, some of which, by the evidence of their style, can be dated well back into the middle ages. Their subjects were manifold. There were ballad versions of many popular mediaeval European stories, such as the Charlemagne legends and the story of Sigurd the Völsung (i.e. the Scandinavian version of the *Nibelungenlied*). Some of the ballads contained English themes, as for instance one called *Grímur á Bretlandi* (not the same as the story of Havelok the Dane). There were ballad versions of several Icelandic sagas. Some of these *kvæði* are of great length: one has nine parts and over 600 stanzas. Surprisingly few of the ballads deal with Faroese themes, although in *Sigmundar kvæði* is to be found a fragmentary version of the *Færeyinga saga*.

The circumstances in which these ballads were sung can best be described in the words of a Faroese novelist, Heðin Brú, who early in the present century grew up in a village where ballad-singing was still a living tradition. He writes:

The weeks between Christmas and Shrovetide were the only time in the year when there was dancing. Yes, it was Faroese ballad-dancing, other kinds being unknown. There was no dance hall in the village. During the afternoon of the day after Christmas, some of the young men would go into the village to try and borrow someone's living-room in which to dance. They always found one. Now biddings were sent to every house. I can still remember how glad we youngsters were to get this message, which we had been awaiting for so long ... During these weeks there was dancing every Sunday evening, as well as on New Year's Eve, Twelfth Night, Candlemas, and the night before Shrove Tuesday, which was the last time there was a dance before the following Christmas ...

During the dancing period each village had its special festival night, when folk visited from the neighbouring villages; one village might have New Year's Eve, another Twelfth Night, and so on. On such an evening the whole village was ready to receive guests ...

The dances and the ballads were held in high honour. People would take care that the different ballads were not sung too often, lest they should become commonplace. Likewise every singer stuck to particular ballads; no-one would take up a ballad that someone else in the village was in the custom of singing. The ballads were really the more important, the dance being regarded more as a form of expression that one used to bring to life the narrative material in the ballad. In this connection, it ought to be mentioned that if it was rumoured in the village some evening, that a well-known singer was going to sing some very well-loved ballad, it might happen that aged men who had not been to a dance in years, would suddenly be all fire and flame. "I'm going to dance *that* ballad once more before I die." A lesser song would not tempt them, nor yet the dance itself; it was the dramatic narrative of the great ballad, brought to life in the dance, that set them aflame.

A genre cultivated everywhere in the islands during the seventeenth and eighteenth centuries, and in some villages preserved to this day, is that of the satirical ballad *(táttur)*. These *tættir* are composed in the high style of the *kvæði* but deal with the unlucky encounters or ridiculous actions of people known in the village. One account tells how sometimes two strong young men would grasp the victim himself, drag him into the ring, and compel him to dance to his own discomfiture. The usual practice is to refer to people in a *táttur* by nickname, but in small communities like the village of Faroe nicknames are only too well known to everyone. The tradition of the *táttur* has remained particularly strong in some villages. In the summer of 1957, I collected a Nólsoy specimen based on a strike that took place during the Second World War.

From the seventeenth century onwards, Danish folk songs *(folkeviser)* began to spread in the islands, learned either from Danish priests or from early song-books, and sometimes coming to form an important part of the oral tradition of some villages. These Danish songs are usually much shorter than the Faroese ballads, and it has been suggested that when a Faroese ballad on a heroic subject met the competition of a shorter Danish version, the former rather than the latter tended to be lost.

The visual arts hardly flourished in Faroe at all : opportunity was lacking. A certain amount of decorative wood-carving was done, but not on a scale comparable with Iceland. The craftsmanship involved in making objects of everyday use, however, was often considerable.

There were some printed books in the islands during the seventeenth and eighteenth century, largely religious works in Danish such as J. R. Brochmand's *Huspostil*, a seventeenth-century collection of sermons. Some Icelandic books were read in Faroe, the Icelandic language not being too difficult for a Faroeman to read. Indeed, a late mediaeval Icelandic religious poem, *Ljómur,* was still known to oral tradition in the 1780s. Of secular works, there may have been a few copies here and there of such works as Peder Claussøn's *Norske Kongers Chronica,* published in Copenhagen in 1633.

The Faroe Islands are the home of one of the remotest communities of Europe, and it is hardly surprising that ideas and new cultural forms were slow to penetrate there. Changes that did take place came largely through the Danish priests and officials, though partly, too through the work of Dutch and English smugglers. The isolation imposed by distance and by commercial monopoly thus preserved in Faroe a cultural pattern that had long since become extinct elsewhere.

CHAPTER III

WINDOWS OPEN ON THE WORLD

RYBERGS HANDEL

The first considerable influence of the outside world on traditional Faroese society came through the establishment of a smuggling depot in Tórshavn.

In the series of bitter struggles engaged in by England and France from 1689 to 1815, an important prize was mastery of the East and West Indian trades. Whatever other motives for conflict may have been present from time to time, control of the East Indian trade in tea, coffee, spices and luxury goods and the West Indian trade in sugar, tobacco and rum, was seldom far from the minds of the combatants. The prize was a glittering one. In the eighteenth century, for the first time in human history, imported produce was being consumed by whole populations, instead of merely by the rich; successful merchants could now reap immense profits.

The struggle between the two chief maritime nations of Europe gave for those of the second rank, Holland and Denmark, a golden opportunity. From 1755, in particular, Denmark pursued a profitable policy of neutrality. The wars sent freight rates up to magnificent levels, to the benefit of neutral maritime powers, though the latter did consequently run the risk of being drawn into the conflict. It was at this time that the Norwegian merchant fleet first began to assume world importance; and that the Danish colonies in the East and West Indies, although tiny in extent, became especially profitable.

The surge of neutral prosperity reached Faroe in 1767, when the great Danish merchant Niels Ryberg founded a transit depot at the head of Tórshavn's western harbour,

which became known as Friedrichs Vaag, or Rybergs Handel.
This depot flourished for twenty years on the flaws in the
British taxation system. The long wars with France were being
financed partly from import duties, and the rates rose so high
that smuggling became a lucrative business. The Isle of Man
had been the chief base for the contraband trade until 1765
when the Duke of Atholl parted with his sovereign rights as
Lord of Man for a capital payment. The way was now clear
for the opening of a new smugglers' base. Indeed, Niels
Ryberg recruited some of his staff from the Isle of Man.

Goods came to Rybergs Handel chiefly in three of Niels
Ryberg's ships, but also in American vessels and ships plying
from Bergen. Often as many as twelve or fourteen ships were
to be seen at one time in Tórshavn harbour, either bringing
goods to the depot or taking them away. Sloops and luggers
came for cheap dutiable goods from many parts of Ireland
and Scotland. By 1782, their number was so great as to make
it worthwhile for the company to maintain a lighthouse on
Nólsoy to guide the smugglers. The company even maintained
a commercial agent in Ayr, a town well-placed on one of the
best smuggling coasts in Scotland.

Trade flourished particularly during the American War of
Independence, when Britain, France, Spain, Holland and
the American states were all at war, and the Danish-Norwegian kingdom was the only neutral power with interests in
the East and West Indies. Great quantities of rum were
exported from Rybergs Handel during these years, supposedly
the produce of the Danish West Indies, but probably including
much that had been smuggled *into* St. Croix or St. Thomas
in order to take advantage of a transatlantic passage in a
neutral hold. The port of St. Thomas, moreover, was one of
the principal markets where the belligerents sold their prizes
taken in American coastal waters. The tea that passed through
Rybergs Handel may likewise have been shipped in from
Tranquebar, after being smuggled there from the Dutch,
French and British settlements in the East Indies.

Besides rum and tea, the chief transit goods that passed

through the warehouses were gin, brandy and tobacco. The quantities of tobacco sold in the years 1779—81 were enormous. This was purchased mostly from England, Rybergs being able to claim drawback of import duty on the re-export of the goods — which were subsequently sent back by the smugglers into the northern parts of Britain. When the British government stopped the payment of drawback on tobacco consigned to the Faroe Islands, Ryberg obtained Danish government sanction to take it to Bergen for trans-shipment there.

When Rybergs Handel closed in 1788, the causes were twofold. In 1784, the import duty on tea entering Britain was reduced from 119 to 12½ per cent. This was a mortal blow to an important branch of the contraband trade. Also, after the American war ended in 1783, Britain at last had its hands free to put diplomatic pressure on Denmark to close down the Tórshavn depot. Ryberg started sending his rum stocks from Faroe back to Copenhagen in 1787, and after 1788 only a few of his staff remained in Tórshavn to dispose of the last remaining stocks.

The depot was important to the Faroe Islands in a purely economic sense, since many Faroemen were employed about Ryberg's workshops and warehouses, and they and the foreign staff were a source of demand for such goods and services as Faroe could supply. More important, however, were the skills which the Faroemen learned through the depot. Coopers, carpenters, clerks, shipwrights, tobacco-curers and many other craftsmen were plying their trades in Tórshavn for almost a generation.

For the first time, too, foreigners became a familiar sight in Tórshavn. These, besides Ryberg's resident staff, were the crews of his transatlantic merchantmen, and the smugglers. The latter were mostly Scots and Irish, and so numerous that English was widely understood in Tórshavn for many years afterwards. One of the most colourful of the smugglers was Carmichael, a Scotsman who skippered a sailing vessel brilliantly adapted to the contraband trade. It looked

different every time it came to Tórshavn; it had different sets
of sails, and might be painted white on one side of the hull and
black on the other. A quickly retractable mast enabled it to
slip rapidly into hiding-places among the cliffs. Many tales
were told of Carmichael's escapes from the revenue cutters.
Among the smugglers were also to be found kilted High-
landers, whose bagpipe music became a familiar sound around
Tórshavn.

In 1772 Rybergs Handel received a government licence to
carry on cod and herring fishing from Faroe, the catch being
salted and cured, and sent to Spain, the Mediterranean
countries, the Baltic, or elsewhere. Ryberg's men taught the
Faroese how to salt herring, which had previously been
thrown back into the sea after more had been caught than
could be eaten fresh. The Faroemen also learned to make
klipfish (split, salted and dried cod), but this skill died out in
the islands and had to be relearned in the 1830s and 1840s.

Rybergs Handel was an imaginative undertaking, which
deserved more fortune than it eventually achieved — though
a venture based on the profits from smuggling must necessarily
be highly speculative. Ryberg intended that Faroe should be
developed, both commercially and agriculturally, and he was
tireless in his attempts to introduce improvements; however
the period of twenty years when his company was in Faroe
hardly sufficed. In spite of this, the company did have a deep
influence on Faroese life. It gave the islanders their first
window on the world. They learned new crafts, and they
heard about the outside world. Captain Born, the commandant of the Tórshavn garrison, commented:

> All the Agricultural Development Society's encourage-
> ments, subsidies, inducements, homilies, pamphlets and
> other promptings towards an improvement and a broaden-
> ing of the economic life of the islanders will not produce as
> much progress in fifty years, as the transit depot and the
> foreigners in Tórshavn, by their example, have produced
> in ten.

NÓLSOYAR-PÁLL

During the latter years of Rybergs Handel, one of the most talented and remarkable Scandinavians of his age was growing to manhood. Only the outbreak of war between England and Denmark in 1807 prevented him, almost single-handed, from bringing about the entry of Faroe into world commerce more than half a century earlier than it actually took place. Almost every one of the necessary steps which the Faroese were painstakingly and individually to take during the first half of the nineteenth century had been foreseen by the most brilliantly imaginative of all Faroemen, Poul Poulsen Nolsøe.

The talented family from which Poul Nolsøe descended had long been settled in Eysturoy, but his father married and settled in Nólsoy, and there Poul was born, the fourth of seven children, in October 1766. His baptismal name was simply Poul Poulsen, but in addition to the patronymic he and his brothers took the name of Nolsøe, after their native island. In Faroe he is commonly referred to as Nólsoyar-Páll, i.e. Páll from Nólsoy.

Three of the six Nolsøe brothers, Poul, Johannes and Jacob, were forward in teaching themselves to read. It is said that they scraped their first letters in the ash of the hearth, and later scratched them on a roof-slate with the stem of a clay pipe. When they were older, the king's bailiff, Wenzel Hammershaimb, often lent them books and helped with their education; but they probably had little or no regular schooling. However, Nólsoyar-Páll and his brothers grew up during the great days of Rybergs Handel, when Tórshavn, only three miles away, was full of craftsmen and sailors, many of them foreigners; thus the opportunities for self-education by gifted adolescents were never better. Johannes taught himself medicine, partly from an old book he managed to obtain, and partly by questioning Rosenmeyer, one of the resident managers of Rybergs Handel. He remained on Nólsoy, a skilful farmer and noted boat-builder. Jacob Nolsøe was the most studious of the three brothers. He learned sufficient of

the art of navigation to become a competent instructor —
although he himself had never been to sea. His chief study,
however, was accountancy. Starting as a clerk, he made his
way in time to the highest commercial position in the islands—
that of resident manager of the Royal Monopoly.

Poul's ambition was to go to sea, and he too studied navigation, from one of the Monopoly accountants. Only when his
father, who opposed his plans, died in 1786 was the young
man able to procure a place on board a ship. For a year or
two he sailed with the ships of Rybergs Handel, and after the
closure of the depot with the vessels of the Royal Monopoly. In
1791 or 1792, he took to deep-sea voyaging, and for five or
six years, Faroe saw and heard no more of him.

Oral tradition has a few colourful tales to tell of Nólsoyar-
Páll's "lost years". It is said that he was in Marseilles and
Paris during 1793, and that he served in both the French and
the British navies and later sailed as a skipper for a large
American merchant firm. However, all that is known for
certain is that somewhere he picked up an acquaintance with
the poetry of Robert Burns, and that, as a ship's captain, he
visited America, the West Indies, England, France, Portugal,
Norway, Denmark and several other places. In March 1798
Poul was back in Copenhagen, and had probably already
revisited his native islands. In September 1798 he married
a Nólsoy girl, and settled in Copenhagen for a couple of
years, sailing in the service of the Royal Monopoly. He
returned to Faroe to live in 1800. A few months later his wife
died, but in 1801 he remarried. His second wife was the
daughter of a wealthy crown tenant on Borðoy, whose farm
was not far from the site of the flourishing modern fishing port
of Klaksvík. Poul took over a crown tenancy of 7 marks near
that of his father-in-law, and soon proved to be the ablest farmer in Faroe as well as the best seaman, and he was awarded
a silver medal by Det kongelige Landhusholdingsselskab, the
Danish Royal Society for the Advancement of Agriculture.

Nólsoyar-Páll's inventive mind now turned to improving
the technical resources of the Faroese peasant-fisherman. His

native island of Nólsoy had long been renowned for the skill
of its boat-builders, a skill that he and his brothers shared.
Poul now showed that a boat would hold its course better in
the strong currents round Faroe if the keel timber were longer
and rose from the water more sharply than was the traditional
practice. He also modified the almost square sail of tradition
into something with more of a lateen cut about it, that would
enable a boat to go closer to the wind. Both these features
were rapidly adopted throughout Faroe. An ingenious
improvement he made to the spinning-wheel, did not,
however, come into general use.

But Nólsoyar-Páll was concerned with more than the shape
of a sail or the angle of a keel. He had seen Rybergs Handel
at work, and later, as a ship's captain, he had seen something
of the world's commerce. He conceived the idea of preparing
his countrymen for free trade and an economy based on
commercial fishing: the Monopoly had to go.

Although monopolies are generally unpopular, this was
not true of the Royal Faroese Monopoly. It was not oppressive,
although it may at times have been inefficient. Indeed, in the
last quarter of the eighteenth century, it had been running at
a loss, and a royal commission of 1789–90 had recommended
that within a few years the trade should be freed, like the
Iceland trade at that time. Opposition, however, came from
the Faroese. The inhabitants of Eysturoy, on hearing rumours
that the fixed-price trading was to be abolished, rapidly
circulated a petition from village to village, and got it to
Captain Born, commandant of the fort and a member of the
commission, just before he left for Copenhagen. The ultimate
result was that the crown monopoly was retained, but that
certain reforms were introduced.

First, a new price list was drawn up — almost a hundred
years after the now out-dated and unsatisfactory tariff of the
1691 ordinance, by which the Faroe trade was still governed.
The new tariff was expressed in Danish currency — rigsdalers
and skillings — instead of the old gylden and skind. Goods not
listed in the export tariff might be sent to Denmark for sale by

private commissioners. Such goods were to be carried in the
Monopoly's vessels at fixed freight charges. Priests and
officials whose children or families were in Copenhagen were
even allowed to send them goods listed in the tariff provided
these were for private use and not in trade quantities.

The new tariff was based on the average prices of the goods
over the previous five years, plus a charge for handling and
freight. However, corn and other necessary provisions, and
articles needed for the productive work of the islands were set
at a specially low price. The payments for exports were
calculated on the basis of the previous five years' auction
records, again with a charge for handling and freight. The
tariff as it now came into force was as follows:

EXPORTS

	Rigsdalers	Skillings
1 bundle of 40 sheepskins	2	8
1 lispund (17½ lbs) of washed wool	1	1
1 pund (1.1 lbs) of washed wool	—	7
1 lispund of unwashed wool	—	88
1 pund of unwashed wool	—	5½
1 lispund of feathers	1	—
1 pund of feathers	—	6
1 lispund of smelted tallow	1	32
1 pund of smelted tallow	—	8
1 tun (26 gallons) of butter in cask	13	—
1 lispund of dried fish	—	48
1 pund of dried fish	—	3
1 barrel of salted cod	6	—
1 pund of coal-fish	—	1
1 pot (approx. 1 litre) of train-oil:		
shark or fish oil	—	8
whale or seal oil	—	7
1 alen (2 feet) of homespun cloth,		
2 alen in width	—	20
1 pair of stockings of top quality	—	25
of lowest quality	—	10

IMPORTS

	Rigsdalers	Skillings
Barley, per barrel (about 4 bushels)	3	—
Barley flour, per barrel	8	—
Oatmeal per barrel	7	48
Malt, per barrel	3	48
French spirits, per anker		
(about 120 litres)	14	24
per pot (about 1 litre)	—	36
Danish spirits, per anker	10	—
per pot	—	24
French wine, per anker	5	—
per pot	—	12
Salt, Spanish, in the cask, per barrel	3	32
French	2	8
Lüneburg	6	—
Ship's biscuit, best quality, per barrel	4	—
lower quality	2	48
Complete timbers for a boat	3	72
Hemp, per pund	—	8
per lispund	1	32
Iron bars, per lispund	—	72
Lead, per pund	—	6
Tobacco, better qualities, per pund	—	44
lesser qualities	—	36
Wool carders, per pair	—	48
Tarred fowling-line, per pund	—	8
Millstones, largest size, per pair	2	8
lesser size	1	84
Kingo's hymn-book, per copy	—	32
Danish Catechism, per copy	—	4

N.B. — The above lists are selective only. Comparison with the tariffs given on pages 36 and 39 is not easy, since the accounting units, as well as the usual units of weight and measure, were changed. Prices may be compared, however, by reckoning 4 skilling = 1 skind, or 1 rigsdaler = 1 gylden 4 skind. There are 96 skilling to the rigsdaler.

The continuance of the Monopoly, even in improved conditions, slowed the growth of the only economic resource available to the islanders that was capable of significant expansion — namely, the fishing industry. The Monopoly tariff put a premium on knitting — making it a more lucrative and more certain, as well as a physically safer way of earning a living than fishing. The lack of out-stations of the monopoly trade meant, as we have seen, that much fine fishing weather was wasted in trading journeys to Tórshavn. Every inhabitant of the islands had a running account with the Monopoly, and few were ever prosecuted for debt. This measure of social security inhibited any enterprise not along the old and tried lines.

Among other hindrances to the growth of fishing, an important one was the primitive nature of Faroese fishing equipment and curing methods. Another was the right of certain farmers to man their boats for the spring fishing from among their poorer neighbours, making the latter less mobile and less able to obtain full value from their own smaller boats.

Finally, there was the restriction on marriage. An ordinance of 21 May, 1777, forbade the priests in Faroe to marry any couple unable to show that they had the means of maintaining themselves. This was defined as follows: they must either possess $\frac{1}{2}$ - 1 mark of land or, after both man and woman had shown diligence, skill and faithfulness for five years in farm service, some craft by which the man could support the family, such as carpentry or blacksmithing — fishing or knitting did not count. This measure was designed to discourage any further increase in the indigent population of Tórshavn, who at midsummer used to tramp to every village in Faroe begging for wool. The government wanted to secure to farmers instead an adequate supply of labour, enabling extra corn to be grown, and the unprofitable corn imports to be kept at the lowest level possible; but the law prevented the growth of landless families in which the men fished while the women knitted. The measure, incidentally, was an intolerably oppressive one when extramarital sexual relations remained a criminal offence. It was not repealed until 1846.

The key to progress in Faroe lay in the training of the islanders in the management of larger vessels than the open boats from which they were accustomed to carry on their fishery. As soon as the Faroese were handling schooners in their fishing, there was no longer any moral reason why they should not conduct their own carrying trade. Niels Ryberg, indeed, had shown that sloop fishing was commercially possible, and he had not lacked successors, such as the king's bailiff, Wenzel Hammershaimb, although no one had made it a complete commercial success.

Soon after his return to Faroe in 1800, Nólsoyar-Páll, together with two wealthy Suðuroy farmers, his brother-in-law Per Larsen of Gerðar in Porkeri and the so-called Learned Peasant, Jacob Jacobsen of Toftir in Vágur, applied to the Danish exchequer for a loan of 1500—2000 rigsdaler to purchase a ship. But, although the application was supported by both the king's bailiff and the resident manager of the Royal Monopoly, it was turned down. Undiscouraged, Nólsoyar-Páll and his associates bought at a district sheriff's auction at Hvalbøur, Suðuroy, the wreckage of a ship that had drifted in to the islands. They removed the materials to Vágur, and there, with the help of Poul's brothers, they built a schooner — the first seagoing vessel to be constructed in Faroe, and the first Faroe-owned ship since the early middle ages. It was launched on 6 August 1804, and called *Royndin Fríða* — 'the beautiful trial'.

It was not a large vessel: its length was about 45 feet, its breadth 14 feet at the widest, and the deck stood a mere $7\frac{1}{2}$ feet above the water. But the schooner was seaworthy, and as the *sorenskriver*, Lauritz Olsen, remarked, if one remembered that it had been built from wreckage, without any of the normal equipment or tools of a shipyard and by persons almost

completely without shipbuilding experience, it might be
called a masterpiece.

Within two and a half weeks of its launching, Poul was out
on the fishing-banks with his schooner. In September, he did
very well off Svínoy. When the bad weather came, he laid up
the *Royndin Fríða* for the winter, and resumed fishing the
following April. However, 1805 was a poor fishing year, and
Poul resolved instead to make trading journeys.

During the summer of that year, Poul took his vessel on
voyages first to Bergen and later to Copenhagen. Each time
his cargo was Suðuroy coal which, since 1777, had been mined
experimentally; its carriage, consequently, was not an
infringement of the monopoly laws. In Copenhagen, Poul
wanted to pick up a return cargo to the Faroe Islands, but
this was refused by the Monopoly authorities there; instead,
he had to return carrying ship's stores and a few personal
purchases only. He arrived in Faroe early in September, and
laid up his ship for the winter near his farm on Borðoy.

If Nólsoyar-Páll had that summer been denied the chance
of bringing a cargo to the Faroe Islands, he nevertheless
managed to bring something of far greater importance:
smallpox vaccine. Four previous attempts to bring vaccine
material to Faroe had failed, the scabs losing their efficacy
during the long voyage. Poul had one of his crew vaccinated
in Copenhagen by a Danish doctor just before the schooner set
out on its return journey. When the scab of the first man had
matured, Poul used it to vaccinate the second man in his
crew, and so on. In this way fresh vaccine material came to the
islands for the first time. His brother Jacob helped to spread
the practice of vaccination through the islands.

During the winter of 1805-6, Poul bought up knitted
sweaters, train-oil and dried fish, all goods which could be
exported on private account.[1] His intention was to take
a cargo to Copenhagen, but his right to do this was contested

---

[1] Train-oil and dried fish were permitted for private export by a royal resolution
of 22 May, 1805.

by the resident manager of the Royal Monopoly, Mads Mørch, whose view was that export of the goods was permissible only in the Monopoly's ships. However, in spite of Mørch's protest and the warning of the *sorenskriver,* he took the cargo, to Denmark, arriving in Copenhagen on 7 June.

Mørch wrote to the Monopoly directorate in Copenhagen by the first ship, claiming that Poul had infringed the royal privilege. The Danish exchequer, which handled Faroese administrative matters, upheld Mørch's protest, and while permission was given to Poul to dispose of the cargo he had brought on this occasion, he was forbidden to make further trading voyages. A few days later, however, this ruling was relaxed "until further notice" in the case of Faroe coal and dried fish.

Despite the prohibition on taking goods to Faroe, Poul took on a cargo of provisions with the intention, as he claimed, of disposing of them in one of the Norwegian ports on the way home. Instead, he later maintained, he sold them to a Swedish brig he had encountered in the Kattegat. He thereafter returned to Faroe, reaching the islands by the end of July, and bringing with him only a few articles for the personal use of Jacob Jacobsen of Toftir and himself.

Soon after his return, Nólsoyar-Páll found himself summoned before the Tórshavn court by the district sheriff, Joen Christiansen Øre. There were three charges. He was accused of not calling at Tórshavn to hand in the papers certifying his ship to be free from infection, of disposing of goods in a place other than a lawful port (contrary to a little-known law of 1797) and, most serious of all, of importing goods unlawfully into Faroe. He was convicted on the first two charges and fined, but cleared of smuggling. Poul seems to have taken this case as a demonstration that the officials in Tórshavn had become his open enemies.

It is understandable that the Tórshavn officials should have come to dislike Nólsoyar-Páll. First, there was the usual fear that mediocrity has of genius. Emilius Løbner, the commandant, and others like him, accustomed to dealing with a submissive and respectful peasantry, must have been disconcerted when faced with the great talents and natural powers of leadership of Poul, whose achievements had already brought him favourable notice in the highest government circles in Copenhagen. Secondly, the Tórshavn officials made a practice of supplementing their incomes by private, and illicit, trade. Probably only the commandant, Løbner, had made a serious business of it, but the introduction of free trade would present a certain financial threat to all of them, and make likely the eventual rise of a moneyed merchant class that would tend to overshadow them socially.

The high-spirited Poul decided to retaliate for what he believed to be the mischievous court action that had been brought against him. He laid a summons against his prosecutor, Joen Christiansen Øre, the Tórshavn district sheriff, charging him with smuggling on a considerable scale. It seems that Christiansen and the other Tórshavn officials were receiving supplies of goods from their Danish friends via the Monopoly's vessels, and sending in return, knitted sweaters (not listed in the 1790 tariff) for sale in Denmark. Poul's witnesses brought much inconvenient evidence to light, but no existing documents on the case bear a later date than 4 June, 1806, and Poul may well have let the case drop after showing his antagonists that vindictiveness by way of lawsuit was a double-edged weapon.

Poul had another way of punishing his antagonists, in which they could hardly retaliate in kind. He was a highly talented poet. During the winter of 1806-7, he composed a satirical ballad about the officials of Tórshavn, presenting them in the guise of birds of prey, while he himself, as the *tjaldur* (oystercatcher), warned the smaller birds of their evil intentions. This was not Nólsoyar-Páll's first satirical ballad — his best-known effort in the genre hitherto having been *Jákup á Møn*, about the misfortunes of an unlucky wooer, and the *Fruntatáttur*, satirising the current women's fashion for wearing the hair in a fringe. But the *Fuglakvæði* (Ballad of the Birds) is undoubtedly his masterpiece.

Both for the quality of its versification, and for the way in which the birds remain birds, yet unmistakably portray their human counterparts, *Fuglakvæði* is an extraordinarily skilful piece of writing. It is a long work — there are 229 stanzas of four lines each, besides the chorus sung after each stanza — but the ballad was soon being performed throughout the country, and there was a brisk trade in manuscript copies, which fetched nearly a rigsdaler each.

At the same time as this psychological weapon was having its effect, Poul waged a campaign on constitutional lines. During the summer of 1806, petitions were organised on Suðuroy and in the Northern Islands, requesting that the trade be freed, at first for an experimental period of three years. These petitions, which were presented at the annual session of the Løgting at the end of July, met opposition from every district sheriff, and except those from Suðuroy, by all the jurymen present, who maintained that there was no desire in the country for anything other than the traditional Monopoly trade. Since there was no possibility of having an official request for free trade forwarded to Copenhagen with the blessing of the Løgting, Poul called a public meeting of all the islanders on 25 August, 1806. Here it was agreed that a deputation of five, including Nólsoyar-Páll and Jacob Jacobsen of Toftir, should go to Denmark to petition the government in person.

The problem now arose how to finance the deputation. Few of the islanders had ready money, although many were prosperous enough in goods. It was finally agreed to make up a consignment of woollen sweaters, and to seek permission from the Tórshavn authorities for their export on the *Royndin Fríða,* on which the deputation was to sail. This was refused, a decision in keeping with law and precedent. The petitioners next asked that their sweaters should be sent to Copenhagen by Monopoly ship, as the law permitted, but that because of the urgency of the need to provide funds in Copenhagen for the expenses of the deputation, they should be despatched by the first possible ship. This request was also refused, despite a series of safeguards and compromises proposed by the petitioners. It was clear that the officials in Faroe, particularly Løbner the commandant, who had lately been appointed acting *amtmand* (chief civil officer), were determined to delay and obstruct the deputation as far as lay in their power. So the 1806 sailing season passed by, and it was June 1807 before the *Royndin Fríða* was able to sail for Copenhagen, Even then, the journey had to be financed partly by the illegal sale of 2,600 sweaters and some other Faroese goods to a Norwegian merchant.

The Faroese deputation was well received in the Danish capital, and its requests won the sympathetic attention of various ministers of state, and of Crown Prince Frederik (regent for his father, Christian VII, who for many years had been insane). Far-reaching reforms in the administration and trade of the Faroe Islands seemed imminent; but negotiations were brought to an abrupt halt by the sudden outbreak of war between Denmark and England. Hostilities began at the end of July 1807, and Nólsoyar-Páll and his friends were present during the terrible British bombardment of Copenhagen (2—5 September) and the subsequent capitulation of the city and surrender of the Danish fleet to the British. The war naturally prevented the government from considering petitions of a domestic character from Faroe or anywhere else; moreover, Denmark's age of neutral prosperity was now at an end. The last year of Nólsoyar-Páll's life was spent grappling with problems very different from those on which he had hitherto been engaged.

WAR AND HUNGER

After removing the Danish fleet, the British withdrew their land forces from the Danish mainland, but the British Navy blockaded the coasts of Denmark and Norway for six years. For the Faroe Islands, heavily dependent on imported grain, the blockade brought an immediate threat of starvation. The annual consumption of barley in Faroe was about 10,000

barrels (about 670 tons). Before the war, a fifth of this had
been grown in the islands, and the balance of 8,000 barrels
(545 tons) had been brought in by the Monopoly. If the grain
import fell below 5,000 barrels (335 tons), distress would be
caused. Nobody in Copenhagen saw the implications more
clearly than did Nólsoyar-Páll. He secured 250 barrels of
barley from the Monopoly directorate, and by representing
the plight of the Faroe Islands to the British naval authorities,
he obtained a pass from Admiral Gambier to take his cargo
unmolested to Faroe. Early in October he unloaded the grain
in Suðuroy, where need was already felt, the inhabitants
subsequently paying the Monopoly station in Tórshavn in
Faroese goods. It was Poul's ship which brought to Faroe the
first news of the bombardment and capitulation of Copenhagen. No more corn was to come to Faroe until 5 July, 1808,
and before that time, the islands were to receive other
visitors.

The first was the *Clio,* a British naval brig based on Leith,
commanded by Captain Thomas Folliot Baugh. The *Clio*
arrived in Faroese waters on 30 April, 1808, and cruised round
the islands for two weeks in search of Danish merchantmen on
their way home from the East or West Indies. Such ships
might make for Faroe in the hope of meeting a Danish naval
convoy for the risky passage through the North Sea; and
might even be unaware of the outbreak of war between
Denmark and Britain. Captain Baugh was careful to conceal
the identity of the *Clio,* but when the brig was off Borðoy,
Nólsoyar-Páll, dressed as a peasant, visited the ship, and
correctly identified it as a British naval vessel. When asked by
Baugh about the strength of the Tórshavn garrison, Poul said
that it was 300 men — nine times its true strength. (It is
probable, however, that Baugh was not deceived.) On his
return, Poul immediately sent a message to Løbner, the
commandant, warning him to put the fort at Tórshavn into
readiness, as an attack by the *Clio* was imminent.

Late in the evening of Sunday, 15 May, the *Clio* appeared
off Tórshavn. A landing party of about fifty men was sent

ashore, and an officer went ahead to demand the surrender of the fort. Løbner immediately complied, without the smallest show of resistance, although he had a strong redoubt with nineteen cannon, eight of them 18-pounders, and a good supply of powder, shot and small-arms. By the capitulation, Løbner agreed to surrender the fort and all warlike stores; the garrison were to march out as prisoners-of-war, although they were to be released on their parole not to serve against Britain for the term of one year. Government property was to be at the disposal of the captors, but all private property in Tórshavn was to be respected.

The *Clio* stayed off Tórshavn for two days. The arms, ammunition and powder were removed from the fort, the guns were spiked and their trunnions broken off, and the powder magazine was blown up. On the evening of Tuesday 17 May, the *Clio* weighed anchor and returned to Leith, leaving Tórshavn and the Faroe Islands stripped of all fortifications, but still in the charge of the Danish officials. Nólsoyar-Páll later immortalised Løbner's cowardice and incompetence in yet another satirical ballad, the *Gorplandskvæði*.

A fortnight later, another warship arrived in Faroe, the 20-gun privateer *Salamine*, commanded by Thomas Gilpin, but owned and fitted out by one Baron Charles von Hompesch. Hompesch, black sheep of an illustrious family, had had a colourful career in many countries. He was born about 1760, the son of one of the small German sovereigns, who had also held high positions in the court of Bavaria. His uncle was the last Grand Master of the Knights of St. John, who had surrendered Malta to Napoleon in 1798. Earlier in his life Hompesch himself had been influential as a Hungarian noble and had served in the Austrian Imperial Army until 1792 when he became involved in political intrigues and had to flee the country. As a major in the Prussian army, he served with distinction against the French, and in 1796 he fought through the fever-ridden San Domingo campaign with the British army. By 1808 he held the rank of lieutenant-general, but had not seen active service for some years. He now fitted out the *Salamine* and secured British letters of marque. Like all privateering, this was doubtless a speculation.

The *Salamine* left England in April or May, sailing first into the Bay of Biscay, and afterwards round the west of Ireland and north of Scotland, where Hompesch hoped to fall in with returning Danish Indiamen. At the end of May, finding himself in northern waters, Hompesch recollected that there was a small fort in Tórshavn. Passing Vágar island, he picked up two Faroese fishermen, who piloted him into the town early in the morning of Tuesday, 1 June, only to find the fort already disarmed.

In Tórshavn, he tried to secure a pilot for the coast of Norway. A sixty-three year-old retired skipper, Peter Hansen, who had sailed both for Rybergs Handel and the Monopoly, and knew the Norwegian coast, lived in Tórshavn, but was unwilling to go with the *Salamine*. Hompesch had to threaten bombardment of the town before he could be found and persuaded.

When Hansen had been secured, Hompesch sailed north. In the Northern Islands, however, he learned that there were Danish government funds in Tórshavn, and that the extensive trading establishment there was a Danish crown undertaking. (His informant was either the priest of the Northern Islands, or Peter Hansen himself.) Hompesch thereupon turned the *Salamine* southwards again, anchored off Tórshavn on the evening of Sunday, 6 June, and at once sent landing-parties ashore to occupy the Monopoly warehouses and the houses of all the officials, especially Løbner. Hompesch took possession of all the public money, including the funds of the church and the school, and the goods in the Monopoly warehouses. As it was represented to him that the islanders were short of grain, he allowed $17\frac{1}{2}$ barrels of barley remaining in the warehouse to be distributed to the poor and sick without charge. On 8 June, the *Salamine* took part of the capture to Lerwick, while an armed party was left to guard the remainder. Hompesch now made his way to London, but sent the *Salamine* back to

Tórshavn to collect the remaining stores. On 27 June, these were removed from the Monopoly warehouses, and a few days later were lodged with the money and other goods in Lerwick custom house. Hompesch now applied to the Admiralty Court to have these goods condemned to him as lawful prize of war.

While Hompesch was in London, the *Salamine* sailed to Reykjavík, and stayed there from 23 July to 8 August. No fortifications were found but, as at Tórshavn, all money and goods that could conceivably be called Danish government property were carefully removed. Peter Hansen had sailed with the *Salamine* to Iceland, but he was dropped off in Faroe as the privateer passed on its way to London, which was reached about mid-September.

Towards the end of July, Hompesch found himself in ill odour with naval officers and others. Rumours of his misdeeds and harshness in the Faroe Islands had begun to circulate. These rumours originated in a report sent by Løbner to the British Admiralty. The *Clio*, under Captain Baugh, had returned to Tórshavn on 10 July 1808, with the sole object of obtaining a true account of Hompesch's activities. The Admiralty probably initiated this voyage considering itself entitled under the capitulation to the prizes claimed by Hompesch. Løbner, however, who had been contemptuously treated by Hompesch, saw in this an opportunity of making trouble for the baron. As well as exaggerating some petty thefts by some of the *Salamine's* crew, Løbner accused Hompesch personally of robbing him of various articles which he had in fact sold to him.

Hompesch had, indeed, done nothing illegal in Tórshavn. Løbner and the other officials had concealed the existence of Danish government money and property from Captain Baugh at the time of the capitulation. Hompesch had found this public money and property and removed it, and so doing he had acted properly. He had respected private property, returning a stock of sweaters found in the Monopoly warehouses belonging to Nólsoyar-Páll and awaiting shipment in a Monopoly vessel, as soon as Jacob Nolsøe, Poul's brother, represented to him that it was not government property. Hompesch even refrained from taking the *Royndin Friða* which, as an enemy ship, he was entitled to seize. Indeed, he wrote Poul a letter of recommendation to assist him with the British naval authorities in securing further grain cargoes for the islands. The baron was, however, to reap no benefit from his seizures, because he claimed them as prize. Instead he should have claimed a share of the goods as salvage. The prize laws allowed privateers (or for that matter, naval vessels) to seize enemy ships, or enemy property in fortified places on land. Iceland was totally unfortified, so he was unable to make out any case for prize there; and the money he had taken was returned. As for his Tórshavn seizures, the naval authorities interposed a claim under the third article of the capitulation to the *Clio*. By this, all Danish government property became property of the British government; it was not, therefore, lawful prize for Baron Hompesch. Had the baron claimed as salvor, he could have been awarded a share for his recovery of property wrongfully concealed under the capitulation. In bidding for the whole, he failed to secure the part. The case was without precedent, and Hompesch appealed. The case dragged on until 1811, when the original decision — that public property among the seizures belonged to the British crown, and private property (Tórshavn was unfortified at the time of the *Salamine's* visit) must be returned to its owners — was upheld. After the appeal, the money and the value of the goods were claimed as private property — under the fiction that the Monopoly was run by the King of Denmark not as king, but in a private capacity. The British crown did not contest this claim, and the value of what Hompesch had removed, less legal expenses, was returned to Tórshavn in 1812 and 1815.

By a strange chance, Nólsoyar-Páll was present in London at the prize court hearing, and some of his evidence was actually in the baron's favour, although their meetings in Faroe had been anything but cordial. This chance was the outcome of Poul's attempt, soon after the final departure of the *Salamine,* to secure grain supplies for his fellow-countrymen.

Løbner had every reason to hate Nólsoyar-Páll, but the circumstances in Faroe were such that he was compelled to seek the help from the only man in the islands with a seagoing vessel. Poul left Faroe on 29 June with a cargo of woollen sweaters, and set out in search of the British commander in the Skagerak, to know where he might proceed. On 8 July, off the Skaw, he fell in with H.M.S. *Fury,* which seized the *Royndin Friða* as prize, and took it in to Gothenburg, where Poul and his crew were lodged in an English prison ship. Poul's ship was damaged beyond repair as it was being brought into harbour.

Poul secured an interview with Admirals Keats and Bertie and represented to them the distress that already existed in the Faroe Islands, which he was able to substantiate from the letters Løbner and other officials had given him. They sent him at the earliest opportunity to London, where he and his crew were released, and where the Privy Council gave him a fresh ship, the *North Star,* in exchange for the one he had lost.

It was now November, and the prize court case over the Tórshavn seizures was in progress. Hearing that Poul was in London, Hompesch had him, much against his will, summoned as a witness. Poul was able to authenticate the signatures of Løbner and others, and he bore witness to the tithe laws in force in Faroe. Most important, he confirmed the baron's release of his private property on the application of his brother Jacob. The baron had had difficulty proving that what he had seized was indeed public and not private property, and this instance of his having refrained from removing private property was useful to him.

The last time Nólsoyar-Páll testified in court was on 17 November, 1808, when he was already on board the *North Star,* at anchor in Milwall Dock, and ready to sail to Faroe with the first of what was intended to be a series of grain cargoes. He never arrived in Faroe. During late November and the whole of December 1808 there were violent storms off the east coast of Britain. The *North Star* doubtless foundered in the heavy seas, and no trace of it was ever found.

Poul Nolsøe's memory has always been held in high honour by his countrymen. He failed in his efforts to secure the abolition of the Monopoly, but his achievements were nonetheless remarkable. He was one of the most talented poets Faroe has ever known, and he brought to Faroe many new ideas of economic importance. In particular, by building the *Royndin Friða* and using it to train Faroemen as deep-sea sailors, he blazed a trail that many were to follow in the next half-century until the deep-sea fishery had become the source of Faroese prosperity; and Klaksvík, where he made his home and hauled up his schooner for the winter, has become one of the many thriving fishing ports of the islands. Finally, his patriotism, both for his native islands and for the whole Danish state, was an example to all.

However, his most enduring achievement in Faroe was to teach his countrymen to value men for their personal qualities, rather than honouring them merely because they were government officials or had come from Copenhagen. He achieved this partly through his poetry and partly by the sheer scale of his personal achievements. Of course, he aroused the envy and hatred in the Tórshavn officials at the same time. Løbner, especially in reports to Copenhagen, was constantly accusing him of seditious activities, and in a letter of April 1809 expressed his great satisfaction at the continued absence of Poul from the islands. This manifest hatred has led many Faroemen, from that time to this, to conclude that Løbner was somehow instrumental in compassing Poul's death. It has been suggested that the *Odin*, a Norwegian privateer, commissioned by the Copenhagen directorate of the Faroese Monopoly, lay in wait for the *North Star*'s arrival south of Faroe, and sank it with all hands, being sunk itself in the process. Although this theory does not stand up to scrutiny, its appearance at the time indicates how deep was the personal antagonism between Nólsoyar-Páll and Løbner, just as its persistence in modern times indicates the ardent and reverent affection in which most Faroemen still cherish the memory of their great compatriot.

The years 1808–10 were a period of distress in Faroe, due to the continuance of the blockade, and the death of Nólsoyar-Páll. In 1808, only 1,570 barrels of grain arrived in Tórshavn. In 1809, there were 2,720 barrels, and in 1810, 3,550 barrels. The Faroese barley harvest of 1808 was a failure. Løbner introduced a rationing system, but it was badly conceived in some of its details, and failed to encourage those with land to extend their cultivation of barley. In the summer of 1808 several parts of the islands were in a state of near-insurrection. On 5 August the men of Skúvoy believed they had been unjustly treated when they were claiming their barley ration from the Monopoly warehouse at Tórshavn; they bound and insulted both the resident manager of the Monopoly, Mads Mørch, and the commandant Løbner, and threatened that if their demands were not met, they would be taken back to Skúvoy, lodged in a byre, and fed on bread and water.

As a result of Hompesch's actions in Faroe, which roused great indignation in England, Sir Joseph Banks and others secured an Order in Council excluding the Faroe Islands, Iceland, and Greenland from hostile action. This Order, published on 7 February, 1810, also gave inhabitants of the Danish north Atlantic dependencies neutral status when visiting British territory, and ordered that vessels plying between the dependencies and Leith or London should not be liable to seizure as prize. The order gave verbal encouragement to navigation to Faroe, but as no explicit provision was made for the supply of the islands, want was still felt there that year.

In July 1810, a second schooner was built in Faroe. The largest open boat in Suðuroy (where the islanders kept specially large craft for trading journeys to Tórshavn) was decked in, and converted for deep-sea sailing by a group of Nólsoy and Suðuroy men. The schooner had a displacement of 14 tons, and a length of some 33 feet: it was thus much

smaller than the *Royndin Friða*. On most of its voyages it was
skippered by Peter Hansen, and it was named *Nødvendighed* —
necessity. Besides local trips, it made two journeys to Leith in
search of supplies. The first was a complete failure, since the
high duty on the Faroese goods carried in the ship made them
unsaleable. The second journey, made under the direction of
Jacob Jacobsen of Toftir, at least succeeded in bringing the
distress of Faroe to the notice of the firm in Leith which had
managed the Danish vice-consulate until its closure at the
outbreak of war. This firm contacted the Admiralty, and the
gun brig *Forward* was sent to Faroe in July 1811. On its return
the commander, Captain Bankes, made a detailed report on
the provisioning situation in the islands. As a result, two ships
were allowed to carry corn and other articles from Denmark
to Faroe, provided they called at Leith each year to have
their licences renewed.

For the rest of the war, Faroe was reasonably well supplied,
although the islands were drained of all currency; even the
gold and silver ornaments on the traditional bridal dresses were
sold to secure grain during these hard years. The laws against
smuggling were put in abeyance during the war, and this
too led to windows being opened on the world. The minister
of Suðuroy, Johan Henrik Schrøter, established a trading
connection with a Liverpool merchant house, and kept his
island well supplied for some years. Schrøter was a channel
through which many new ideas flowed into Faroe. He was
one of the first to encourage the cultivation of the potato,
which grows well in Faroese soils and never fails to produce
a crop — in marked contrast to Faroese barley, which fails
almost completely one year in every three or four. In 1811,
only two of the islands grew potatoes; but within a generation
their culture had become general, largely through Schrøter's
propaganda.

Thus in the period from the founding of Rybergs Handel to
the seven years' war between Denmark and England, the
people of Faroe became ever more aware of the outside world,
and the ancient isolation of the islands had almost broken

down. The career of Nólsoyar-Páll showed the islanders that change for the better did not need to wait for a new royal ordinance or an enlightened governor from Copenhagen, but that initiative could come from within the islands themselves. The physical and social change in Faroe during the half-century which ended in 1814 was not perhaps impressive; but the psychological atmosphere had become very different. However, a final period of stagnation was yet to intervene before the great changes which Faroe experienced in the nineteenth century.

CHAPTER IV

ABOLITION OF THE MONOPOLY

HARD TIMES FOR DENMARK

The Danish kingdom paid dearly for its alliance with Napoleonic France. The financial needs of the war led to the printing of great numbers of banknotes and wild inflation, and finally to the state's bankruptcy in 1812–13. Towards the end of 1812, paper money was passing for only 6 or 7 per cent its face value, and speculation in foreign exchange was heavy and constant.

At the same time, the fortunes of war were turning against Napoleon. The winter of financial crisis in Denmark concided with Napoleon's disastrous retreat from Moscow. On 16–19 October, 1813, the decisive Battle of the Nations was fought near Leipzig, after which the Danish army in Germany separated itself from the French and retreated towards Jutland, pursued by an army of Prussians, Swedes, and Russians. The Danish king, Frederik VI, although fond of military parades and manoeuvres, was no general, and faced with overwhelming odds was forced to the conference table. The Treaty of Kiel, signed on 14 January, 1814, ended the war for Denmark.

By its terms, Norway was surrendered to the Swedes, and Heligoland to England. The Swedes renounced in favour of the Danish monarchy all rights to Swedish Pomerania and the island of Rügen, territories which, a few months later, Denmark exchanged with Prussia for the small duchy of Lauenburg, adjacent to Holstein. Denmark retained the ancient tributary lands of the Norwegian crown, the Faroe Islands, Iceland and Greenland. She also undertook to enter the war against France, but a few months later Napoleon was in Elba, and the war had ended.

The period from 1814 to 1830 was economically the hardest in Denmark's modern history. The inflation took a quarter of a century to control, Danish paper money reaching parity only in 1838, and not becoming officially convertible until several years later still. The post-war slump adversely affected trade throughout Europe, and Danish agriculture suffered through a heavy drop in prices. Denmark had also the burden of a vast external national debt, entered into by Denmark on behalf of the Danish-Norwegian kingdom as a whole. By the Treaty of Kiel, this debt was supposed to be divided according to the populations and resources of Denmark and Norway respectively, and it would have been reasonable for Norway to assume about a third of the obligation; but Norway had also suffered economically from the war. Besides, the Swedish crown had been able to assert authority over Norway only by acceding to the most free constitution in Europe, leaving Norway as an independent country which only shared a king with Sweden; the Norwegians refused to recognise the Treaty of Kiel, to which they had not been a party. By a compromise agreed in 1819, the Norwegians agreed to pay only one-tenth of the debt, over a period of ten years.

With the kingdom in this condition, there was little demand in Faroe for free trade. A royal commission set up in 1816 to report on Icelandic and Faroese commerce was informed the following year, when taking evidence from Faroe, that "the Faroe Islands are not accustomed to, and the inhabitants would not be benefited by, a freed trade." The signatories on this occasion included not only the Tórshavn officials like Løbner, who would have been expected, due to timidity and personal interest, to resist change, but also the district sheriffs, all Faroemen in touch with opinion throughout the country, and even pastor Schrøter, who was later one of the staunchest advocates of opening Faroese commerce to the world.

In the depression period of 1814 to 1830, only one attempt was made to fish commercially off Faroe from a decked vessel. This was in 1824, when a wealthy Eysturoy man fished from a small sloop, but the attempt was a financial failure. Only when conditions were once again favourable to such attempts did Faroese opinion swing once again in favour of free trade. By that time, political as well as economic developments were working strongly in its favour.

THE RISE OF THE FAROESE FISHERY

The Faroese open-boat fishery began to have importance in the 1830s and 1840s. Subsistence open-boat fishing ("rowing out" as the picturesque Faroese phrase puts it) had been practised from the first settlement of the islands, and in good years some fish had been exported. But the old proverb *Seyða ull er Føroya gull* (sheep's wool is Faroe gold) — almost incomprehensible to the modern Faroeman — is evidence of how subordinate was the part played by the fishery in the earlier commerce of the islands.

The new development may be illustrated by a few figures. In the eighty-year period 1709 to 1788, only 1748–50 could be called good export years for fish. Only in those years, and in 1757, 1766 and 1788, did more than 2,000 *vog* of fish (that is, more than about 36 tons) leave the country. Out of the forty years 1789 to 1828, there were eleven years when more than 2,000 *vog* left the country.[1] From 1829, there was only one year (1839) in which less than 2,000 *vog* were exported, and on four occasions in the 1830s the annual export rose above 4,000 *vog*. From the 1840s onwards, 4,000 *vog* made a bad year, and 20,000 *vog* a good year. The change in the percentage distribution of exports was equally impressive, as the following table shows.

There were two main causes for the rise of the open-boat fishery at this period. One was that from shortly before 1800 the population of the islands, after centuries of stagnation or very slow rise, began to expand rapidly, which it has continued

---

[1] During the war years 1808 to 1813 inclusive, there was no export, and the fish were consumed in the islands to save corn. Strictly speaking, therefore, these six years should be left out of account.

Percentage of Total Exports

Period	Raw Wool	Woollen goods	Tallow and Sheepskins	Fish	Other sea produce	Butter and feathers
1712—21	14.8[1]	67.2	6.4	5.2	3.7	2.7
1767—76	0.1	92.5	4.3	1.2	0.5	1.4
1792—1801	—	78.6	11.1	5.8	3.9	0.6
1841—50	—	55.1[2]	4.2	19.3	19.7	1.7

to do into modern times. Until the late eighteenth century, the population of Faroe had never exceeded 5,000, but in the mid-1830s it was past 7,000, and by 1850 it was over 8,000, a growth rate that has been well maintained since that time.[3] The other cause was the enlightened administration in this period by both the government officials and the Monopoly directors.

The population rise in itself compelled an increasing number of Faroemen with only a small amount of land, or with no land at all, to turn to the sea for a living. At the same time, the land was more intensively cultivated, especially around Tórshavn. Originally a mere fortified trading post with a tiny population of officials, soldiers, warehouse labourers and paupers, Tórshavn began in the 1830s to develop into a fishing port, and the broad, shallow valley behind the harbour was rented out in small plots by the two crown tenants who held the leases. In 1836 Pastor Schrøter wrote to Sir Walter Calverley Trevelyan, who had visited the islands fifteen years before:

---

[1] The Faroese never liked exporting raw wool, as they thereby lost the opportunity of winter earnings; but at this period a proportion of raw wool had to be tendered with knitted goods brought for sale to the Monopoly.

[2] Consisting of 48.5 per cent sweaters and 6.6 per cent stockings. The earlier figures refer almost exclusively to stockings.

[3] Population rose as follows: 1769, 4,773; 1801, 5,265; 1834, 6,928; 1840, 7,314; 1845, 7,781; 1850, 8,137; 1855, 8,651. In 1911 it was about 18,000 and in 1970 well over 38,000.

If you could see the territory around Thorshavn, I am convinced you would find upwards of 100 acres English now better cultivated than the former infield of the King's Farm; and for all that the sheep are more numerous and fatter.

By 1847, he remarks on the change in the physical appearance of the Tórshavn area:

The prospect of the enclosures around Thorshavn is now really charming if compared with its wild aspect formerly. I hope it will increase hastily. I suppose it is most of the stones cleared away, and the land well drained.

By 1851, 200 acres were under cultivation, and the question of the purchase of this land was beginning to be argued out. The plots were being tilled largely by open-boat fishermen who thus provided their families with potatoes and milk, both to supplement their fishery earnings and as a standby in bad fishing years. Potato cultivation increased dramatically between 1811 and 1830. In the former year only 120 barrels of potatoes had been grown throughout the islands, 100 barrels on Suðuroy and twenty on Streymoy. By 1830, the crop was nearly 10,000 barrels.

The enlarged population did not result in unemployment or under-employment in the islands. On the contrary, the population was rising partly because of the more promising economic circumstances. By 1844, farm wages had increased to two and a half times what they had been early in the century, but even so farm servants could hardly be found. Pastor Schrøter, even at the beginning of the 1830s, was looking forward to a prosperous future for Faroe with free trade and a population of 20,000. The greater opportunities in fishing and the spread of cultivation were at once causes and effects of the population rise. Potatoes are a far more certain crop than barley, and a poor man with a tiny patch of land is more likely to raise a large family growing potatoes than growing grain. But the chief element in population growth in Faroe, as in the rest of western Europe, was the improvement in medical care (especially midwifery techniques), which probably began to be felt in Faroe from about 1780, coming just at the time when the economy was able to absorb a greater population.

The second main reason why the open-boat fishery rose to importance was the improved quality of both governmental and commercial administration. The improvement in government was probably due less to institutional reforms than to the personalities of a series of able provincial governors who followed Løbner. The institutional reforms were considerable, however. After the Treaty of Kiel there was an obvious need to remodel the administration according to Danish rather than Norwegian practice. The thousand-year-old Løgting, which had fulfilled some of the functions of a parliament, as well as being a court of appeal, was abolished in 1816. Also abolished was the office of lawman, the highest judicial authority in the islands henceforth being the *sorenskriver* (see page 24). Appeal cases now had to be referred to the higher courts in Denmark.

There have subsequently been many regrets over the passing of the ancient Løgting. At the time there were few or none, for it had long been a mere shadow of its former self. For half a century very few appeals had been brought before the Løgting; and its function in giving testimonials to government officials had, with the growth of navigation and the consequent increase in opportunities of sending news or petitions to Copenhagen, become far less necessary than formerly. Likewise, the consideration of the supply position no longer needed to be a ceremonial annual affair. For several decades before 1816, there had been proposals for the abolition of the court. The Icelandic Althing had been abolished in 1798, the Norwegian *Lagtings* in 1798, and the Bornholm *landsting* in 1813, so that by the end of the Napoleonic Wars, the Faroese Løgting was the only such institution left in Denmark and Norway.

But if Faroe lost a higher judicial officer, a resident executive officer, the *amtmand* or provincial governor, was gained. An *amtmand* is the highest civil authority in a province. His responsibilities at this period were to decide the applicability of laws within his province, supervise all the officials under him, control the church estates when there were any, and in general represent the power of central government in the province. Before about 1770 the function of *amtmand* of Faroe had been carried out by various government officials in Denmark as a minor adjunct to their normal duties. From about 1770 the lawman carried out these duties, but in 1806, Løbner was constituted temporarily into the position in association with the king's bailiff, Wenzel Hammershaimb. Wartime experience demonstrated the value of a resident *amtmand,* and in 1821 the office was made permanent. By a royal proclamation of 6 June, 1821, it was ordained that the *amtmand* should be assisted by an advisory committee of the district sheriffs and leading inhabitants in considering the applicability of Danish laws to Faroe.

Løbner was retained in his position when the office of *amtmand* of Faroe was made permanent. His limitations may not have been apparent to those in the capital, and he probably had protectors in high places. Faroe gained little from his governorship, but his four immediate successors were all men of ability who served the islands well, and whose careers will be described in more detail below. They had a number of things in common. All were career civil servants, whose years in Faroe served as a springboard to higher things elsewhere in the kingdom. They were all deeply conscious of the need for economic development in Faroe, especially on the sea. And all had their roots essentially in Denmark rather than in Faroe.

This last was a new development. In previous centuries, priests and civil servants taking up positions in Faroe would usually stay there for a lifetime, marrying locally if they had arrived single. (Løbner married the daughter of a Tórshavn cooper.) Their children would sometimes follow in their fathers' footsteps, or they might marry into the more prosperous farming families, but in either case they would become assimilated with the Faroese population. Now, however, the tendency developed for officials to come to Faroe for a term of years only. This certainly resulted in a more enlightened, broad-minded, detached and impartial official class, but it also meant that, unless they were men of exceptional social gifts, the officials tended to be more remote from the population at large. Late in the nineteenth century there even developed a foolish snobbery amongst certain Danish residents in Tórshavn, and a native Faroeman appointed to the position of *amtmand* was cold-shouldered socially during his period of office from 1897 to 1911, in spite of his fine academic record and brilliant legal gifts.

But if the administration was thus becoming danified, the local control of the Monopoly passed into the hands of a Faroeman, Nólsoyar-Pall's youngest brother Jacob Nolsøe (1775–1869). He had first entered the service of the Monopoly in 1795, and had become its chief accountant in 1808. When Mads Mørch died in the autumn of 1831, Jacob Nolsøe was appointed his successor, despite misgivings in official circles in Copenhagen at the appointment to such a position of a man with local connections.

Jacob Nolsøe's commercial policy was the opposite of his predecessor's. Mørch had lived through an age of financial crisis and disaster, and was ever concerned to avoid loss, even when this meant under-ordering to the inconvenience of the population of Faroe. Jacob Nolsøe, on the other hand, never feared to spend money when he had a reasonable confidence of a corresponding profit. Although he had to act within general instructions that enjoined caution, he had within three years converted a loss into a handsome annual profit for the Danish exchequer. It is true that the course of trade ran in his favour during his twenty years as resident manager of the Monopoly, but, unlike his predecessor, he seized the opportunities as they arose.

One of these opportunities arose through the work of a commission which sat in the winter of 1835–6 with the object of bettering the Monopoly and preparing the inhabitants for free trade. As a result of this commission's findings, Jacob Nolsøe was given the task of opening out-stations of the trade. These were successively set up in Tvøroyri, Suðuroy (1836),

Klaksvík in the Northern Islands (1838) and Vestmannahavn to serve Faroe's westerly regions (1839).

From 1844, the Monopoly retained an Icelandic fish-curer in Faroe, whose efforts, and subsequent instruction of young islanders, resulted in a vast increase in the exports of klipfish (dried and salted cod). Previously, a good deal of the fish caught between mid-June and mid-August had become verminous through lack of knowledge of how to cure it. The purchase of fresh fish by the Monopoly was of particular service to the poorer, landless families who, unlike the peasants, had no means of storing dried fish. By the end of the 1840s, the exports of fish were around, ten times what they had been before the war.

The *amtmænd* following Løbner were Christian Ludvig Tillisch (1825–30), his brother Frederik Ferdinand Tillisch (1830–37), Christian Pløyen (1837–48) and Carl Emil Dahlerup (1849–62). All of these were unreservedly popular figures in Faroe except for Dahlerup who, although no less able, far-sighted and benevolent than his predecessors, was less widely liked. During his tenure of office, paternalism was giving ground to new ideals of popular participation in legislation, and Dahlerup was a man of the old school.

The chief work of Christian Tillisch was in education. He strove to have schools set up in the villages, while in Tórshavn he founded a handicraft school where girls could learn spinning, weaving, sewing and dyeing. With energetic help from some of his subordinates, he founded in 1828 the Faroe Islands Provincial Library, for which — after nearly 2,000 books had been donated by private individuals in the islands, in Denmark and in some other countries — he obtained an annual royal grant. (By the 1850s, when the free library movement was only beginning in Britain, the Tórshavn library already had over 5,000 volumes.) Christian Tillisch also founded the first Tórshavn hospital. The old Argir hospital had only been a primitive kind of leper-house, and after leprosy became extinct in Faroe in 1744, it functioned mainly as a home for the destitute. By 1800, its affairs were in a very

poor state, and when the new Tórshavn hospital was opened
in 1829, the Argir hospital buildings, together with their four
marks of infield, were sold. Christian Tillisch also took an
interest in commercial affairs, and was instrumental in
building two large new warehouses, and installing a machine
for removing dust from the corn.

Frederik Tillisch, who, as Danish administrator for Slesvig
in the troubled years for the duchies between the two wars,
was later destined to play a rôle of European importance,
likewise left enduring marks in Faroe. His work was primarily
economic. Like many another reformer, he tried to introduce
the plough into Faroe, and like his predecessors, he was
defeated by the peculiar local conditions and the prejudice
of the inhabitants. However, to forward this and other schemes,
he founded a Society for Economic Advancement which
experimented with vegetable cultivation, the breeding and
foddering of stock, and even the planting of a species of grass
brought from the Falkland Islands. He brought some order
into the periodical whale-drives by promulgating as law the
system already unofficially in use in Suðuroy for dividing the
kill, so that 200 whales could now be shared out in a couple of
hours, in such a way that no disputes could arise between the
hunters.

His most important achievement, however, was the foundation in 1832 of a savings bank in Tórshavn. If Faroe were ever
to have free trade, it was necessary for capital to be accumulated by islanders on a scale sufficient to finance import and
export — otherwise the islands would pass into the power of
foreign merchants. The bank was at once a great success, and
by 1848 over 400 islanders had accounts. Depositors received
3 per cent annual interest, and their money was freed from
liability to stamp duties and from distraint for public or
private debt. The savings bank deposits were, of course, only
a fraction of the accumulated capital in the islands, much
being held by farmers in the form of valuables or stocks of
goods : money transactions were still less common than barter
— at least outside Tórshavn.

Christian Pløyen, who followed the Tillisch brothers, was the most popular of all the *amtmænd* of the nineteenth century, and his name is remembered in Faroe to this day with gratitude and affection. He was born in 1803 in Copenhagen, his fathers' family being civil service and his mother's clerical. Pløyen passed the usual legal examinations and in 1830 after three years in the Danish chancellery, he was made king's bailiff in Faroe, a post he held for seven years before succeeding as *amtmand*. He remained in the islands until 1848, when he was promoted to a larger province in Denmark.

Although his upbringing was not different from that of any other Danish civil servant of his day, Pløyen managed to enter into the daily life and amusements of the Faroese in a way that endeared him to everyone. He learned to speak the Faroese language like a native, and was not only perfect conversationally, but also knew a number of the traditional ballads which use an older form of the language. His gifts as a singer made him a welcome guest at weddings and other celebrations, and he came to know the Faroese, their aspirations and their fears, as no earlier official had done. His ballad *Grindevisen* has been sung at every whale-killing for over a century. With much humour this ballad tells of a typical Faroese whale-drive, from the first sighting of the school by the crew of a fishing-boat to its final destruction on the sandy shores of the straits north of Hvalvík. Although written in Danish, its style is close to the Faroese idiom, and contains many echoes of old Faroese ballads that Pløyen knew.

Pløyen's many reforms affected nearly every aspect of Faroese life. A considerable number were minor, but they were still significant for the Faroese. He popularised the use of Scottish and Shetland seed-potatoes; he introduced the labour-saving Shetland peat-spade, which soon superseded the native model. He started the first regular mail service, and encouraged intercourse not only with Denmark, but also with Shetland and Leith. He encouraged a new export — of whale and animal bones. These were shipped to Britain, where they were used for manure, especially in Lincolnshire. He

persuaded the farmers to grow oats as green fodder, so that
they could keep their cows at home in the summer, instead of
letting them range the outfield, to the partial loss of their milk
and total loss of their manure. He also tried to encourage the
individual holding of sheep in place of the village joint-stock
system such as had been legally required since 1698, on the
principle, to which he was a firm adherent, that a man looks
best after his own.

The fishery was Pløyen's constant concern. The caaing-
whale fishery became specially important during his term of
office, because schools of whales appeared round the coast in
extraordinary numbers. It was, moreover, the last age in
which whale-oil was used in lamps — the development of
kerosene as a lamp-oil began in 1856, and by 1859 the drilling
of the first Pennsylvanian oil-wells killed this market for train-
oil. But in the thirties and forties, whale-oil was an important
article of export — in the decade 1841–50, indeed, it made up
nearly 20 per cent of Faroe's total export — while whale-meat
became so plentiful that farmers started to feed it to their
cows. Pløyen's chief improvements were a reform in the
laws relating to the division of the catch after a killing,
and the conversion of the harbour at Vestmannahavn into one
of the best whaling bays in the islands. This harbour, though
generally well placed for whale-killing, had a coastline and
sea-bottom of such a form that the schools usually escaped.
Pløyen, in imitation of what he had read of Russian practice
in Spitzbergen with another kind of whale, had a giant net
of strong cordage made, so that their escape route seawards
could be cut off. Vestmannahavn has ever since been one of
the best whaling bays in Faroe.

Pløyen brought about still more important developments in
conventional fishing. His efforts brought to Faroe the long-line,
with its hundreds of hooks left in the sea. He also had some of
the most intelligent islanders sent to Shetland at government
expense to learn the techniques of fishing and fish-curing that
were employed there, while he himself toured Shetland,
Orkney and Scotland in search of ways of benefiting the

Faroese. He tried to encourage fishing from decked vessels, but for a variety of reasons, chiefly accidental, none of these attempts prospered. But Pløyen saw, as clearly as Nólsoyar-Páll, that the future of Faroe lay on the sea. For that reason he favoured the extension of conscription to the Faroe Islands — only Faroese resident in Denmark were then liable — so that Faroemen, through service in the Danish Navy, could be won to sea-going ways.

Pløyen's book describing his journey through Shetland, Orkney and Scotland in the summer of 1839, published in Copenhagen in 1840, and in English translation in Lerwick in 1894 and 1896, is a permanent memorial to the efforts of this diligent and intelligent man. It was written with the motive of making the islanders aware of every possible tool or technique that might help them economically — and to show the benefits of free trade, of which he was a constant advocate.

Pløyen realised that the chief obstacle to free trade was public fear of commercial chaos during the transition period. While he recognised the benefit that the newly-established Monopoly out-stations had brought, he regarded as a surer method of progress the partial freeing of trade in certain products that had existed in Nólsoyar-Páll's time, which he believed, would give the islanders experience in import and export, and would assist the accumulation of native capital on a scale sufficient to manage the trade when the Monopoly was abolished. He urged these views upon a royal commission in the autumn of 1840. Reporting in 1842, the commission recommended that the trade should be freed in the course of the next two or three years. However, constitutional reforms and, later, the Slesvig-Holstein crisis absorbed the energies of the Danish government for the rest of the decade, and the project was shelved.

Thus, by the efforts of the people at large, and the encouragement of the officials responsible for both the general administration and the management of the Monopoly, the Faroe Islands made remarkable economic progress during the first half of the nineteenth century. The abolition of monopoly naturally followed, due partly to this progress and partly to the wave of constitutional reforms that followed in the Danish kingdom in the 1850s. Faroese nationalism, in any full meaning of the term, was not yet a factor in the situation, but was to develop later.

CONSTITUTIONAL REFORM IN DENMARK AND FAROE

In the early nineteenth century, the constitution of the kingdom of Denmark was still, in theory if not in practice, an absolute hereditary monarchy; indeed, it was probably the only one in Europe to have been legally established. The absolute monarchy had been introduced at a time of national crisis in 1660, when all the estates of the realm resigned their privileges unreservedly into the king's hands. The Faroe Islanders swore a public oath to the new form of government in a session of the Løgting on 14 August, 1662. The long-term effect of absolutism was to place power previously wielded by the nobility into the hands of a fairly well-trained bureaucracy.

During the last twenty years of the eighteenth century Denmark had experienced much reform initiated from above. However, like most European countries, she experienced a powerful reform movement from below in the second quarter of the nineteenth century, consequent on the swing of public opinion towards some form of constitutional government. With the growth in influence of the press, a demand arose that representatives of the people should have at least an advisory voice in matters of state. At the same time, with the growth of German national feeling, the associated complication of the relationship between Denmark and Slesvig-Holstein began to be felt.

The Danish government first showed itself disposed to move with the spirit of the times in 1831 when Frederik VI announced his intention of constituting provincial assemblies in both the kingdom and the duchies. These assemblies, elected on a franchise based on ownership of land, came into being in 1835. They were situated at Itzehoe for Holstein, the town of

Slesvig for Slesvig, Viborg for Jutland, and Roskilde for the Danish islands, including Iceland and Faroe. The function of the Roskilde and other assemblies were to examine and discuss existing laws, to present petitions, to propose and draft legislation, and to forward any complaints of maladministration.

The representatives of Faroe at the Roskilde Assembly were all crown nominees. However, they were all men of ability and goodwill, and in their capacity as government officials, had all had first-hand experience of conditions in Faroe. The first two representatives were the former *amtmænd*, the brothers C. L. Tillisch (from 1836 to 1841) and F. F. Tillisch (from 1841 to 1844). From 1844 onwards, Faroe was represented by a former *sorenskriver*, Niels Hunderup.

Iceland and Faroe, relics of the old connection between Denmark and Norway, were in a plainly anomalous position as far as the Roskilde assembly was concerned — both from a legal viewpoint and from considerations of geography and common sense. Iceland's special position was recognised in 1843, when its affairs were removed from the hands of the Roskilde Assembly, and the old Icelandic Althing was revived in the form of a provincial advisory chamber with its seat in Reykjavík. Consistency might have demanded that Faroe should also be given a separate treatment, but it was not easy to see how a constitutional organ could be given to a population of seven or eight thousand, living in scattered communities, few of the people having had any higher education, and with no organs of opinion to ventilate the issues. In 1846, a committee of the Roskilde Assembly did consider a petition, signed by twenty-eight Faroemen, that an advisory elected body might be set up for the islands; and although the committee later reported in favour of the measure, the proposal was carried no further at the time, and Faroe remained, almost inadvertently, among the provinces of metropolitan Denmark.

The unexpected success of the Paris revolution in February 1848 had its influence in the Danish kingdom as in other parts

of Europe. The Germans of Slesvig-Holstein rose in a revolt
which led to a three-year war in Jutland, the insurgents having
the assistance of Prussia. The Danes themselves demanded,
and were readily granted, a free constitution on the lines of
the 1831 constitution of Belgium. Absolute monarchy
officially ended on 21 March, 1848, and by autumn a constituent assembly was in being, three-quarters of it elected by
universal suffrage.

In this constituent assembly, Faroe was once again represented by a crown nominee — this time Christian Pløyen.
Now at the end of his eighteen years of government service
in the Faroe Islands, Pløyen represented the Faroemen's
interests with ability. Yet when Denmark's new constitution
was finally adopted on 5 June, 1849, the Faroe islanders had
still not had the opportunity of helping to draft its decisions, or
express their opinions on whether it should apply to Faroe,
through any *elected* delagate or group. Early in 1850, a special
law was passed — still without Faroese participation —
extending the provisions of the Danish constitution to Faroe.

This decision to include Faroe, willy-nilly, in the constitutional arrangements designed for Denmark proper was
undoubtedly high-handed; yet there was sufficient reason to
believe that the Faroese people identified themselves closely
with the Danes, in a way in which the Icelanders did not.
The public collections for war expenses, for instance, had an
excellent response, considering the poverty of the islands, and
a number of islanders had volunteered for army or navy service
in the Slesvig-Holstein war, in a cause which affected Faroe
only insofar as it affected the Danish kingdom as a whole.
When the leading Danish National Liberal, D. G. Monrad,
said that it would be unreasonable to organise Faroe as a
separate state, and that the Faroemen *ought* to want to be
Danes, he was speaking better sense than later generations
have given him credit for.

And in the event, the Faroe islanders were given a dispro-
portionately large voice in the Danish legislature. They were
granted a seat in both the lower house (Folketing) and the

upper house (Landsting), although the population of Faroe did not exceed 8,000, while the normal Folketing constituency had a 14,000 population basis, and the normal Landsting constituency had one of 30,000,

The first Faroese election for the Danish Folketing must hold the Scandinavian prize for irregularities. No fewer than five breaches of electoral law had to be scrutinised and condoned when the successful candidate arrived in Copenhagen. The first four irregularities were trivial, but the fifth was important, and throughly Faroese in character. In Suðuroy, in accordance with law, it had been decided that voting should take place in Hvalbøur, and it was there that the proceedings were duly opened. Just before polling began, however, there was a cry of "*Grindaboð!*" — the alarm summoning everyone to a whale-drive. Everyone agreed that it was quite unreasonable to deny the election supervisors the chance of joining the drive, so it was resolved that polling should take place when and where the whales were killed, which turned out to be Trongisvágur. The document excusing the irregularity was furnished with an impressive number of signatures.

Thus was Faroese representation secured in the Danish legislature; and amid the press of other business, the Danish parliament now found time to pass reforms for what had become Denmark's most northerly province. The Løgting was revived, albeit in a changed form; and at last, the 300-year-old Monopoly passed out of existence.

FREE TRADE AND A REVIVED LØGTING

Among the first items of business to come before the new Folketing was the question of free trade for Faroe and other parts of the Danish realm. Few were now prepared to oppose it for Faroe. Nevertheless, at least one modern Faroese historian[1] maintains that the decisive factor even then was the pressure of the Copenhagen wholesalers who wished to take

---

[1] Hr. Róland Waag Høgnesen.

the place of government in the supply of the islands. Copenhagen commerce had been in a poor way for some years,
because of competition from provincial centres; and the
Copenhagen merchants, he asserts, saw in Faroe a market
they could make their own. Be that as it may, the principle of
a free Faroe trade was agreed by the Folketing in a resolution
of 17 March, 1851, when the government was requested to
implement free trade by the end of the financial year 1852–3
at the latest. A law was duly drafted, but a further delay
occurred as a consequence of representations by a deputation
from Faroe, led by the provost, Otto Jørgensen, urging that
trade in Faroe should be open to merchants of all countries, not
merely Danish nationals. The deputation further objected to
the proposal that trade should be restricted to the four places
where the Monopoly had operated. Both points were conceded, and the proposals for the complete freeing of the
Faroese trade passed into law on 21 March, 1855.

The Free Trade Law abolished the crown monopoly in
Faroe as from 1 January, 1856, although the government
trading company was to continue in business for a further six
months to dispose of its stocks. From the same date, navigation to and from the islands was opened to ships of all nations
on payment of a low import duty on cargo landed. Any
person over twenty-five and of good reputation might set up
his shop counter anywhere in the islands, provided only that
he had registered with the *sorenskriver* as a merchant for the
place chosen. All former trade legislation, unless specifically
renewed by this Law, was now repealed, with the exception
of laws on weights and measures. In the summer of 1856, the
government trading company disposed of its buildings and
capital assets by public auction. By the end of July, the last
building had been sold, and the trading company which had
supplied the Faroe Islands since 1709 was no more.

Over the years, the Royal Monopoly had become involved
with almost every facet of economic life in the islands, and
a considerable amount of consequential legislation had to be
passed, especially over poor relief and taxation. During the

Monopoly period, poor relief funds had been derived from a 1 per cent commodity tax on goods sold by the Monopoly. The funds had been accounted for by the Monopoly's resident manager. This responsibility had now to be taken over by the government officials, and an alternative source of income found in the import duties.

The taxes of Faroe had been levied in kind and disposed of through the Monopoly trading establishment. An alternative means had to be found of paying taxes and tithes, and the problem was how to assess these in goods when fixed-price trading was no longer in force. This was done partly by an annual price inquisition by the officials each June, and partly by a system of equivalents between goods of various kinds — for money trading was still the exception rather than the rule for the rest of century. The fish tithes and the land taxes were now the most productive imposts; in the years following free trade, many minor taxes were either commuted or repealed.

The merchant houses which now took over the Faroe trade were partly Faroe-financed, but most of the largest were from outside the islands. Some were from Copenhagen, while others were from Slesvig-Holstein or Hamburg. British capital, surprisingly enough, was not attracted to the islands.

The revival of the Løgting occurred shortly before the abolition of the Monopoly. The Løgting which had existed down to 1816 had been a court of appeal with the power also to carry public complaints to Copenhagen. As revived in 1852 it had relatively limited powers, but it had direct authority over certain essentially local matters, such as the administration of church estates and poor-law funds, and the regulations concerning the ferrying of goods and travellers from island to island. Politically, it was only an advisory body, executive power remaining in the hands of the *amtmand* and legislative power being with the Landsting and Folketing in Copenhagen. In 1855 it was officially decided that these houses, and not the revived Løgting, had the power of deciding the applicability of new Danish laws to Faroe. Henceforth any law from which Faroe was to be exempted (because of

Faroese local conditions there were many such) had to spell out this point in its text.

Thus, in the 1850s, largely because of constitutional developments in Denmark, but partly also because of growing prosperity based on the export of fish, the Faroe Islands were at last granted free trade, and in addition they acquired an advisory council at home and representation in the legislature in Copenhagen. Most Faroese regard the Free Trade Law as the most important landmark in their country's history, and speak of it as marking the end of the mediaeval period in Faroe. On economic grounds this could be disputed with the argument that free trade only reinforced tendencies that were already in motion. Yet with the arrival of politics and the growth of trade in every village, the old patriarchal peasant community began to break up, and a new social order came into being.

CHAPTER V

THE NEW AGE OPENS

THE FIRST FAROESE POLITICIANS

The Slesvig-Holstein troubles and the constitutional crisis in metropolitan Denmark had given an artificial stimulus to Faroese political life, which after a stormy beginning, settled into a placid and conservative routine for a quarter of a century. Once the great issue of free trade had been satisfactorily settled, the energies of the Faroese were absorbed rather by the new opportunities of economic development than by political controversy. The ideals of the age did cause a few political ripples in Faroe, but the disputes took place in a tiny world where everyone knew everyone else intimately, and where personalities were more prominent than principles.

The first Faroese representative in the Danish Folketing, however, tried hard to prod the islands into some sort of political consciousness. This was Niels Winther (1822–92), who held the seat from 1851 to 1856. Winther was the son of a Tórshavn joiner. As a boy, he had shown such extraordinary skill in reading and writing that, at the age of eleven, he was taken on by the *sorenskriver*, Niels Hunderup, as junior clerk. Hunderup paid him no salary for several years, but promised that when he returned to Denmark to take up a post there, Winther should go with him, and that he would support him financially to enable him to take the law examinations in Copenhagen. Niels Hunderup was as good as his word, and Winther duly took the first law examination.

In Copenhagen, Niels Winther imbibed from his student friends the new ideal of replacing absolute monarchy and bureaucratic power with representative, constitutional government. He returned to the Faroe Islands in 1849, and settled in

Tórshavn in the dual rôle of solicitor and political activist. He gained a reputation as a friend of the landless and the under-privileged, and as a critic of the officials, whom he regarded as embodying the still-surviving power of the old absolutism. His efforts tended somewhat to polarise public opinion, and although he had made many enemies among the people as well as among the official classes, he won the 1851 Folketing election by a slim majority. Tórshavn, where the influence of the officials was strongest, voted heavily against him, but he won enough support in Eysturoy and Suðuroy to gain a small lead over his nearest rival, one of the officials.

Winther realised that in the long run, political power was a matter of being at the centre of a communication network. Thus in 1850 he visited Copenhagen to learn the craft of printing, and in May 1852 he started the first Faroese newspaper, *Færingetidende*. Hitherto, the only sources of public information about politics had been by word of mouth, or the official newsletters sent out by the *amtmand*.[1] A printed paper was a sensational novelty for Faroe, and if it had survived for long its editor and publisher could hardly have failed to become a man of great influence.

The newspaper was printed on a tiny hand press that Winther had purchased in Copenhagen, a good deal of the capital being supplied by the wealthy Jacob Nolsøe, then lately retired from his position as resident manager of the Monopoly. *Færingetidende* was written in Danish, then universally the language of public business and even of private correspondence, for the Faroese language was not customarily written, and the technical difficulties of producing a Faroese-language newspaper, even if Winther had ever contemplated it, would have been insurmountable.

Færingetidende was not, however, destined to last long. The

---

[1] The issue of newsletters was started in 1849, when the war was in progress in Jutland. *Amtmand* Dahlerup, fearing the spread of groundless rumours, had the principal news items from such Danish and English newspapers as found their way to the islands copied out and promulgated via the district sheriffs and the priests.

first issue appeared on 13 May, 1852, the ninth and last on 27 July the same year. Although many wished the paper well, Winther's vitriolic style, learned from the Copenhagen newspapers of his time, made him enemies. No. 8 contained a sarcastic attack on the quality of the goods in the Monopoly. This article was thought to be defamatory, and Winther was fined 600 rigsdaler (about £70), which he could scarcely afford. After the newspaper ceased publication with No. 9, the Faroe Islands had no press until 1877.

Friends rallied to pay Winther's fine, but as a man of only modest means, just married (to a granddaughter of Jacob Nolsøe), he realised his vulnerability. This blow made him disillusioned with his prospects as a solicitor in the islands, and of having a political career there, so in 1856 he resigned his Folketing seat, and in 1857 moved to Hjørring, in north Jutland, pursuing a legal and political career in that town for the rest of his life. In 1868 he purchased the newspaper *Hjørring Amtstidende,* of which he remained editor for seventeen years. Winther's politics became less and less radical as the years passed by, and he ended up a conservative. He did not lose interest in his native islands, as he wrote a history of Faroe, *Farøernes Oldtidshistorie,* incorporating much material from Faroese oral tradition, which was published in 1875.

Apart from the small part he played in getting the Monopoly abolished, Winther's principal achievement for his native islands was the revival of the Løgting. But his years in Copenhagen had put him out of touch with the rather limited political aspirations of the Faroese of his time, so that he was unable to follow up this success with a radical social policy for Faroe. It was perhaps inevitable that, faced with this situation, Winther should have left the islands a disappointed man and that Faroe should have followed more conservative political lines for a generation.

The first representative of Faroe in the Landsting, elected by the handful of wealthy residents in the islands, was a farmer, the crown tenant Johan Hendrik Wejhe (1786–1868), who in his younger days had been a skipper aboard his own

small trading vessel, and was later known as one of the most
skillful farmers in the islands. At different times, he had been
district sheriff of Eysturoy, and while he was far more conservative by disposition than Niels Winther, he had a variety of
useful experience, and it was partly due to his advocacy that
the law reviving the Løgting passed the upper house. Wejhe
was the only Faroese peasant to sit in the Danish legislature
until the twentieth century. He did not stand for re-election
to the Landsting in 1853, but tried unsuccessfully to enter the
Folketing in 1857 and 1858. This lack of success was unfortunate, since he was psychologically well in tune with his
countrymen, and with further parliamentary experience
might have overcome his diffidence in the House.

The principal scene of Faroese political life soon became the
revived Løgting in Torshavn. Its composition was at first
sixteen, later eighteen elected members, together with two
ex-officio members, the *amtmand* and the provost. Moreover,
the *amtmand*, by a rule which aroused resentment amongst the
democratically-minded, was the Løgting's permanent chairman. Unwise use of the permanent chairmanship was the
chief factor contributing to the protracted strife that took
place in the Løgting's early years between the elected members
of the chamber and *amtmand* Dahlerup.

Carl Emil Dahlerup (1813–90), a native of Hillerød in
Sjælland, was an official of the old school, stiff, correct and
paternal. He was never married, and his lack of domestic life
and the restricted nature of Tórshavn society probably induced
him to give to official business an intensity of devotion that
was excellent from an administrative standpoint, but which
tended to mar his relations with anyone happening to see the
public needs differently from himself. He was *amtmand* of
Faroe from 1849 to 1861. Like his three predecessors, he was
able and conscientious. He had a particular interest in
agriculture, and arranged for young Faroemen to go to
Denmark for training. He made yet another attempt to teach
the islanders ploughing by fetching a ploughman from
Denmark to Faroe. In 1855, he had hares brought from

Norway and set free on Streymoy; they rapidly became common on some of the larger islands and provided the people with both sport and a new kind of meat. To diversify Faroese economic life, he tried to establish the export of paving-stones from Faroe to Copenhagen, but this sensible idea was unsuccessful. He was far-sighted in his wish to move the main seat of Faroese commerce and administration from Tórshavn to Skálafjørður, with its excellent harbour and more extensive hinterland; but it was beyond his powers to achieve this.

Amtmand Dahlerup did not take kindly to sharing his authority with an elected body, although with the weight of the patronage he wielded and the profound respect habitually accorded by Faroese to their higher officials, he need have had no fear of losing control of affairs. However, he tended to treat the Løgting members like schoolchildren as he initiated them into the mysteries of administration; and he had no patience with those he thought fools. He made himself unpopular in the first Løgting by whistling when elected members said things with which he disagreed. The dual task of impartial chairman and guide to the inexperienced members without their realising it was beyond him. He made matters harder for himself by quarrelling with the provost, Andreas Djurhuus; several of the elected members were priests, and their weight tended thereafter to be thrown in on the popular side. The Danish government eventually had to move Dahlerup to a new post and fetch in someone able to make a fresh start.

The members of the Løgting were not, in those early days, chosen along party lines. Political divisions in Denmark proper had no significance for the Faroe islanders; and native parties were not to emerge for half a century. The candidates tended to be the locally literate and articulate, and Niels Winther was the only early member of the Løgting who could reasonably be described as a dedicated politician. The composition of the 1856 Løgting, for instance, was as follows: *amtmand* and provost (ex-officio), three priests, three school-masters, seven farmers, one tailor, one lawyer and one official.

After the departure of *Amtmand* Dahlerup, Faroese politics entered a quiet, conservative phase. The most prominent figure of the next twenty years was Hans Christopher Müller (1818–97), a district sheriff with wide interests and great abilities. Müller spoke fluent English, French and German besides his native Faroese and Danish; he was the only Faroe islander to visit the Great Exhibition in London in 1851; he had many foreign friends who regarded him highly; and he carried on a series of useful scientific investigations in the fields of ornithology and zoology. Müller became the local agent when a steamship connection with Faroe was established and postmaster with the development of a postal service. His political influence in the islands was enormous — from 1858 to 1864 he was the Faroese representative in the Folketing, and from 1866 until 1886 he served in the Landsting, overcoming a redoubtable series of opponents at successive elections. On Danish political issues he was a conservative, though not bigoted. In Faroese matters he maintained the closest possible touch with the Løgting.

Contact with the Løgting was aided by the provisions of the 1866 constitutional changes in Denmark. The Faroese election law now placed the choice of member for the Landsting (upper house) in the hands of the Løgting instead of the well-to-do. This conveniently linked the local elected body to the legislature, while retaining direct popular voting for the Folketing. However, interest in Folketing elections was small. The Faroese electorate was ill-informed about party divisions and public issues in Denmark due to lack of newspapers, and the poor communications between Faroe and Copenhagen made it impossible for the member to be in regular touch with his constituents. Public interest in Løgting affairs was greater, but there was irritation at its apparent impotence, even compared with the Løgting as it had existed before 1816. Within Faroe, despite the rapid development of the fishery at this period, there was no burning political issue or economic difficulty that either united or divided public opinion about what should be done in Copenhagen.

ECONOMIC ADVANCE

During the years following the abolition of the Monopoly, the Faroese fishery made further rapid advances. The spread of the industrial revolution through Europe was bringing about a long-term tendency for the price of fish to rise. At the same time, the fishing techniques of the Faroese were improving. During the decade 1841–50, fish products constituted 39 per cent of the total export compared with 61 per cent land products (mostly knitted woollens). In the period 1895–9, although the export volume of land products was little less than it had been at mid-century, these now formed only 6.3 per cent of the total export, compared with 93.7 per cent fish and other sea products. This boom in fish exports, and the simultaneous stagnation and slight decline in the export of knitted woollen sweaters, the most important land product, can be seen from the following table:

Average yearly Exports from Faroe

(in tons)

Years	Klipfish	Salt fish	Stockfish	Sweaters
1841—50	21	—	186	51
1858—65	581	—	163	?
1866—75	1,520	71	50	46
1876—85	2,023	42	49	52
1886—95	2,510	183	32	42
1896—99	3,869	338	6	39

From 1856 to 1872 the fishery was still carried on exclusively from open boats in the seas immediately surrounding the islands. But open-boat techniques were improving, chiefly through successful application of methods learned from the Shetlanders. Pløyen's visit of 1839 was far from being the last contact between the two island groups.

The chief improvement in technique was the use of the long line. At the time of Pløyen's visit, the Shetland boat's crew of six men employed a line over 5,000 fathoms long, with 1,200 hooks. A similar Faroese crew using hand-lines would have only five hooks in the water, since the sixth man had to keep the boat in position. The baits used were now also improved by reference to Shetland experience, and a smaller and more efficient hook came into use. Hand-line fishermen now used lead weights on their lines in place of the *vaðsteinur*, the prehistoric stone weight. By the 1870s the long line had become the chief technique of the Faroese fisherman, although the hand-line remained important for exploiting the small, very rich fishing grounds off the Faroese coast, which are often only a few yards across, and thus demand accurate rowing and small-scale apparatus.

In 1872 began a new development in the Faroese fishery. In that year three Faroemen bought a wooden sloop, and with it devised a technique for the distant-water fishery. They were Dánjal, Niclas and Petur Haraldsen, three brothers living in Tórshavn. They acquired their ship in Scarborough — a 38-ton vessel called *Fox* — and fetched it in to Tórshavn in July 1872. Before the summer was out, they had it out on the Icelandic fishing grounds. The crew fished from small boats as was their custom at home, and brought their catch in to the *Fox*. The following spring, the brothers took their sloop out to the Faroese fishing banks.

The success of the *Fox* quickly led to the purchase of other sloops. Within five years there were twelve in the Faroe Islands, and by 1900 there were no fewer than eighty-one. In displacement they varied between twenty and eighty gross registered tons. Most of them were purchased in Britain at very low prices; towards the end of the century, the British fishing industry turned over to steam trawling, and the old wooden fishing sloops were sold off cheap. These vessels had a long life. Many of them were still being used in Faroe in the 1950s, and the few last survivors have only recently been taken out of regular service (nearly all had been fitted since the 1920s with auxiliary engines). Together with the small boats of the inshore fishermen, which continued to land a large quantity of fish from the local banks, these wooden sloops dominated the Faroese fishing scene until well into the 1930s.

The chief markets for Faroese fish were the Roman Catholic countries of the Mediterranean. Spain, in particular, was a large customer for klipfish (salted and dried split cod), buying also from Iceland, Norway and France. Klipfish was by far the most important export, as the accompanying table shows.

The rise of the fishing industry brought wealth to the islands on a scale never known before. But it also led to the fishermen becoming financially dependent on the Faroese trading firms now to be found in every village; and these firms were in their turn generally dependent on the large Danish trading houses which had taken the place of the defunct Monopoly as the main importers.

Economic advance was accompanied by social revolution. The farmers — particularly the crown tenants who, until the nineteenth century, had been the leading social group in Faroe — were deserted by their dependants, the landless labourers, who now looked to the sea for their living. The crown tenants had henceforth to rely largely on the man-power of their own families for the work of their farms. On the other hand, privately owned land tended to become divided into small-holdings that could easily be managed by a fisher-man spending seven months away at sea, if he had the help of the younger lads who were not yet ready for the distant-water fishery, or the old men who were past it.

Faroese Exports, 1858-1899

Year	Klipfish (tons)	Salt fish (tons)	Stockfish (tons)	Roe (barrels)	Train Oil (barrels)
1858	315	?	191	?	?
1859	548	?	264	?	?
1860	465	?	210	?	?
1861	490	?	167	?	?
1862	479	?	127	?	?
1863	725	?	99	?	?

Year	Klipfish (tons)	Salt fish (tons)	Stockfish (tons)	Roe (barrels)	Train Oil (barrels)
1864	569	?	192	?	?
1865	1,054	?	56	?	?
1866	1,178	15	15	64	992
1867	1,244	1	9	108	919
1868	828	—	76	83	466
1869	1,105	92	87	170	611
1870	1,828	283	69	361	1,351
1871	1,656	122	13	142	1,331
1872	1,450	106	11	136	1,137
1873	1,449	20	41	170	2,255
1874	1,879	66	66	281	1,113
1875	2,579	—	114	543	980
1876	1,921	55	56	409	1,314
1877	1,812	107	7	402	1,569
1878	1,388	64	22	414	1,512
1879	1,685	57	51	312	1,928
1880	1,981	39	70	331	1,146
1881	2,045	—	67	267	748
1882	2,320	—	21	156	934
1883	2,352	—	14	328	745
1884	2,262	1	46	322	870
1885	2,468	167	65	297	1,409
1886	1,822	159	22	433	1,076
1887	1,962	212	11	203	1,149
1888	1,516	220	4	184	1,105
1889	1,745	14	5	292	986
1890	2,177	1	35	101	810
1891	2,979	8	88	406	463
1892	3,094	308	66	320	2,032
1893	2,708	418	36	442	1,348
1894	3,608	197	21	197	1,374
1895	3,480	291	35	298	1,654
1896	5,158	314	16	432	3,369
1897	3,432	369	8	254	3,024
1898	3,360	278	2	241	7,264
1899	3,524	392	—	317	8,103

Mobility of labour was aided by the repeal in 1865 of the ancient and now anachronistic obligation of the larger farmers to maintain big fishing boats, and for their poorer neighbours to man them for the spring fishing, being paid only by their share of the catch. This obligation was connected with the old communication system used in the islands (and formerly in Norway), known in the Danish language as *skyds*. *Skyds* was the individual obligation to forward travellers — in Faroe principally by boat. Priests and officials on public business travelled free, while other travellers paid according to a tariff fixed by law. In every village a so-called *skydsskaffer* was appointed, who for this duty called in rotation on every able-bodied male between fifteen and fifty. Refusal to comply with the summons of the *skydsskaffer*, except in case of sickness or other sufficient excuse, was punishable by a fine.

The *skyds* was also the official postal service of the islands. The few private letters were generally sent by casual travellers but official letters, if properly sealed and carrying the initials K.T. (*kongelig tjeneste* — on royal service) were carried, like travellers, by the *skyds*. Urgent letters might be inscribed *uopholdelig befordring*, i.e. express delivery. These had to be taken forward stage by stage without delay.

A letter from the king's bailiff in Tórshavn to the district sheriff of Suðuroy would be given first to the Tórshavn *skydsskaffer*, who would find a runner to take it over the mountain ao the *skydsskaffer* at Kirkjubøur. The latter would requisition t boat's crew to take the letter across the sound to Skopun. Until 1836 there was no settlement there, so one of the boat's crew would have to carry the letter over the island to Sandur. It might now go from Sandur to Skúvoy, and from Skúvoy to Hvalbøur on Suðuroy, before completing its journey overland to wherever the district sheriff happened to be.

In 1872 three postmen were appointed, each to make seven journeys in a year. One took the post to the Northern Islands, one to Vágar, and the third to Suðuroy. The boat connections were now paid for. The postmaster was H.C. Müller, whose political activity has already been mentioned. He had a post

office in a house on Tinganes in Tórshavn, and it remained
there until 1908, when it was moved nearer to the centre of
the town. The use of village boats was finally given up when
motor boats became available after 1905. By that time the
post no longer consisted principally of official letters, private
and business correspondence having become considerable.

EDUCATION

Before the nineteenth century Faroese education had had a
long but broken history. The earliest school in the islands,
founded in the twelfth century, was a seminary at Kirkjubøur,
where priests were trained for the mediaeval Faroese church.
All that is known about this school, however, is that one pupil
was the celebrated Norwegian king Sverre (reigned 1184–
1202), who by the standards of his time was a well-educated
man.

At the Reformation this seminary was closed, and in its
place a Latin school similar to those in Denmark was opened
in Tórshavn. From this school young Faroemen could
proceed to Copenhagen University and subsequently enter
the professions. In addition, a Danish school was founded in
Tórshavn about 1630 for pupils whose gifts were insufficient
for them to be taught Latin. These two schools had a chequer-
ed history, their state at any given time being dependent on
the skill and enthusiasm of the South Streymoy priest and his
deacon, who were in charge of the teaching. At times, pupils
proceeded direct from the Tórshavn Latin school to the
university — in the record year, 1660, three Faroese pupils
were thus admitted.

However, it was more usual for a prospective student to
spend a year or two in a Latin school in Denmark before
entering on his university course. Thus Johan Henrik
Schrøter (born 1771), son of the government surgeon resident
in Tórshavn, attended the Tórshavn Latin school from 1784
to June 1790. In August 1790 he entered Slagelse Latin school
for a year, and in November 1791 he was admitted to Copen-

hagen University. There he studied medicine and theology, and took examinations in 1786 and 1797. In the latter year he was appointed curate on Suðuroy, and in 1804, on the incumbent's death, became parish priest of that island. Such a career was typical. Schrøter's predecessor in the Suðuroy living, Christopher Rasmussen Müller (grandfather of the politician H. C. Müller) had been taught first at home, then in the Tórshavn Latin school, and finally at Helsingør Latin school before proceeding to the university.

The Danish school in Tórshavn closed in 1770, and the Latin school took no further pupils after 1794, although the aged schoolmaster continued in office for another ten years until his death.

As might be expected there was little organised schooling in the villages. Attempts were made in the eighteenth century to organise schooling under peripatetic teachers, but with little success, even on Sandoy, where overland communications between the villages were the best. Home tuition was customary, and even about 1670 one of the Tórshavn priests estimated that about half the population could read. The standard of education in certain families was relatively high. Most of the Faroese lawmen, though without formal legal training, were well read in the law and fully competent in their office.

Compulsory elementary education was introduced into metropolitan Denmark in 1814, but was not extended to the dependencies. Yet the Danish example, whereby every parish supported a school in which every child from six to thirteen might be instructed in reading, writing, arithmetic, scripture, gymnastics and gardening, was bound to stir emulation in Faroe as Danish priests and officials with experience of the new system arrived in the islands. Indeed, the Tórshavn Danish school had already been revived in 1806, and the first village schooling began in 1812, when an Icelandic teacher was employed to travel round the villages of Suðuroy to hold classes for the children. Purpose-built village schools followed, in Miðvágur (1829), Nólsoy (1837) and Saltnes on Skálafjør-ður (1844).

The finances available to assist villages in setting up and maintaining schools were not large. In 1818, certain sums accruing from a vacancy in the priest's living in the Northern Islands were formed into a fund for the provision of school books. In 1829, about a third of the proceeds from the sale of the lawman's 24-mark farm on Vágar were applied to Faroese school purposes, and to this was added the income of the defunct Latin school. For the most part, however, the villagers had to find the money for themselves.

In 1845 the Danish government decreed the introduction of compulsory schooling in Faroe, to take effect from the beginning of 1846. This was not a success. Control of the schools now became less democratic, the children were kept in school at times when their help was needed in the fields or at sea, and a school rate was imposed which it was the teacher's invidious task to collect. Petitions to both the *amtmand* and the government stressed that the decree failed to provide sufficient income for full-time teachers, yet was economically burdensome to the villagers. It was finally revoked by a law of March 1854, which merely placed upon everyone the duty of ensuring that in some way every child over seven should be given sufficient instruction in reading and religious knowledge. Unfortunately, the tradition of home instruction had already been upset by the 1845 order and by the economic revolution then in progress.

During the next twenty years, however, the school situation became a good deal brighter. A high school *(realskole)* was opened in Tórshavn in 1861, which in 1870 started a course for teacher training, at first of two years but in 1878 extended to three. Women were admitted to teacher training in 1884.

A law of 1872 established a system of local government in Faroe and each commune (parish or municipal council) was allotted the duty of seeing that all children received instruction, either from full-time or part-time teachers, or by some other means suited to the locality. By the end of the century, nearly all except the smallest of Faroese villages possessed village schools, and, moreover, more advanced educational institutions were growing up, at least in Tórshavn. Important among these was a school of navigation, founded in 1893. The rise of Faroese nationalism in the last years of the nineteenth century also led to the foundation of a Faroese folk high school in 1899.

By the end of the nineteenth century, democratic institutions existed in Faroe that were as extensive as the population could then well use; economic progress was well under way, drawing the islanders increasingly into world commerce; and public education was providing a standard of enlightenment that often surprised the foreign observer. An intelligent British visitor to the islands wrote in 1905:[1]

> The priests, as a rule, are well-educated men, and several of them have in past times contributed largely to our knowledge of the islands. The very peasants, too, although comparatively few of them can read or write Farish, are, in very many cases, exceedingly well informed, often surprising the traveller by their knowledge of history, geography, and even foreign literature. Some years ago, at Kollefjord in Stromoe, I met a man who had never left the islands, but could speak excellent English and Danish, and could read German, French, and Icelandic. He had learnt them in the winter evenings, in order that he might have something to read; and what was even more extraordinary, he knew how to apply what he had learnt. From some vegetable seeds which he had procured from Scotland a plant of the common ragwort had come up. Struck by the beauty of the yellow flower, and considering it a rarity, he was even more pleased with it than if it had been the cabbage he expected. On my telling him its English name he gave me, in a very modest way, a little discourse on the etymology of the word 'wort'. He told me that his great ambition was to see a real diamond, and he seemed quite at a loss to understand what a country could be like where all the fields were level.
>
> Such men are by no means rare in the Faroes.

---

[1] Nelson Annandale, *The Faroes and Iceland*, Oxford 1905, pp. 29—30.

CHAPTER VI

NATIONAL AWAKENING

THE AGE OF ANTIQUARIANISM

It was a growing public interest in the language and oral literary heritage of Faroe that gave the first impetus to Faroese nationalism. What began as a form of antiquarian research gave rise, in time, to a new pride among the Faroese people in their language and a desire to employ it for all the purposes of modern life. There was an urge, in consequence, to build up a modern, printed literature. By the end of the nineteenth century, this cultural struggle had begun to spill over into Faroese politics.

The first known occasion when Faroese literary texts were set down on paper was in 1639, when the versatile Danish antiquarian Ole Worm received from the Faroe Islands a transcript of twelve *kvæði*, but the manuscript was unfortunately lost in the great Copenhagen fire of 1728, and only a few verses were preserved through a copy.

The earliest considerable work on the Faroese language and the oral literature of the islands was done by the philologist and naturalist Jens Christian Svabo (1746–1824). Svabo was the son of the parish priest of Vágar, and until he was thirteen, his father educated him at home in Miðvagur. He was then sent for six years to the Latin school in Tórshavn where he became friendly with another gifted young Faroeman, Nicolai Mohr (1742–90), whose life, though shorter than Svabo's, was destined to greater worldly fortune. Mohr undertook a number of investigations for the Danish government as a naturalist, and for the last few years of his life was manager of the royal porcelain factory in Copenhagen.

Svabo and Mohr were the first Faroemen to pursue studies

at the university that were not in theology. Both went to Copenhagen in 1765, and studied political economy and natural history. Svabo possibly had the idea of giving service to this native country by assisting its economic development. In 1769 the office of lawman became vacant, and Svabo applied for it. He was unsuccessful, doubtless because he was considered too young. To support himself, his father by this time being dead, Svabo took a number of humble positions in Denmark.

During the 1770s, influenced by the prosperity of the rest of the Danish-Norwegian kingdom, and prompted also by the physiocratic theories of economics which he had imbibed at the university, Svabo submitted a number of papers to the Danish government on the improvement of husbandry in Faroe, one or two of which were printed. From 22 May 1781 to 1 September 1782, with financial aid from the government, he undertook a survey of the physical resources and economic life of the islands. He returned with a collection of immensely valuable material, but from this point good fortune deserted him. His journey left him in debt, he became chronically ill, and his friend Nicolai Mohr died. In 1800, a broken man, he returned to Faroe, where in his latter years he was assisted by a tiny government pension. His account of the Faroe Islands, a truly magnificent piece of work, was not printed in full until 1959 although, almost from the time it was written, the manuscript was used by other writers on Faroe.

Svabo's philological labours, which probably began about 1771 were continued throughout his life and are his enduring title to fame. He prepared a monumental Faroese-Danish-Latin dictionary, which remained in manuscript until 1966. He was helped initially by Mohr, who had the advantage a thorough command of Icelandic. Svabo wrote down the words in the way they were pronounced on his native island of Vágar. His intention, as he says, was to give to posterity an account of the Faroese language as it existed in his time, for he thought it likely to become replaced progressively by Danish. The ultimate effect of his work was that the reverse happened: Faroese replaced Danish in fields where the latter had been used for centuries.

Svabo, besides preparing his dictionary, made an important collection of Faroese traditional poetry. His great manuscript contains fifty-two poems, four of which are satirical ballads, one is a late mediaeval religious poem composed in Iceland, and the remainder are *kvæði*. Like his work in lexicography, his ballad collection went unregarded by the learned world in Svabo's lifetime, and the manuscript gathered dust in the Royal Library in Copenhagen. Only one of the ballads was printed in Svabo's lifetime — in 1814, in a Swedish collection of folk poetry. This was the first time a Faroese text was printed.

No further work was done on the ballads of Faroe until 1817. In that year, the Danish clergyman H.C. Lyngbye (1782–1837) came to the islands to study the algal vegetation along the coasts. Faroese ballad dancing aroused his interest, and after some instruction in the language from the aged Svabo, Lyngbye began to collect *kvæði* whenever the weather prevented his botanical excursions.

After returning to Copenhagen, Lyngbye showed his material to Professor P. E. Müller (1776–1834), who recognised among the ballads a version of the *Völsunga Saga*. Müller wrote to both Pastor J. H. Schrøter (1771–1851) and Provost Peter Hentze (1753–1843) for help in gathering further ballad material. The recording of Faroese oral poetry now began with great energy. Schrøter was soon able to send to Lyngbye the Suðuroy text of the *Sjurðarkvæði*, the ballad which Müller had recognised as being on the *Völsunga Saga* theme. From Schrøter's copy and his own, Lyngbye published in 1822 *Færøiske Qvæder om Sigurd Fofnersbane og hans Æt* ('Faroese ballads about Sigurd the slayer of Fafnir and his line'). This, the first book printed in Faroese, brought Scandinavian scholars to appreciate the quality of the literature preserved by oral transmission among the Faroese peasants — some of it undoubtedly dating from the middle ages.

Schrøter continued to collect ballad material for the rest of his long life. He also made two important translations into Faroese: of the Gospel according to St. Matthew (1823) and the Icelandic *Saga of the Faroemen* (1832).

Provost Hentze, working on Sandoy, made a collection of eighteen ballads which in 1819 he sent to Lyngbye in Denmark. His assistant and amanuensis, Johannes Klemensen, or Jóannes í Króki (1794–1869), continued recording Faroese *kvæði* for his own interest, and between 1821 and 1831 wrote down the largest collection of ballads ever made — his manuscript has nearly 900 tightly-written pages. In 1872 it was bought by the Danish scholar Svend Grundtvig, who gave it the name *Sandoyarbók* (the Sandoy Book), and it has since passed into the keeping of the Royal Library in Copenhagen. In 1968 this great collection began to appear in print.

Others now began to collect ballads, notably Hans Hansen, a farmer of Hattarvík on the island of Fugloy, and Napoleon Nolsøe (the son of Jacob Nolsøe), who had a medical practice in Tórshavn. Hans Hansen's large collection now has the name of *Fugloyarbók*; like *Sandoyarbók,* it is a collection of considerable size, although its contents are less consistently high in quality than those of its predecessor.

Venceslaus Ulricus Hammershaimb (1819–1909), who was to give the Faroese language its orthography, collected further ballad texts during his year-long visit to Faroe in 1847–48. These appeared in print at various times from then until 1891.

The various ballad collections were collated and edited as a whole between 1872 and 1905 by the two Danish scholars Svend Grundtvig (1824–83) and Jørgen Bloch (1839–1910). The resulting manuscript of eighteen quarto volumes entitled *Føroyja Kvæði: Corpus carminum Færoensium,* contains almost the complete body of Faroese traditional poetry. It consists of no fewer than 234 items with a total of about 70,000 stanzas. It is now in course of publication.

Collections of Faroese traditional prose literature were undertaken much later than the recording of the poetry. The

pioneers were Hammershaimb and Schrøter, but the work
of the latter was largely vitiated by his not leaving the
material as he had collected it, but assembling different
accounts, which he amplified from his own vivid imagination,
often translating the result into Danish. Hammershaimb's
collections appeared in the periodical *Antiqvariske Tidsskrift*
(1849–51) and in his *Færøsk Anthologi* (1886–91). However,
the greatest collector of Faroese prose stories was to be the
philologist Jakob Jakobsen (1864–1918). His major collections of historical tales of villagers of former times and of
fictitious tales with a magical content were made in the 1890s,
and published as *Færøske folkesagn og æventyr*, between 1898
and 1901. A few of the historical tales are of pre-Reformation
date, with accounts of the Black Death, for example. The
fictitious tales are mostly variants of the common north
European stock — stories of witches, giants, trolls, and the
farm lad who wins the princess.

The recording of this wealth of oral literature demanded an
orthography. The first man to devise a convention for
writing the Faroese language was Svabo, who wrote down his
texts, and the words in his dictionary, in a manner closely
related to Danish orthography. Faced with a diversity of
dialects, Svabo selected that of his native island of Vágar.
Related systems were used by Jóannes í Króki for the
Sandoyarbók, by Lyngbye for *Sigurd Fofnersbane*, and by Schrøter
for his translations, but these were adapted to the dialects of
Sandoy and south Streymoy.

To penetrate the diversity of Faroese dialects and arrive
at an orthography serviceable for all of them equally was a
problem of great importance to those working on the Faroese
language in the first half of the nineteenth century. One way
of reaching ground common to all the dialects was to base the
orthography on the etymology of the words. The first to work
along these lines was Jacob Nolsøe, a poet and lover of the
Icelandic sagas, which he used to read to the crews of boats
waiting to be served at the warehouses of the Monopoly, of
which he was manager. About 1830, he wrote a grammar of

the language, in which the orthography was more etymological than Svabo's — with the side-result that Faroese written in this way becomes closely akin to Icelandic.

The orthography that finally gained general acceptance was devised as a result of the deliberations at the Roskilde Assembly that led to the ill-fated Faroese school law of 1845. The Assembly delegates took it for granted that the medium of instruction in the new schools would be Danish. Many of them indeed, believed that Faroese was not a true language at all, but a corrupted dialect of Danish and Icelandic. To refute this view and lay the foundations of a written Faroese literature was the major achievement of V. U. Hammershaimb.

In an article in the *Kjøbenhavnsposten* of 19 December 1844, over the signature "A Faroeman", Hammershaimb, then a theological student at the university, pointed out that Faroese had all the characteristics of an independent language, however much it might have been influenced by Danish during the centuries that the latter had been the medium of religion and public business. A few months later, Hammershaimb's close friend Svend Grundtvig wrote, under the pseudonym S. Frederiksen, a pamphlet entitled *Dansken paa Færøerne: Sidestykke til Tysken i Slesvig* (Danish in the Faroe Islands, a parallel with German in Slesvig). Grundtvig's point — a very telling one in the political atmosphere of the time — was that just as Danish was under pressure from the German-language elementary schools in the Danish-speaking parts of Slesvig, so, by the proposed school law, the Faroese language would be oppressed by the Danish of the schools in the islands. Danes who objected to the former could not in justice support the latter.

About this time, spurred on by a Danish critic, Hammershaimb became convinced that in order to promote the Faroese language, an orthography was needed, firmly based on etymological principles, that would be common to all the Faroese dialects. With the help of the Icelandic scholar and patriot Jón Sigurðsson (1811–79), he devised the system of rendering Faroese that in essentials is the one used today.

Behind the word for "day", pronounced *dæ-avoor* or *dee-oor*,
Hammershaimb saw the Old Norse form *dagr,* and wrote
dagur. The difference between Svabo's system and Hammershaimb's may be seen from the following conversation, first
as Svabo originally wrote it, and then as modern orthography
renders it:

Svabo's Orthography

Géuan Morgun! Gud signi tee! Kvéat eru Ørindi tujni so
tujlja aa Modni? Ee atli méar tiil Ûtiréurar; Kvussu eer
Vegri? kvussu eer atta? Téa eer got enn, men Ee vajt ikkji
kvussu téa viil téaka see up méuti Deï. Viil tû ikkji féara vi?
Naj! Kvuj taa? tuj Ee vanti méar ajnkji aa Sjéunun, o téa eer
betri à féara éat Sejï.

Hammershaimb's Orthography (as used today)

Goðan morgun! Gud signi teg! Hvat er ørindi tíni so tíðliga á
morgni? Eg ætli mær til útroðrar; Hvussu er veðrið? hvussu er
ættað? Tað er gott enn, men eg veit ikki, hvussu tað vil taka seg
upp móti degi. Vil tu ikki fara við? Nej! Hví tað? tí eg vænti
mær einki á sjónum, og tað er betri at fara at seyði.

English

Good morning! God bless you! What is your business so early
in the morning? I intend to row out (i.e. go boat-fishing).
What is the weather? What is the wind direction? It is still
good, but I don't know how it will be later in the day. Won't
you come along? No! Why so? Because I don't expect to
catch any fish and it's better to go to look after the sheep (i.e.
in the outfield).

Hammershaimb's orthography made Faroese texts easily
comprehensible to the many scholars and others in Scandinavia
who could read Icelandic or Old Norse. Hammershaimb
also wrote the first Faroese grammar to appear in print (1854).

Besides achieving recognition for Faroese as an independent European language, Hammershaimb's work in time enabled a native literature to develop, which in turn aroused a new national self-consciousness within the islands.

THE BEGINNINGS OF FAROESE LITERATURE

In a letter dated 5 November 1879, written to catch the last ship of the year, a seventeen-year-old Faroese boy, in the final year of his Danish school before going on to Copenhagen University, wrote to his father:

In the library I got hold of Hammershaimb's Faroese Grammar; it interests me very much, especially now that I have made fair progress in Old Norse; it is truly fascinating to see how the language has developed and how little difference there is in reality between the older and the newer language. I wonder whether it would not be possible for Faroese to become once again a written language, to supersede Danish as the official language? It does seem to me a rather remarkable thing that even so small a people as the Faroese should use one language in speech and another language, as remote as Danish really is, in writing, in church and in the law-courts. I would like to learn to write Faroese; I have several times tried it, and really it is not difficult. Even by writing the words in Old Norse one comes fairly close to the correct form.

His father replied:

You tell me in your letter that you have got hold of Hammershaimb's Faroese Grammar, in which connection you advance the question whether it is not an unnatural linguistic situation that is to be found here, in that the population speaks one language in the home and a quite different one in the church and the law-courts, and whether it might be possible to get this position altered so that one might elevate Faroese into a written language and as the official language, and that of the church and courts. It is after all an old idea that is coming up here once again, and as I learn from Finsen that this is something which haunts the minds of most of the Faroese who study in Denmark and has even been discussed in *Morgenposten*, I should rather like to give you my detailed opinion about the matter, since I would very much wish to discourage you from engaging yourself deeply in this chimera, since even though for a short period it should work itself through to a reality, yet instead of bringing the Faroese population a new vitality, by isolation it would so weaken it that it would soon go down before the powerful English nationality, which geographically lies so very close to us ... The Faroe Islands have a population of only about 10,000 people, the same as a medium-sized market town in Denmark; how should it be conceivable that so small a population would have the power to support a literature that would content other than spiritual Lilliputians? ...

It seems to me that the spirit of the time is, moreover, working towards the union of the related into larger nationalities, instead of searching out with microscopic delicacy particularities by which to define a new people — for behind a literary language must stand a people who in any event have enough spiritual if not physical power to guard it against destruction ... Yet I once certainly did think of the possibility of the Faroese language being used up here in all public *speaking*, as well in church as in the Lagting and the law-court, since as the customary language of the people, it influences the emotional life more readily than the more remote Danish ...

The father was Enok Daniel Bærentsen (1831–1900), descendant of a long line of farmers who had leased a crown tenancy at Sund, a few miles north of Tórshavn. But he had left the land, obtained a commercial education in Copenhagen, and after the abolition of the Monopoly had settled in Tórshavn as a merchant. He was also an active politician. He sat briefly in the Danish parliament, and for twenty-four years was an active member of the Løgting, having been in the 1850s one of the members chiefly responsible for the removal of *amtmand* Dahlerup. The son, Christian Bærentsen (1862–1944) studied law and became the first and only native-born *amtmand* of Faroe (1897-1911). Their exchange shows very clearly the dilemma facing patriotic and intelligent Faroemen. If Faroese were to be launched as a written language for all public and literary purposes, would it lead to the isolation and eventual destruction of the Faroese nation, as commercial links with Britain steadily developed? The blossoming of Icelandic literature earlier in the century gave the Faroese some hope of success, but the population of Faroe was only a fraction of that of its northerly neighbour.

Although a generation had passed since Hammershaimb had published his orthography and grammar, his youthful dream of a Faroese literature at last came to pass owing to the efforts of the very students referred to by Enok Bærentsen. In his son's lifetime, a printed literature took its place beside the oral literature that Faroe had known hitherto.

In the 1870s, Faroese students, fired by an ambition to raise the status of their native tongue, began to write Faroese drinking and patriotic songs. Many were fired by the political success of the Icelanders, who in 1874 attained a large measure of home rule: there was much contact between Icelandic and Faroese students. The most important of the Faroese students was Frederik Petersen (1853–1917), who attended school in Reykjavík before entering Copenhagen University to study theology. It was Petersen, later provost of the Faroe Islands who wrote the first Faroese national anthem *Eg oyggjar veit* (I know of islands) ; after his return to his native country he wrote three Faroese hymns of great beauty, which in time took their place beside the Danish hymnal which was used in the churches. The old ballad style was now no longer the sole Faroese poetic idiom — lyric verse had begun to blossom. The social gatherings of the Faroese students in Copenhagen led in 1881 to the formation of the *Føroyingafelag* (Faroese Union), devoted to the advancement of Faroese culture amongst Faroemen resident in Denmark.

The example of the students was later taken up in Faroe itself. A group of Faroemen concerned for the building of a new national culture to replace the traditional one, now perishing with the old peasant community, called a meeting in the Tinghus (parliament building) in Tórshavn for the afternoon of 26 December, 1888. The aim of the meeting was announced as being "to discuss how to defend the Faroese language and Faroese customs".

Amongst the convenors of the meeting was Enok Bærentsen, who in nine years had modified his views on the practicability of maintaining a national literature in the islands. There was also Rasmus Effersøe (1857–1916), agricultural consultant and poet, and the farmer's son Jóannes Patursson (1866–1946), then making one of his first appearances in public. Those present at the meeting were aroused to great enthusiasm and emotion reached its height when Effersøe recited a poem written by the young Patursson, *Nu er tann stundin komin til handa* (Now the moment is with us), which contains an impassioned appeal to Faroemen to defend their language against foreign (i. e. Danish) influences that were threatening to corrupt and overthrow it. (On this occasion the poet himself was too shy to recite his own work, though in later years he became anything but a shy man.)

The outcome of the meeting was the formation, early in 1889, of the *Føringafelag*[1] (Faroese Union), with the twofold aims of bringing the Faroese language into honour, and of working for the unity, progress, and self-sufficiency of the Faroese people. The society hoped that in time the language would be used for all public business, and that a strong Faroese literature would develop.

The most important work of the society was the issue of a newspaper, *Føringatíðindi,* written exclusively in Faroese. The only newspaper published in the islands at that time was *Dimmalætting* (first regularly printed in 1878, after a trial issue had appeared the previous year). Although *Dimmalætting* bore a Faroese title (meaning 'Daybreak'), it only occasionally carried articles in Faroese, and the public were generally unacquainted with the conventions of writing their own language. However, *Føringatíðindi,* which appeared from 1890 to 1901, can without exaggeration be said to have taught

---

[1] Distinct from the earlier Copenhagen society of the same name and slightly different spelling.

the Faroese nation to read and write its own language.

Learning to read and write Faroese was more than simply mastering an orthography. The new Faroese authors, like those of Tudor England, had to invent a whole range of new words for the purposes of literature, scholarship and modern life in general. But instead of borrowing foreign words (as the English writers often did), the members of the Føringafelag preferred to develop the language from its own internal resources. The old ballads were ransacked for useful linguistic material, and ingenious compounds were devised to take the place of Danish words in current vernacular use. Yet when Rasmus Effersøe, the first editor of *Føringatiðindi*, claimed that he could not think a thought that he was unable to express in his mother tongue, it was reckoned a very bold statement. For Faroese, rich and vivid as it might be for anything tangible, say for the work of field or fjord, was poor in words for expressing abstract conceptions.

Danish influence, though abhorrent from a linguistic point of view, was a powerful cultural element in shaping the Faroese national movement. Most important as an influence were perhaps the ideals propagated by the Danish folk high schools. These schools arose in Denmark from 1844 onwards in response to the growth of democracy within the country, and the outside threat that Danish culture might be overwhelmed from the German south. The folk high schools aimed at giving the Danish peasantry a liberal education and making them aware of the cultural inheritance which was now passing into their protection. The situation in Faroe at the end of the century was obviously analogous. Several leading members of Føringafelag had attended folk high schools in Denmark, and two of them, Símun av Skarði (1872–1942) and Rasmus Rasmussen (1871–1962) founded the Faroe folk high school in 1899. For many years this was the only school in the islands in which the Faroese language was either a subject or the medium of instruction; it shared with *Føringatiðindi* the task of building a literary language and bringing to life a national culture. For ten years the school remained in a remote corner of the island of Borðoy, but in 1909 it was removed to Tórshavn, the country's natural cultural centre.

The charismatic leader of the Føringafelag was the young Jóannes Patursson, who in every way was fitted to become the leader and hero of the national movement. He was the eldest son of the crown tenant of Kirkjubøur, and himself inherited the lease — the largest in the Faroe Islands — in 1891. Patursson had close links with Iceland and Norway, the countries with closest cultural affinities to Faroe. His wife was an Icelander, and he had attended agricultural college in Norway. In Norway he had become deeply involved emotionally with the linguistic struggle there, which had many similarities with that in Faroe.[1] His home had been the palace of the mediaeval bishops of Faroe. So daily he was surrounded by the most impressive monuments of Faroese antiquity; and in his farm the *sagn* and the *kvæði* had for centuries been diligently cultivated.

Jóannes Patursson was an accomplished poet in both the traditional ballad idiom and in the lyric style of the new Faroese literature. His output consisted mostly of patriotic songs, but he also wrote hymns. For nine months he edited

---

[1] During the period of Danish rule, the town-dwellers and official classes of Norway, especially in the less sparsely populated eastern parts of the country, came to speak a language that was very close to Danish. The rise of national romanticism led the self-taught philologist Ivar Aasen (1813–96) to study the peasant dialects of Norway, in which he recognised the true descendant of Old Norse. From these country dialects Aasen worked out a common literary standard — what in fact the Norwegian language would have become had the union of crowns with Denmark never taken place — and from 1853 he tried to propagate it as the vehicle of a truly national literature. The struggle between the proponents of Danish-Norwegian and those of Aasen's *landsmaal* has been long and bitter. Aasen's language has been an inspiration to many Norwegian writers; but the attempt to introduce it nationally has led to much confusion and controversy in Norway's educational system. But the *landsmaal*, being heavily dependent on the valley dialects of west Norway, has a good deal in common with Faroese, and it is easy to understand Patursson's enthusiasm for it.

Føringatiðindi. His public work included projects as diverse as an attempt to have trees planted in the islands and, with his brother Sverre and others, the foundation in 1895 of a Faroe Islands museum. He was above all a political figure, and as we will see later, he was principally responsible for the later development of the national movement along political lines, with demands for home rule accompanying the struggle for cultural autonomy.

A dispute about orthography finally broke up the Føringa-felag. In the 1890s the philologist Jakob Jakobsen, who was no mean stylist in his native language, proposed changes in the Hammershaimb system of writing Faroese to bring it closer to the pronunciation, particularly that used in south Streymoy, which was tending to become the Faroese standard. The proposals led to bitter disputes within the society, and when in addition differences of temperament led to quarrels between Rasmus Effersøe and Jóannes Patursson, the society ceased to function and the newspaper survived it by only a year.

By the beginning of the twentieth century, Faroese was established as a literary language, although no works of genius had yet appeared in it. Vernacular journalism did not flourish, however, and the next newspaper to be published in Tórshavn was written principally in Danish. Of the considerable quantity of miscellaneous journalism in Faroese published about this time, most lasted only a short time. The most notable publication was the first Faroese literary review, *Búreisingur,* which went through six numbers in 1902. Its editor was the minister of Sandoy, A. C. Evensen (1874–1917). It has recently been republished as part of a series of the classics of early Faroese literature.

There was somewhat more success in other literary fields. From 1889 a small amateur theatre in Tórshavn was producing Faroese plays, many of them from the pen of Rasmus Effersøe. A. C. Evensen was a pioneer of island historiography by publishing a collection of documents relating to the sixteenth-century history of Faroe, accompanied by a Faroese

commentary (1908–14). He also made a translation of St.
John's Gospel, which was published in 1908 by the Scripture
Gift Mission of London. From 1911, even scientific works
began to appear in the Faroese language.

Of fundamental importance for the development of the
language was the production of vernacular literature for
children. A. C. Evensen wrote school readers and anthologies,
while Jacob Dahl (1878–1944), a teacher who became a
priest, and succeeded Frederik Peterson and A. C. Evensen
as provost, brought out a Faroese school grammar. Nothing
brought written Faroese to the consciousness of children
growing up in the early years of the present century more
forcibly than the children's magazine *Ungu Føroyar*, published
in 1907–8 and 1914–15; it was the work of Símun av Skarði,
assisted during the first year by Símun Pauli úr Konoy
(1876–1956). The magazine contained poems, traditional
and modern stories, articles on world affairs, historical
personages and natural history, jokes, riddles, pictures and
a small amount of religious material. It was well-written, and
the children used to await its monthly appearance with great
eagerness. It was from *Ungu Føroyar* that most children of
this period learned to read and write their mother tongue.
Their school books were, of course, exclusively in Danish.

The outbreak of the 1914–18 war saw the Faroese language
widely used as a vehicle of literature. Little had yet been
printed that would have repaid the trouble of translation
into any other tongue, with the exception of the traditional
ballads and prose stories; but there could no longer be any
doubt that in time Faroese would take its place among the
literary languages of Europe.

NATIONALISM BECOMES POLITICAL

Faroe had been politically quiescent since the early days of
the revived Løgting and the struggle leading to the removal
of *Amtmand* Dahlerup. This was probably because the natural
leaders of political life in the islands in the latter half of the

nineteenth century were few in number, well-known to one
another personally, and united in economic interest. Nearly
all the politically active were either officials (not, as in
Britain, debarred from political activity) and merchants. The
Danish political group most closely approximating to the-
political outlook of these men was the *Højre*, or Conservative
Party; and although the politically active never felt any need
for formal political organisation during this period, the Faroe
Islands could be considered a safe conservative constituency.
Only once, in 1884, was a member elected to the Danish
parliament who belonged to the *Venstre*, or Liberal Party.
Polling for the Folketing elections was always extremely low,
reflecting the lack of information available to the Faroese
electorate on Copenhagen politics.

At this time the work of the Løgting was generally non-
controversial, so that there was no stimulus to the growth of
political parties on the basis of local issues. Those elected to
seats on the Løgting were nearly always local personalities,
and the electoral divisions were small enough for a choice
on the basis of personality to be real. The problem of primary
education, for example, was solved in 1872 on non-partisan
lines by the introduction of a system of local government
(see page 104).

Another important but non-controversial issue typical of
the work of the Løgting was the legislation proposed by the
Faroese chamber and passed through the Danish parliament
for increasing the area of cultivated land. It had become the
custom, particularly around Tórshavn, for landless fishermen
to rent stretches of outfield from farmers, usually crown
tenants, for use as allotments (*traðir,* singular *trøð*). On these
they would grow hay and potatoes to assist the household
economy. It was considered to be in the public interest that
these allotments should pass into the absolute ownership of
those who cultivated them, and negotiations led finally to
two allotment laws being passed. The first, dated 19 January,
1863 enabled all the Tórshavn tenants to purchase their
allotments at twenty-five years' rental, which sum could be

converted into a state mortgage at an interest rate of 4 per cent. The second law, dated 13 April, 1894, permitted allotments to be purchased on similar terms from crown land anywhere in the islands, although not in smaller areas than were sufficient for the winter foddering of one cow. Sometimes such a *trøð* might carry with it the rights of summer pasture for the cow on the village outfield, sometimes not. These technical but highly useful measures are typical of the type of legislation for which the assistance of a locally-elected body is essential.

The allotment acts had not long been on the statute book when Jóannes Patursson burst upon the political scene with romantic and patriotic aims and a quite new type of politics. In the Danish Folketing elections of 1901, the conservatives, after a long period of power, were ousted from office, and a Venstre government, supported by a landslide majority, took over. The member for Faroe, now for the second time in its history returning a Venstre candidate, was Jóannes Patursson. Patursson, probably because he was seen as a romantic young peasant-patriot from the distant Faroe Islands, was given a warm reception in Copenhagen.

Patursson was of the Venstre, yet he was not particularly interested in or well-informed about matters in metropolitan Denmark. Politics for him were Faroese politics. His intention was to promote Faroese home rule, giving to the Løgting in Tórshavn a central position in legislation for the islands.

After his re-election in the 1903 Folketing elections, Patursson advocated his cause very skilfully in a little book entitled *Førøsk Politik*, published the same year. He produced an abundance of evidence to show that the Faroe Islands had formed an administrative and judicial entity separate from Denmark throughout their history, down to the time of constitution-making in Denmark. Next, by a masterly use of quotations from the speeches of the founding fathers of the Danish constitution, particularly those of whom the Venstre politicians regarded themselves as the spiritual and political heirs, Patursson showed that the constitutional arrangements incorporating the islands in the Danish kingdom had never received Faroese consent. He concluded that the extension to Faroe of the 1849 constitution had been irregular and remained so.

Patursson's programme for the future was based on five main demands: (i) that the Løgting should consist only of elected members, and that it should choose its own chairman; (ii) that the Danish government representative (i.e. the *amtmand*) should have the right to speak in the Løgting, but not to vote, unless he himself were an elected member; (iii) that no law applying to Faroe alone should be valid unless it were ratified in its entirety by the Løgting; (iv) that the Løgting should have the power to submit draft laws direct to the Danish government, instead of through the Danish parliament; and (v) that the Løgting should have financial control of moneys both raised and spent in Faroe.

This programme, particularly its last point, raised a storm in the Faroe Islands — especially when Patursson claimed that the Danish government had declared in support of his policy. The merchants and officials in the islands feared, on good grounds, that such a measure of autonomy for the islands would bring about a vast increase in direct taxation. For many years the Faroe Islands had been costing the Danish exchequer more than they had yielded in tax, and with the prospect of expensive new capital projects like a telephone system and improved harbour facilities, Faroese home rule could at this time have been a heavy burden economically.

The opponents of Patursson's policy therefore joined together in 1906 to defeat him at the polls in the elections for both the Folketing and the Løgting. The leaders of this movement were Frederik Petersen, Oliver Effersøe (1863–1933),[1] and Andreas Samuelsen (1873–1954). After a convincing electoral victory they constituted themselves into the *Sambandsflokkurin,* or Unionist Party, dedicated to the defence of the existing constitutional link with Denmark, and to economy in the management of the Løgting's finances.

---

[1] A brother of Rasmus Effersøe of the Føringafelag.

The Danish government withdrew support for Patursson's policy after his electoral defeat. They were unwilling to force on the Faroese people any constitutional arrangements that were clearly unwanted. The very offer that had previously been made of Danish government support for a Faroe Islands home rule bill was later represented as having never been more than the private scheme of one of the Venstre ministers, P. A. Alberti, who in 1908 fell from office as the result of a major financial scandal. So as to clinch matters, the new Folketing member Oliver Effersøe, although known hitherto as a conservative in Danish politics, now diplomatically declared his adherence to the ruling Venstre party. Some Venstre members might still feel much affection for Patursson and his aims, but by his action Effersøe initiated an alliance between the Faroese Samband and the Danish Venstre which has now lasted for well over half a century.

The natural reaction of the Løgting minority which supported Patursson was to found its own party with the aim of recovering the ground that had been lost. Thus came about the formation of the *Sjálvstýrisflokkurin*, or Home Rule Party later in 1906. Its members were far from being the separatists as which their political opponents often represented them. The policy of the Sjálvstýri was indeed moderation itself compared with some of the notions that were to be current later in the century. They wanted a greater degree of autonomy for the Løgting, with increased financial powers and the right to approve or reject any legislation passed in the Danish parliament and applying solely to Faroe. They wanted a continuation of the ancient system whereby affairs in the islands were administered by a single minister in the Danish government instead of being spread among the different departments. Finally, they wanted as wide a use as possible of the Faroese language and its admission to equal status with Danish for all uses within the islands.

The two newspapers in Faroe ranged themselves on opposite sides in the political struggle which now began. The old-established *Dimmalætting* supported the Samband, and

Tingakrossur, which had begun publication in 1901, became the organ of the Sjálvstýri. With the formal organisation of political parties personal animosities began to grow in Faroese politics, and through the pages of these two newspapers, a sharp note of controversy became apparent.

The strongest card of the home-rulers was the emotional pull of the Faroese language and the impetus of the national movement. In 1912, the Sjálvstýri acquired a useful martyr in this cause, Louis Zachariasen (1890–1960), a young and skilful teacher in Velbastaður, just over the hills from Tórshavn. He insisted on using the Faroese language in the classroom, contrary to a school regulation issued earlier that year that Danish should be the medium of instruction, while Faroese was to be used only as an aid to understanding the Danish of the lessons. For the instruction of the younger children, Faroese was inescapable, which made the regulation nonsensical. For teaching many subjects to older children, Faroese still lacked a suitable vocabulary, and as there were no Faroese schoolbooks, Danish would have been necessary, with or without the regulation. Everybody knew this, but Zachariasen not only broke the regulation but proclaimed that he was doing so. When the *amtmand*, Svenning Rytter, tried to force him to follow it, he resigned on the issue. It was, of course, Rytter's duty to enforce regulations, and this was far from being the only occasion when he had to use strict measures with recalcitrant teachers; however, his involvement made it seem that the Danish government was bent on oppressing the Faroese language, and maintaining the existing state of affairs, with Faroe as the northernmost province of Denmark, by means of Faroese linguistic and cultural subordination. This made good propaganda for the Sjálvstýri.

But despite the emotional strength of the appeal the Sjálvstýri was capable of making, the Samband dominated the Løgting in at least the proportion of three to two right up to the first world war; and the Folketing elections of 1909, 1910 and 1913 gave a convincing mandate to candidates who were Samband in Faroe and Venstre in Denmark.

CHAPTER VII

THE FISHING INDUSTRY, 1900–1939

THE INDUSTRY ABOUT 1900

The first fishing sloop came to the Faroe Islands in 1872 (see pages 98), and its success soon led other Faroemen to buy up the vessels that the British fishing industry was then selling off cheaply as it turned over to steam trawling. The great age of sloop buying was the twenty-year period 1890 to 1910, during which the Faroese deep-sea fishing fleet rose from fourteen to 137 sloops. At the turn of the century over 1,000 men were employed on these sloops, and by 1910 the figure was 1,823. (Over the same period, the population as a whole was growing from just over 15,000 to nearly 18,000.)

There were several reasons why the boom in sloop-fishing should have begun in the 1890s. An important factor was the nature of sloop finance. No trading banks or other sophisticated financial institutions existed in Faroe, and these sloops were bought principally with the savings of the more thrifty fishermen. It happened that 1891 was a particularly good fishing season, and world market conditions kept prices for the catch high. The 1891 season set in motion much capital investment that continued through the succeeding years, as sloop income was reinvested.

A second stimulus to sloop buying was the foundation in 1892 of a Faroese scheme of mutual insurance for sailing vessels. Insurance premiums with *Færøernes gensidige forsikrings-forening for sejlfartøjer til fiskeribrug* (The Faroe Islands' mutual insurance union for fishing vessels under sail) were only one-third of those charged by foreign insurers. A further reason was a modification made in 1892 to the law concerning the certificates needed by fishing skippers, which had previously been needlessly strict. At the same time it became possible for the relative examinations to be taken within the Faroe Islands instead of abroad. This measure quickly multiplied the number of sloop skippers available for the fishery.

The first sloop brought to Faroe, *Fox,* was of only 38 gross registered tons; but the vessels purchased later were usually of between 70 and 100 gross registered tons. They were from about 80 to 100 feet long, and loaded they would draw about 12 feet of water. They were handsome craft, slender and deep, built of oak, and with a sharp stem rising straight out of the water. The rigging consisted of a main-mast and gaff, supporting a foresail, jib, mainsail, topsail, stern-sail and stern-top-sail. For fishing off Iceland, they carried a crew of eleven to fifteen, which was one or two more than were needed for operations on the banks near the Faroe Islands.

In March, the sloops would make for the Faroe Banks, a rich fishing-ground some 100 miles south-west of Suðuroy. Later in the year, when the weather was more reliable, they would go north to Iceland, especially to the south and east coasts. As the cod were caught they would be cleaned, split and salted on board, and packed into the hold. When twenty to forty tons were aboard, a sloop would return to Faroe; at the port where it discharged, the women would be waiting to spread the catch out on the rocks to wind-dry it into klipfish. The sloop then returned to Iceland for more. The season ended in September; the sloop would return to its home port, and the crew would strip it and lay it up for the winter.

The customary payment system was for the sloop-owners to take two-thirds of the catch and the crew one-third, with the ship's provisioning to be at the expense of the owner. In a good year a fisherman might make 250 to 400 kroner in six or seven months. But life on board was hard: in fair weather when the fishing was good, the men might be working all round the clock, and in bad weather, they would be confined to the two cabins with a floor space of only a few square feet. Several Faroese novels have been written by men who went out on the sloops, and these vividly depict the cramped quarters, the snatched meals and the ceaseless fishing when the sloops were out on the Iceland banks.

Despite the rapid growth in the number of sloops, inshore fishing from small boats was still important to the economy at the turn of the century, as the following table will show:

Salt fish landed in the Faroe Islands, 1895-99
(tons)

Year	Inshore fishermen	Sloops		Total
		off Faroe	Iceland	
1895	3,152	1,264	1,383	2,647
1896	4,619	2,719	1,067	3,786
1897	2,862	862	2,024	2,886
1898	2,562	939	2,031	2,970
1899	2,790	1,108	2,002	3,110

Indeed, the tonnage landed by inshore fishermen did not noticeably decline until after the 1914–18 war, although by that time the annual catch being landed by the deep-water fleet averaged over 9,000 tons. In 1898 there were an estimated 2,000 rowing-boats in Faroe, although the number was tending to decline. From about 1911 onwards there were about 1,500.

But the growth point at the end of the century was clearly the Iceland fishery. After 1898, the waters around Faroe were being progressively invaded by steam trawlers from Britain, which the Faroese accused of over-fishing and depleting fish stocks, fishing inside territorial waters, and operating trawls with a complete disregard for the inshore fisherman's long-lines. The Danes, at Faroese request, kept a small gunboat in the islands to protect Faroese fishing rights, and from 1900 the British found it necessary to have a resident Englishman appointed as their consul in Tórshavn to settle the inevitable disputes. There was consternation in Faroe in 1901 when an agreement between the British and Danish governments set the fishing limits round the Faroe Islands at three miles only, and there were predictions of the utter ruin of the Faroese inshore fishery. Off Iceland, however, there was still room for all.

POWERED FISHING VESSELS

The installation of engine power in Faroese fishing vessels began in 1904, when auxiliary engines were installed in some of the sloops. After the 1914–18 war, more powerful engines were used, until it was the sail rather than the engine that was the auxiliary power source; but capital was never plentiful, and as late as 1927 there were still only sixty Faroese fishing vessels powered with internal combustion engines, as against 112 relying on sail alone. Six years later, however, the position was transformed, with only sixteen vessels lacking engine power. The immediate motive was that the most profitable fishing-grounds were now even further afield.

The first steam trawler owned in the Faroe Islands was bought in 1911, and other purchases followed, but Faroe possessed no considerable trawler fleet until the very eve of the second world war, as the following table shows:

Steam Trawlers in the Faroe Islands, 1911-38

1911	— 1	1934-5	— 1
1922	— 2	1936	— 5
1926	— 3	1937	— 3
1927-30	— 1	1938	— 10

All these trawlers were bought in Britain, and all were fairly old when purchased.

The inshore fishery also felt the effects of the internal combustion engine. Its first motor-boat went into service in 1905, by 1911 there were 120 powered boats, and by 1914 there were 186. Many of these were quite large craft with decks; but from the 1920s, as outboard motors became available, there was a gradual decline in the number of decked boats with fixed motors. The small rowing-boat powered with an outboard motor is of particular service in the many Faroese villages that lack proper harbour facilities, where the boats have to be hauled ashore, often in a heavy sea. Such small boats are often not only fishing-boats, but also the villager's principal link with his town or with the mail-boat that once a week will lie off his village for goods or travellers to be ferried ashore.

The installation of petrol engines has to a certain extent modified the traditional lines of the Faroese boat. Petrol-driven boats are longer, broader and deeper than comparable rowing-boats used to be; but Faroese boats still preserve the shape of miniature long-ships and have excellent sea-going properties in the difficult tidal currents round the islands.

It was in this manner that the islanders, in both their inshore and their distant-water fisheries, began to enter the machine age. The growth of a modern, power-based fishing industry now led to a multitude of social changes, and to the growth of institutions already well-known in other parts of Europe, but not previously found necessary in Faroe.

THE INDUSTRIAL REVOLUTION

The years from 1900 to 1928 might be called the period of the Faroese industrial revolution. From this time on, the mainstay of the Faroese economy — the deep-sea fishing industry — instead of being village-based and heavily dependent on the personal and family relationships between villagers, became much more of a capitalised structure, in which the relationship between employer and employee became less close, and based principally upon a monetary link. The old sloops that had been bought in Britain from 1872 onwards had each cost only about 10,000 kroner, a sum which could be raised by individual men or groups of men. As the new century advanced, ships became dearer to buy and fit out. Average prices rose first to 25,000 kroner and then to 50,000 kroner.[1] Credit institutions had to be founded, so between 1900

---

[1] I have tried to avoid burdening the reader with the complexities of Danish monetary history, but an explanation of the new unit is necessary. From 1625

and 1928, Faroe became a country of limited liability companies, banks and government credit for industrial development.
At the same time, it became a country of trade unions, employers' associations and government intervention in industrial disputes. Yet the impersonality of relations between employer and
employee or between investor and entrepreneur usually found in
countries with populations of many millions did not develop to
the same extent where the population only numbered thousands.

Up till this time the development of financial institutions
had been slow. The first Faroese bank had been Faerø Amts
Sparekasse, the savings bank founded in 1832. This, however,
had not been designed as a sophisticated organ of industrial
finance but principally as an aid to thrift amongst the ordinary
people. The Sparekasse gave depositors an interest of 3 per
cent, and kept a fair proportion of its deposits either on
mortgage loans locally or in 4 per cent Danish government
securities. After the introduction of free trade in 1856, the
level of depositors' balances dropped sharply to about 60 per
cent of the 1855 level, since many Faroemen now preferred
to lend their savings to the local merchant who would be
prepared to give 6 per cent interest, although the security for
such a loan was far less.

By the turn of the century, the larger merchants were
carrying out many of the functions of banking houses. Any
company exporting fish or importing merchandise on a
considerable scale had necessarily to deal in foreign bills, and
would often be used as an intermediary when payments were
being made abroad. Indeed, an English handbook of 1880
lists two Faroese business houses as banks.

---

until the Napoleonic war, the monetary unit had been the rigsdaler, divided
into 96 skillings, one rigsdaler being equivalent to about 4s 6d sterling in the
late eighteenth century. In 1813, after the inflation and state bankruptcy,
a new monetary unit, the rigsbankdaler, was introduced, which was equivalent
to about 2s 3d sterling. From about 1850 this unit was commonly termed the
rigsdaler. The krone, divided into 100 øre, was introduced in 1873 as a common
monetary system for the whole of Scandinavia. It was equivalent to half the
rigsdaler it was superseding.

A proposal that a trading bank should be established in Faroe was put forward by the Løgting in 1904. It was subsequently agreed that a branch of the Danish Landmandsbank should be set up in Tórshavn with a share capital of 300,000 kroner, Faroe residents having the right to contribute up to half this sum over a period of five years. This bank, Føroya Banki, duly opened its doors on 1 March 1906, though the Faroese response to advertisements in *Dimmalætting* and *Tingakrossur,* inviting investment in the shares of the new enterprise, was disappointingly small, and over 90 per cent of the capital came from Denmark. No purely Faroese bank existed until 1932. Føroya Banki was, however, soon working on the finance of local business to the limit of its modest resources, usually lending its money against security in real estate. By 1914, deposit balances in Føroya Banki totalled 840,000 kroner, and 178,000 kroner were on loan to local business houses, either in the finance of local trade or to assist ship purchase.

Also in 1904, the Løgting drafted the first law giving government credit for the purchase of fishing vessels. According to the law as it was finally passed by the Danish parliament, 60,000 kroner were to be made available for loans for the purchase of vessels costing at least 1,000 kroner each. These loans were not to exceed two-thirds of the cost of new vessels, nor half the cost of old ones. The interest rate was 3 per cent and the repayment period ten years. This law came into operation in 1905 for a trial period of five years, and was periodically renewed. From 1920 the Løgting tried to get this scheme greatly enlarged to finance trawler purchase, but negotiations with the Danish government brought no results until 1928. However, more funds were available from 1923 onwards for the purchase of sloops and the fitting of engines into them.

Despite improved public and private credit facilities, capital remained tight, and the fishing fleet consisted largely of old vessels. In 1908, only ten out of 133 vessels were less than twenty years old. Renewal of the fishing fleet usually took the form of buying old ships to replace still older ones. Nevertheless, as a result of bank loans and government assistance, but most of all through continued vigorous home investment, the Faroese fishing fleet attained a capital value by 1926 of nearly 3,000,000 kroner.

It was only to be expected that in an industry employing so many men and so much capital, collective bargaining would develop for the determination of the rates of pay for fishermen. As early as 1896, the Faroese fishing skippers had an association, Færøernes Skipperforening, to protect their interests. It was only with the formation in 1909 of the shipowners' association, Færøernes Rederiforening, that institutionalised bargaining between masters and men began in earnest.

In a meeting at Tvøroyri on 4 December, 1909, the shipowners agreed on a standard form of contract for the employment of fishermen. The basis of this contract was existing practice, which in turn stemmed from the old Faroese idea of one-third to the man who supplied the labour, and two-thirds to the man who provided the means. On the sloops, as we have seen, the crew were paid the price of one-third of the catch; from the owner's two-thirds came the crew's provisioning, all operating costs, and payments to the skipper, the mate and the cook. Expenses connected with bait, however, fell on the catch as a whole.

Although sound in many ways, this contract had certain flaws, the biggest being the uncertain scope of the clause governing bait expenses. Since on any fishing expedition part of the catch is used as bait, it was a reasonable extension of this principle that the cost of any bait that had to be bought and of preserving it on ice should fall on the catch. In practice, the wording of the provision that on the joint catch should fall "*every* kind of expense on the acquisition of bait and its storage" proved capable of being interpreted in a sense far beyond the herrings and ice it was probably intended to cover. It is said that in the 1910 and 1911 seasons, some owners financed the purchase of ice-boxes and other capital items — even ship's boats — out of the joint catch; and provided these were used in the acquisition of bait or its storage, no legal redress could be had by the wronged crew, even if they had the resources to bring an action.

It was a natural result that a fishermen's union should be formed as a counterweight to the shipowners' association. The initiative was taken by the fishermen of Gøta on Eysturoy, who in December 1910 circulated letters to the fishermen of every village in Faroe. The outcome was the formation, on 1 March, 1911, of the Føroya Fiskimannafelag, or Faroese fishermen's union. It was too late for action over the 1911 fishing season, but by autumn the union was at work.

Prominent among the early members of the union executive were certain sympathisers who were not themselves fishermen: A. C. Evensen, the minister of Sandoy; Rasmus Rasmussen of the folk high school, and the lawyer and poet J. H. O. Djurhuus. The union's chairman for fifteen years was the Gøta schoolmaster, Símun Pauli úr Konoy. The reason for this close involvement of non-fishermen was twofold. First, in so intimate a community as that of Faroe, and especially in a Faroese village, every man, regardless of his own occupation, tends to feel a personal involvement with the fate of his fellow-men. And from the viewpoint of the fishermen themselves, it was an advantage to have at least part of their excutive ashore in the Faroe Islands when most of the union members were at sea.

Joint bargaining with the owners over the contract began for the 1912 season. The fishermen deliberately made their earliest demands modest and reasonable, concentrating on clauses that lacked close definition. The regulations concerning bait were sharpened to the advantage of the fishermen, and there were other small changes. In subsequent years the fishermen's battle-cry was "the pure third" — a claim to a third of the catch, free of all deductions.

The union's most difficult negotiations in its early years were for the 1918 contract. War conditions were causing sudden and unexpected changes in the whole pattern of expenses of fitting out fishing vessels. Costs were high, although the prices at which fish could be sold were also very favourable. The 1918 difficulty arose from the German proclamation of unrestricted submarine warfare, which quickly resulted in a tenfold rise in the price of salt. The shipowners proposed that the cost of salt should fall on the joint catch. When the union proposed an alternative concession to help the shipowners, based on fixed fish prices for calculating the crew's payment, the Suðuroy fishermen were dissatisfied with the principle involved, and a strike in that island seemed imminent. At the last minute, the Suðuroy fishermen's leader requested the *amtmand* to intervene, and after two days of hard and very technical negotiation, a separate Suðuroy agreement was signed — about a week before the start of the fishing season.

After the return of more normal conditions the following year, the "pure third" principle was restored, and negotiations thereafter tended to revolve around fringe duties and fringe benefits. The crews' unpaid contractual obligations were gradually reduced, a travel allowance to and from the ship was introduced, special conditions for engine-room and galley crew were negotiated, and an end was put to the old system whereby fishermen were paid only after the sale of the catch. By the mid-1930s, the crew's share of the catch had risen to 35 per cent, and a small monthly wage was paid in addition.

In several years after 1918, the union and shipowners found themselves deadlocked around the months of January or February, and a strike threatened, but throughout the period we are considering no fishing season was lost. There seem to have been three reasons for this. In the first place, the shipowners were not usually unidentifiable agglomerations of anonymous share capital, but known individuals or groups of individuals. The belief that vast wealth is being accumulated through the heartless exploitation of the labouring man is not unnatural in a community so large that people do not know each other personally. But when the mode of life of a shipowner is plain for all to see, a truer estimate of the resources from which both capital and labour get their reward is possible.

A second reason is the nature of the industry itself. A fishing vessel is a small, closed community, and its expenses cannot be kept a secret from anyone. The price at which the catch is sold is common port gossip. Thus the economics of fishing are better known to the crew members than are the economics of factory production to the average shop-floor worker. This results in a far greater realism in negotiations between owners and men, especially when the payment system is based on the size of the catch.

The third reason for the lack of strikes was the success of the government machinery for mediation. In the Suðuroy troubles of 1918, the *amtmand* intervened and acted as mediator, but this was exceptional in the light of subsequent events. After discussions in the Løgting in 1926 and 1927, a bill passed the Danish parliament on 31 March, 1928, bringing into force a regular system of industrial conciliation for Faroe. The official mediator is nominated a by committee consisting of two men from the fishermen's union, one from the skippers' association, two from the Føroya Arbeiðarafelag (Faroe general workers' union), two from the shipowners' association, two from the Færøernes Købmandsforening (Faroe chamber of commerce), one from the employers' associations, and a neutral chairman. The chairman is nominated by the highest official of the islands' judiciary, the *sorenskriver*. To elect a mediator requires seven votes out of the eleven on the committee. If by 1 September each year, the committee has failed to make a choice, the *amtmand* or his nominee fills the post until the committee finds itself able to make a decision.

When a strike or lockout is threatened, the official mediator has the power to call the two sides together. In this he may act either on his own initiative, or at the request of a party to the dispute. He has also the power to delay the cessation of work for one week. The first step in his conciliation work is to conduct discussions with both sides, which they may not refuse. If there is deadlock, he may draft his own conciliation proposals, which then have to be submitted to the membership of the two organisations for secret ballot. The organisations are bound by law to acquaint their members with the conciliation proposals in their entirety, and to report to the mediator the total votes for and against. No one may publish any details of the voting until the mediator has announced the result. If the ballot of both organisation is in favour of the proposals, they come into force at once. The mediator was called upon in the years 1930, 1934 and 1938; in 1934 agreement was secured only on a second ballot, the mediator's first proposals being rejected by a large majority of the fishermen.

The growth of a power-based fishing industry, sophisticated financial institutions, trade unionism, and government conciliation machinery, may be considered to have brought the industrial revolution to Faroe. However, the scale of the industrial working groups and of the community as a whole were so small that generalisations about the nature of industrial society need to be examined with care before they are applied to Faroe. The institutions of an industrial society do not necessarily imply a full measure of its psychology.

GREENLAND

Although a skipper from Faroe visited Greenland waters as early as 1906, regular Faroese fishing there began only in 1925. During the seasons 1925–28 only a few vessels took part; but their success led to thirty-five vessels making the journey in 1929, and throughout the 1930s there were never fewer than fifty Faroese vessels per season sailing to the West Greenland coast. In 1934, the record year, no fewer than 110 vessels out of a fishing fleet of 156 made the journey. Ever since that time, Greenland fishing has been a regular part of the yearly round for all the better-equipped and more modern Faroese fishing vessels.

Greenland waters had not hitherto been subject to the

intensive trawling that had been the fate successively of the
North Sea banks, the Faroe banks, the Norwegian coast and,
by this time also, Icelandic waters. The difference in produc-
tivity between Icelandic and Greenland waters is plain from
the following table, which summarises the performance of
the eighty-one Faroese vessels which visited both Iceland and
Greenland in the 1937 season.

1937 Fishery: Iceland and Greenland compared

Ground	Catch	Total Days Fishing	Men Engaged	Man Days	Tons Per Man	Kgs. per Man Day
ICELAND						
Best ship	57	50	24	1,200	2.48	48
Worst ship	10	79	36	2,844	0.28	4
All ships	2,730	5,697	2,015	142,990	1.35	19
GREENLAND						
Best ship	137	55	25	1,375	5.48	99
Worst ship	111	100	30	3,000	3.70	37
All ships	9,694	7,810	2,019	197,362	4.80	49

It is necessary to remember in interpreting these figures that
the Iceland fishery came earlier in the year, and the working
day would be somewhat shorter. But the attraction of the
Greenland fishery should be clear from these few statistics.
Besides, by the early 1920s the fishing on the Faroe banks had
begun to fail completely — doubtless because of unrestricted
trawling by British and other foreign vessels. Thus the sloops
now had to begin with an Iceland season, moving over to the
more productive Greenland waters as soon as the weather
allowed.

Some difficulties were, of course, unavoidable. Greenland
is a long way from Faroe, and its coastline is contorted and
difficult to navigate. Furthermore, it was then a closed land.

In order to protect the native Greenlander against sudden, overwhelming contacts with the rougher side of modern world commerce, which had been the ruin of so many aboriginal peoples of the world, the Danes kept trade in the hands of a government monopoly, and severely restricted the scale of contacts between Greenlanders and those from outside — including Danish citizens. Thus the Danish government looked with disfavour upon the growing Faroese fishery off the Greenland coast.

There was a long-standing prohibition in force against ships of all nations landing in Greenland without special licence, and even against their taking shelter in Greenland harbours. In 1925, the year in which the Faroese began regular voyages to Greenland, a further law was passed restricting fishing within the three-mile limit to the Greenlanders themselves, and prohibiting it to other subjects of the Danish crown. The Faroese regarded these regulations as harsh. Even if fishing were to be restricted to the high seas, it was less than reasonable that the tiny Faroese sloops, after a long journey from their home ports, should be denied the chance of carrying out repairs or taking on water, even in an uninhabited fjord. The Faroese also pointed out that if shore depots were permitted in the inhabited parts of Greenland, the Greenlanders might learn the art of working klipfish, to their considerable profit.

The Danish government refused the Faroemen any access to the settlements, but offered them instead a small harbour on the island of Ravns Storø as a place for refuge and refit, and for taking on supplies of fresh water. The Faroemen were not satisfied with this concession. Ravns Storø lay 70 miles from the best fishing banks; its harbour was often full of ice, and it was exposed during south-west storms. In 1927, therefore, the Faroemen sought and obtained the use of a harbour in the uninhabited Kangerdluarsorusek Fjord, in latitude 63°41', where besides being able to refit and take on water, the Faroemen could work up their salt fish. This harbour became known as Færingehavn, the harbour of the Faroemen.

These concessions led to a vast increase in the number of Faroese ships going to Greenland each summer, but they had been made grudgingly and the Faroemen were still dissatisfied. The Danish motives for restricting access to Greenland were regarded by many Faroemen as insincere, while from the Faroese point of view, the development of the Greenland fishery seemed a matter of economic life or death for the islands. The Greenland question, repeatedly raised between 1925 and the outbreak of the second world war, was the first issue since the introduction of constitutional government which found Faroese opinion as a whole pitted against the attitude of the Danish government.

Compared with its two predecessors, the 1932 season was a poor one for the Greenland sloops. In 1930, sixty-six vessels had caught 8,921 metric tons (135.2 tons per ship and 5.9 tons per man). In 1931 fifty-two vessels had caught 7,933 metric tons (153.3 tons per vessel and 6.7 tons per man). In 1932, however, sixty-one ships caught only 6,007 metric tons (98.5 tons per ship and 4.3 tons per man). The Faroese skippers were convinced that fish were still swimming about as plentifully in Greenland waters as ever before, only that during the summer of 1932 they had been closer inshore, largely within the three-mile limit. That autumn the skippers' association took the initiative in drawing up a petition to the Danish government on the conditions regulating the Greenland fishery. It was supported vigorously by the shipowners' association and the fishermen's union, and carried a total of 5,915 signatures.

The Faroemen argued that the fish resources of Greenland were so vast that hand-lining within the three-mile limit could do no harm to stocks. The Greenlanders themselves were not suffering harm. In 1925, the first year of regular Faroese fishing off Greenland, native fishermen had landed only 355 tons; but by 1929 their catch had increased to 2,300 tons, and in the seasons 1930 to 1932, they had landed 8,000 tons each year. In 1933, the Faroese Løgting took up the issue and requested (i) that Faroese hand-line fishing be

allowed in all Greenland waters; (ii) that in addition to
Færingehavn, Faroese vessels be allowed to use harbours
in the neighbourhood of Holsteinborg or Sukkertoppen as
depots; (ii) that the Faroemen should be allowed to carry on
an inshore boat fishery from Færingehavn and if possible
other Greenland harbours.

The Danish government came only part of the way to meet
these requests. After 1934, two more harbours were opened
to Faroese ships, one on the Umanak peninsula in the north
and the other at Tovkussak just north of Godthåb. Inshore
fishing from boats was now allowed for the first time, from
Færingehavn. (This last concession was not used on any
considerable scale until the 1939 season, as we will see later.)

The battle for further Faroese rights in Greenland was now
fought every year. The Løgting struggled over the technical-
ities of their case through years that were difficult enough
anyway because of the world economic crisis. The average
fisherman was mortified and angered by the sight of the
fishery protection vessel enforcing the three-mile Greenland
limit against him, when its proper duty would have been to
save the inshore fishery round Faroe by enforcing a fifty-mile
limit against British trawlers whose depredations, the Faroese
believed, had destroyed the breeding-grounds and driven
the Faroese fishing sloops to distant northern waters.[1] Not
until 1939 was a solution found which the Faroemen could in
any way accept. From 1939 onwards they had the right to use
four harbours: Ravns Storø, Tovkussak, Færingehavn and
Færinger Nordhavn in the Egedesminde district. From the
first two of these harbours a boat fishery might be carried on,
within territorial waters but not within the fjords; and for
a certain stretch of the coast, Faroese sloops might fish in
Greenland waters also.

The Greenland boat fishery was carried out only on an

---

[1] The Faroese had good reason for this belief. During the 1914–18 war, when
British trawling round Faroe declined to negligible proportions, the Faroese
inshore fishery increased year by year, and in the 1918 and 1919 seasons was
over 10,000 tons. After 1928 it only once exceeded 2,000 tons.

experimental scale in the five seasons 1934 to 1938. In 1939, however, an inshore fishermen's co-operative was founded, Útróðrarfelagið Grønland. A ship was chartered to carry forty boats and 225 fishermen to Greenland. Materials for huts and boat-houses were taken, as were supplies of provisions, petrol, oil and fishing equipment, together with 1,000 tons of salt. Half the fishermen were settled at Tovkussak and half at Ravns Storø. Fishing lasted from the end of June until the beginning of October, after which the ship came to take the fishermen and their boats back home to Faroe.

The catch amounted to 1,194 metric tons, 671 tons from Tovkussak and 523 tons from Ravns Storø. The 106 fishermen stationed at Tovkussak thus caught an average of 6.3 tons per man, while each of the 119 at Ravns Storø caught an average of 4.4 tons. Although in terms of weight of fish caught, these figures were satisfactory enough, the costs of the expedition proved higher than expected, and the total profit was only about 91,000 kroner, or 400 kroner average per man for four months' work. A similar period on the sloops would have brought in twice as much. All the same, with the experience gained and the prevailing shortage of fishing vessels compared with the number of fishermen, many resolved to give boat fishing in Greenland a further trial; but the outbreak of war in the autumn of 1939 prevented any expedition during the 1940 season. This method of fishing the Greenland waters has, however, been resumed since the end of the war.

In the 1930s, the base at Færingehavn was developed from a mere port of refuge to an international fishing port with a range of amenities remarkable in view of their geographical location. Until 1933 there was nothing in the fjord but bare rocks. In that year the first improvements were made when the skippers' association set up navigation lights to guide vessels into the fjord in the hours of darkness. The Danish government later took over their maintenance. Between 1933 and 1937, the harbour was supplied with a ship repair yard and slipway, oil and salt depots, klipfish warehouses, a small hospital and a seamen's home. In 1937, when the Danish government opened Færingehavn to ships of all nations, the facilities were extended, and a larger hospital was built, the old one being taken over as a seamen's mission.

Throughout this period, the principal equipment used on the Iceland and Greenland fishery was the old-fashioned hand-line with five baited hooks. For an industry chronically short of capital it was a reasonably productive method, and certainly could cause no harm to the fishing-grounds, as was constantly held against the trawl, by stirring up the sea-bed. Yet the hand-line made tremendous demands on the fisherman's endurance. His way of life during the spring and summer months has been portrayed by a Faroese author, Jørgen-Frantz Jacobsen, in *Færøerne, Natur og Folk*:

This is the fishery. It is a migration, a war. It is repeated every year in two campaigns: the spring fishing from February to May off south Iceland, and the summer fishery from June to October off east Iceland, and now mostly off Greenland. Like all wars, this too costs human lives. In 1920 the Faroese lost sixty-two men at sea, that is to say 2 per cent of the participants.

At the end of February the fleet puts to sea, about 200 ships. The north Atlantic is amongst the roughest and most dangerous oceans of the world, but the deck of a Faroese ship is as a rule scarcely bigger than the dining-room of a prosperous man's house. Here the work is carried on in storm, snow and fog off the god-forsaken, treacherous coast of south Iceland. Wrecks and collisions occur almost every year. In these conditions, the crews stand day in and day out hauling in cod.

And yet this bitter springtime has its advantages. The night is so long, and in the darkness one cannot fish. It gives a trifle more time for rest and sleep. But in the light summertime there is no night. The days flow into one another, everything is lost in a rhythmless monotony. The fishermen stand along the gunwales, every man in his place fishing. As long as there is a catch, they fish. Nobody worries about watches. The cook can take care of the watches, just as he takes care of the meal times. The crew have something else to think about, for every single man's return from the trip depends on how much he himself can catch, and he has, therefore, a personal interest.

In summer, when the ship has found a good and safe fishing-ground, the skipper can take it easy. He can lie in his bunk and listen to the curious music of the hand-lines running over the gunwales, and of cod being hauled in and smacking on to the deck. If it goes on without a break, he can sleep at his ease, but if the intervals become long, his peace is over. Then he must rise and manoeuvre the ship to a place richer in fish, for on the leadership of the skipper the whole outcome of the trip depends.

Even when the ship is under sail, the crew do not always have rest. For the fish have not merely to be caught. They have also to be cleaned, split, salted and packed down in the hold, and this is a very considerable proportion of the work.

Off Greenland, where at times as many cod can be caught as one can haul aboard, the crew may allow themselves six hours of sleep per day; but this is reckoned to be a singularly easy life.

In October all the ships return home, unless any of them has been lost. Then they are stripped down, and proceed to winter harbour, and there they lie, *Britons' Pride*, *Star of Hope*, *Bearnaise*, *Mignonette*, and whatever else these former English and French sailing ships may be called. In the course of the winter the fishermen may rest in the bosom of their families, until in February they once again arm themselves for the spring battle.

As the same author later remarks: "The Faroese have the choice between fishing and starving. So they fish."

FISH PROCESSING AND EXPORT

The salt fish brought home from the Faroe banks, Iceland or Greenland was either sold as such, or worked into klipfish. Klipfish used to be made entirely by sun-drying the salt fish on the cliffs, or on specially-prepared drying-grounds near the harbours. The method employed a good deal of labour, chiefly women and children, since the fish had to be turned frequently and fetched under cover if rain came on, which in Faroe was not infrequent. The money the women and children earned at this work was an important factor in many a Faroese family's economy, and was often more than the man of the house would earn at the fishery.

During this process, the salt fish loses about 35 per cent of its weight and becomes a board-like object, with good keeping qualities, especially in reasonably temperate and dry conditions. It can be conveniently exported in hessian bales. The eventual customer restores it to something of its original fleshiness, and makes it fit for eating, by prolonged soaking and subsequent boiling.

Until after the first world war, almost all Faroese klipfish was sun-dried. But as fish landings increased, the available space became too small and the summertime too short for all the salt cod that was to be processed in this manner. Artificial drying had been tried in Suðuroy as early as 1911, but it was after 1926 that drying houses came to be built on a large scale. They were of simple construction, with the fish either hung up or laid on gratings, while coke-fired stoves heated the air which dried out the fish. Because of the shortage of capital, open-air drying was still widely in use at the outbreak of the second world war, and a frequent method was for the initial drying to be carried out in the open, and for the final drying to take place in the drying house.

No other methods of processing fish, apart from the extraction of the oil from cod livers, were of any importance in the Faroese economy before the second world war. Exports of frozen fish were inconsiderable, although some firms were installing refrigeration plant.

Faroese fish exports in 1910 and from 1915 to 1939 were as follows:

Year	Klipfish metric tons	Salt fish metric tons	Other fish products metric tons
1910	3,689	2,539	414
1915	4,080	3,072	512
1916	3,945	4,992	217
1917	3,156	2,989	142
1918	3,225	5,617	113
1919	6,415	1,813	162
1920	5,395	4,689	67
1921	5,001	5,887	21

Year	Klipfish metric tons	Salt fish metric tons	Other fish products metric tons
1922	5,018	6,379	171
1923	5,224	4,208	561
1924	5,103	5,269	30
1925	4,712	3,821	377
1926	9,220	5,780	294
1927	7,990	3,970	1,888
1928	9,353	6,018	174
1929	8,525	8,283	96
1930	10,629	9,512	253
1931	12,319	8,260	237
1932	14,397	3,132	467
1933	15,596	3,406	362
1934	15,625	2,650	485
1935	11,324	1,793	727
1936	7,928	11,126	448
1937	9,205	11,345	1,715
1938	10,217	7,349	1,083
1939	13,756	5,698	613

The prices obtainable for Faroese fish were sensitive to the general conditions of world trade, as the statistics for salt fish prices for the period 1901–38 show:

Salt fish prices
(in kroner per metric ton)

1901 — 198	1914 — 319	1927 — 256
1902 — 202	1915 — 450	1928 — 344
1903 — 217	1916 — 472	1929 — 313
1904 — 230	1917 — 523	1930 — 250
1905 — 266	1918 — 739	1931 — 191
1906 — 261	1919 — 796	1932 — 185
1907 — 283	1920 — 800	1933 — 236
1908 — 245	1921 — 622	1934 — 277
1909 — 201	1922 — 438	1935 — 311
1910 — 245	1923 — 370	1936 — 289
1911 — 237	1924 — 549	1937 — 286
1912 — 238	1925 — 529	1938 — 297
1913 — 301	1926 — 318	

The chief markets for Faroese fish were Spain, Britain, Denmark, Italy, Portugal and Greece. The general tendency was for Denmark and Britain to decline in importance as markets, while Spain bought increasing quantities of klipfish, and Italy of both klipfish and salt fish. The Portuguese and Greek markets made a notable advance just before the second world war. Exports from 1924 to 1939, broken down by country, were as follows:

Klipfish exports
(in metric tons)

Year	Denmark	Britain	Spain	Italy	Other countries	Total
1924	2,579	636	1,674	1	213	5,103
1925	1,300	1,077	2,294	41		4,712
1926	1,620	897	6,660	42	2	9,221
1927	874	806	6,159	152		7,991
1928	1,044	1,205	6,795	104	205	9,353
1929	563	1,070	6,705	49	138	8,525
1930	845	1,147	8,156	266	215	10,629
1931	1,171	710	9,216	1,064	158	12,319
1932						14,397
1933	329	682	13,751	499	336	15,597
1934	258	816	13,942	510	99	15,625
1935	122	914	10,090	135	64	11,325
1936						7,928
1937	223	786	5,205	1,990	1,001	9,205
1938	125	546	2,727	4,840	1,979	10,217
1939	33	596	6,816	4,421	1,890	13,756

Of the "other countries", Portugal took 1,854 tons in 1938 and 1,840 tons in 1939.

Salt fish exports
(in metric tons)

Year	Denmark	Britain	Spain	Italy	Other countries	Total
1924	2,021	2,457		630	160	5,268
1925	792	1,966		696	367	3,821

Year	Denmark	Britain	Spain	Italy	Other countries	Total
1926	1,309	2,589		1,738	144	5,780
1927	1,015	1,081		1,442	441	3,979
1928	1,397	1,266		1,466	1,972	6,081
1929	655	2,938		1,519	3,171	8,283
1930	945	1,881	109	2,769	3,808	9,512
1931	366	2,021	536	2,892	2,445	8,260
1932						3,132
1933	740	454	359	1,838	2	3,493
1934	57	297	388	1,909		2,651
1935	124	399	238	1,029	3	1,793
1936						11,126
1937	107	157		7,618	3,463	11,345
1938	10	170	114	5,553	1,501	7,348
1939	48	192		3,459	2,000	5,699

Of the "other countries", Greece took 1,500 tons in 1938 and 2,000 tons in 1939, becoming the second most important salt fish customer.

N. B. Figures for fish exports to individual countries are not available for the years 1932 and 1936.

Despite the apparently satisfactory tonnages exported during the 1930s, the Faroe Islands shared in full the world economic crisis, as might be expected of a country so dependent on a single industry. First came the catastrophic fall in fish prices in 1931, and as prices began to recover a little, there were other troubles. After the invasion of Abyssinia, the League of Nations imposed economic sanctions against Italy, which came into force for Faroe in the autumn of 1935. Italy was one of the chief outlets for Faroese fish, and the sanctions had the side-effect for a time of locking up a large amount of Faroese money in Italian banks. Immediately afterwards, her other principal customer, Spain, became involved in her long civil war, and purchases and payments by that country were badly affected. Many Faroese businesses went bankrupt, and many fishermen were in bad circumstances for years on end.

The Danish government, as a crisis measure, created a fund of 850,000 kroner to help companies with bad debts in Spain, and a further 300,000 kroner was loaned for the re-equipment of the Greenland fishing fleet.

As a further crisis measure, the export of salt fish and klipfish was rationalised in an exporters' co-operative, Føroya Fiskaexport, set up in 1936 with some government support and a grant of monopoly rights over the export of these two staple products. This co-operative, with its ability to deploy larger resources than those available to individual firms, was the chief factor in opening up the new markets in Portugal and Greece; and experimental shipments of Faroese fish were also sent to South America, Germany and West Africa.

WHALING

The Faroese whale fishery, while never of major economic importance to the country, has flourished intermittently until its inevitable decline with the severe depletion of the north Atlantic whale stocks. The first whaling-station in Faroe was started by a Norwegian lighthouse-keeper in 1894, and early in the present century seven were in operation. A record year in 1909 was followed by a decline, and after a two-year interval in the first world war, whaling was resumed only a much reduced scale, and in 1931–2 it ceased altogether. The two stations in operation at the outbreak of the second world war were those of við Áir on Streymoy and Lopra on Suðuroy. Both had started in 1936. On the outbreak of war, whaling ceased altogether and was resumed only in 1946.

The most valuable quarry of the Faroese whalers was the blue whale, the largest animal species ever known. It is born 20 feet long, and at full maturity will attain a length of 80 or 90 feet and a weight of 150 tons. In the period 1903–16, 178 of these giants were taken off Faroe, but stocks became much reduced, and from 1920 to 1938, only fifty-two were killed. The whalers' chief attention between the wars was given to the fin whale, of which a considerable number still remained.

Small steam-powered vessels were used for the chase, armed with a harpoon cannon in the bow. The harpoon carried a grenade which exploded after the whale had been struck, killing it instantly. At the whaling station, the blubber would be cut away and smelted into whale-oil for export, while the meat was generally sold off cheap within the islands for human consumption.

Since the second world war, Faroese whaling has become uneconomic. There were some good catches in the immediate post-war years, but throughout the seasons 1954–8 only the station at við Áir was in operation. Whaling ceased in 1959–61, to be resumed at við Áir in 1962 and abandoned altogether in 1966.

THE FISHING FLEET IN 1939

At the outbreak of the second world war, the Faroese fishing fleet still consisted largely of wooden ships. There were also ten trawlers with a total of 3,264 gross registered tons, but the sailing vessels numbered 162, making a total of 16,843 gross registered tons. It was a fleet of old vessels. Of the ten trawlers three had been built before 1920, and the rest between 1920 and 1928. Well over half the sailing ships were more than fifty years old, and had been in continuous service in Faroe since the turn of the century. The sailing vessels bought after 1924 were generally larger than the old British sloops, and carried crews of over twenty men. Some of these were schooners from France and Norway, and a further supply of old vessels arrived when the Icelanders modernised their fishing fleet. By the outbreak of war in 1939, few of the Faroese ships relied totally on sail, but many of the older vessels had only small engines — often less than 50 h.p.

The slow development of the sailing fleet may be seen from the following table:

Faroese Fishing Fleet, 1910–1939

Year	Ships	Total tonnage	Average tonnage
1910	137	10,546	77.0
1915	146	10,262	70.3
1920	144	10,369	72.5
1925	145	11,948	82.4
1930	165	15,917	96.5
1935	155	16,314	105.1
1939	162	16,843	104.0

The Faroese owners, skippers, fishermen and government alike were conscious of the need to replace the old craft with more modern and efficient vessels, but by 1939 the problem had scarcely begun to be tackled.

The Danish government loan scheme started in 1904 and was renewed at intervals with little substantial change until in 1923 the available funds were altogether inadequate for the purchase of new ships. The more generous scheme begun in 1923 assisted the modernisation of the old ships and their fitting out with engines. But it was not until 1928 that there was a scheme which served for the purchase of modern vessels. In that year the Danish government provided for annual funds of 500,000 kroner for ship purchase loans, and of 150,000 kroner for shore installations. New ships of over 100 gross registered tons were eligible for loans of up to 80 per cent of their value. These loans were at $4\frac{1}{2}$ per cent interest, and were repayable in stages of twenty years, the security being a first mortgage on the vessel. However, as a new powered sailing vessel would cost more than 50,000 kroner and a trawler more than 300,000 kroner, even this new measure was severely limited in its scope.

The 1930s were full of discussions and proposals for the renewal and modernisation of the fishing fleet, but the successive external crises compelled government help to be limited to emergency measures only. In 1932, the Faroese themselves, particularly those politically in favour of home rule for the islands, founded a fishery industries' bank, Sjóvinnubankin, which made a special point of aiding trawler purchase. The initial share capital was 300,000 kroner, of which 60,000 kroner were subscribed by the Løgting. Sjóvinnubankin was the first Faroese bank to be floated entirely on Faroese capital.

A far-reaching loan scheme for the renewal of the Faroese fishing fleet was finally negotiated in 1939, but the occupation of Denmark by the Germans and of the Faroe Islands by the British in the spring of 1940 prevented it from coming into full operation.

At the outbreak of the second world war, the Faroese fishing fleet was largely in the hands of a multitude of small undertakings. The following table gives the ownership position in 1937:

Numbers of Faroese fishing ships owned by undertakings of different sizes in 1937

Ship-owning concerns	No. of ships owned per concern	Total of ships	Percentage of entire fleet
1	14	14	8.3
2	9	18	10.7
1	7	7	4.2
1	6	6	3.6
4	5	20	11.9
4	4	16	9.5
5	3	15	8.9
6	2	12	7.2
60	1	60	35.7
Totals: 84		168	100

This distribution points once again to an under-capitalised industry, ill-adapted for meeting crises arising from sudden falls in the world prices of fish. Indeed, probably the only fishing craft in the islands that were suited to the modern conditions were the five seine-net ships in the fleet — small-sized craft compared with trawlers, but well adapted for middle-distance fishing and with effective equipment. All the other ships were either old trawlers or still older sloops and schooners. A further slump would have hit the industry hard. However, the Faroese fishermen were destined rather to encounter a wartime boom on a scale that even the older fishermen who remembered the prices of 1915 to 1921 would have found incredible.

CHAPTER VIII

FAROESE POLITICS, 1906–1939

THE TWO-PARTY PERIOD, 1906–28

The issue on which the first Faroese political parties were formed was whether to maintain or loosen the constitutional link with metropolitan Denmark (pp. 95-6). For twenty years there was no other line of party division in Faroe. Later, however, economic issues invaded political life, complicating the political scene, until today there is a fragmentation of parties, resulting from the mathematically possible combinations of attitude to economic affairs on the one hand and to the relationship between Faroe and Denmark on the other.

Until the first world war, the dominant force in Faroese political life was the Unionist Party, the Samband. Its leaders played their cards with skill. In 1909 Oliver Effersøe, the Folketing member, managed to secure a declaration from the Danish government implying that no change in the status of Faroe was contemplated, regardless of any possible temporary Løgting majority favouring home rule or secession — a change from the earlier attitude, expressed by the now fallen minister Alberti, that the Danish government would normally be sympathetic to the wishes of the majority party in the Løgting. The Samband was also active in securing reforms of various kinds. A commission on agriculture and land tenure sat from 1908 to 1911 and produced a report of great value which has formed the basis of much subsequent action on agriculture. The telephone and telegraph systems were enlarged and extended, and plans were laid for harbour works in Tórshavn and elsewhere, and for a road network on Sandoy. The medical service was improved with the opening of a sanatorium near Tórshavn and the enlargement of medical insurance schemes. The Danish government was the more easily persuaded to undertake the heavy expense invol⁄ed because at this time Faroese support was sorely needed for the enlargement of a very narrow parliamentary majority.

The Sjálvstýri came nearest to power during the first world war. The ruling party in Denmark was now the Radical Left — a party supported chiefly by Danish smallholders, which had come into being through a split in the Venstre in 1905. In this administration, the Radicals had the support of the Social Democrats. At the outbreak of war, the Samband still had a two-thirds majority in the Faroese Løgting, and the party leader, Andreas Samuelsen, a Venstre supporter when in Denmark, was the Faroe Islands member in the Folketing. However, things were soon to change.

The Sjálvstýri did not contest the 1915 Folketing elections, but the Samband leader was opposed by an independent, the young solicitor Edward Mortensen,[1] son of a wealthy Suðuroy shipowner. His father might, in the ordinary way, have been expected to be a strong Samband supporter; but because of disappointment over proposals for harbour works at Tvøroyri, he supported his son's candidature, and the combination of local interest and Sjálvstýri support won him the seat by a narrow majority in a low poll. After his victory he joined the Sjálvstýri, while in Denmark he declared his allegiance to the Radicals — in accordance with what was becoming the standard Faroese practice of supporting the government party. He gained in return the powerful political support of the Danish prime minister, C. T. Zahle.

This alliance led to an unfortunate state of tension between the Danish prime minister and the *amtmand* of Faroe, Svenning Rytter. Rytter had been appointed by the previous, Venstre administration, and was an able and industrious civil servant. Apart from his personal feelings in the matter it was his duty to maintain the existing relationship between Faroe and

---

[1] Mortensen, born in 1889, changed his name in 1923 to Mitens.

Denmark. Zahle, valuing Mortensen's support in the Folketing, showed sympathy to some of the aspirations of the
Sjálvstýri. Rytter, on the other hand, had to work closely with
the majority party in the Løgting, the Samband. All the
ingredients for misunderstanding were present, and sus-
picions were aroused on all sides. Rytter was sometimes
openly accused of partiality, and of being the true leader of
the Samband. Mortensen once referred to him as a "new
Dahlerup" — striving to maintain bureaucratic rule in an age
of democracy. Two transactions in particular caused hard
feeling.

In April 1917, the provost of Faroe, Frederik Petersen, died.
Petersen, although the writer of hymns and lyrics in Faroese,
and a pioneer of the national literature, had been politically
a firm advocate of close constitutional links with Denmark,
and had been a leader of the Samband. His successor, A. C.
Evensen, appointed in July, himself died in October. Zahle,
acting partly on information supplied by Mortensen, pushed
through the appointment of the minister of South Streymoy,
Jacob Dahl (1878–1944). No-one doubted Dahl's fitness for
the post, but he was a member of the Sjálvstýri, and when,
before his ordination, he had been a master at the *realskole* in
Tórshavn, he had been a notable campaigner for the use of
Faroese for purposes of instruction. Coming so soon after the
Louis Zachariasen affair, this appointment looked to Rytter
like a political favour to Mortensen and a deliberate snub to
himself.

Zahle had probably been motivated by the wish to show
some sympathy to the cultural aspirations of Faroese nationalism, lest Rytter's somewhat stringent attitude over the
language issue should lead to a sharp anti-Danish reaction
amongst the people at large. On the other side, the political
allies of the Samband in the Danish parliament — the
Venstre — mounted a sharp attack on Jóannes Patursson,
going to the length of accusing him of treason. This arose from
Patursson's activities during the period of unrestricted German
submarine warfare.

Until 1917 the supply position for Faroe had been good. On 1 February, 1917, however, Germany proclaimed that all ships in a wide area of sea around Great Britain would be sunk on sight. This area reached almost to Faroe, and included part of the Faroese fishing banks. However, the British contraband regulations demanded that all ships bound to or from Faroe should call at Kirkwall — well within the danger zone — for contraband clearance. For two months no supplies came to Faroe, and there was a shortage of margarine, petroleum products, matches, and salt for the fishing industry. Patursson, recalling the attempt of his great-grandfather Nólsoyar-Páll to secure provisions for his country-men during the Napoleonic war, now resolved on a dramatic unofficial gesture to improve the provisioning of the islands. He organised a petition to the British government requesting that navigation between Iceland and Faroe should be free from British contraband inspection, so that supplies might be able to reach Faroe from the United States via Iceland, inspection having been carried out on the western side of the Atlantic, say in Halifax. Although the Løgting voted against the promulgation of this petition and the *amtmand,* Rytter, warned people not to sign it, Patursson managed to collect 3,242 signatures. In the event, the petition was not sent to the British government, an act which technically might indeed have been treasonable, but to the Danish ambassador in London, who referred to Copenhagen for instructions.

Breaking-point came during the 1918 election campaign. Zahle, in an interview with a Danish newspaper, commented on the case, referred to the unfairness of certain press attacks on Mortensen, and expressed the hope that he would be re-elected, partly because of his skill in representing Faroese interests in the Folketing, and partly because of his support for the administration. Zahle further expressed the hope that the Faroese would choose a Landsting representative of whom the same might be said — meaning, of course, Jóannes Patursson.

With incredible ineptitude, Zahle telegraphed this newspaper interview to Rytter, and requested him to supply a copy to Mortensen, who was then in Faroe for the election. Rytter, irate at being treated as a mere party functionary when he was the senior civil servant in the islands, did as requested, but resigned his post. Two other senior civil servants in the islands, the king's bailiff and the *sorenskriver*, followed his example.

This conspicuous act of protest led to the Landsting, in which there was a majority of members of the opposition parties, setting up a commission for the investigation of Faroese political affairs, and of the actions of the government in connection with Faroese politics. The Radicals, in a provocative gesture, voted Patursson on to the commission. This commission was in time to produce one of the most voluminous reports in Danish parliamentary history.

The elections took place meanwhile. Mortensen narrowly lost his Folketing seat, and was replaced by the Samband leader Andreas Samuelsen. Ironically enough, the Løgting elections produced for the first time a narrow majority for the Sjálvstýri, although from a slight minority of the votes cast. Thus Samuelsen's Landsting colleague, elected by the Løgting, was Jóannes Patursson, his chief opponent in twelve years of hard political struggle.

The Landsting investigating commission's report came out in 1919, and made some sharp comments about both Zahle and Patursson. The Landsting, in which the opposition parties were in the majority, voted a reprimand on Zahle — but as long as his Folketing majority was secure, the prime minister's position was unaffected. The criticism of Patursson in the report tended to turn the home rule leader more and more into an anti-Danish frame of mind and, if anything, increased rather than diminished his popularity in Faroe. As for Svenning Rytter, he gained such popularity in Venstre circles that when the Venstre won the 1920 elections, he became minister of justice in the government headed by Niels Neergaard. It was ironic that as minister of justice he had overall responsibility for affairs in Faroe.

The 1920 Løgting elections produced a clear majority of votes for the Samband, but because of the working of the electoral system, an equality of elected members. However, the new Landsting member, chosen by lot, was the Samband candidate, Oliver Effersøe. The Sjálvstýri's run of good fortune was over, and the Samband dominated the scene once again until the election of 1936.

The Neergaard administration which had now come to power in Copenhagen adhered in general to the Venstre policy of support for the Samband's view that Faroe should be a province of Denmark and share the constitution of the state in the ordinary way. They did, however, make certain changes in the laws governing the composition, election and powers of the Løgting, thus making it a more democratic body in the spirit of the twentieth century. By an act passed on 18 March, 1923, and coming into force on 1 January, 1924, the *amtmand* and the provost were excluded from ex-officio membership of the Løgting. Henceforth the Løgting was to elect its own chairman and vice-chairman; and although the *amtmand* was permitted to take part in deliberations and to address the assembly as often as he wished, he now had no vote unless he happened to be an elected member in his own right. The number of Løgting seats was fixed at eighteen, with the possible addition of up to five supernumerary places. These latter were seats unattached to any electoral division, but allotted on a basis of popular votes cast, to produce in the Løgting a voting strength proportional to the number of votes cast throught Faroe. Thus a party with a widely scattered following would still be able to win a fair number of seats even though it did not win many electoral divisions outright. Elections were to be held every four years.

It was not necessary to include any measure for the emancipation of women, since Faroese women shared the benefit of the general Danish emancipation in 1915. Women cast their first Løgting votes in 1918.

The 1923 reforms granted the Løgting a much enlarged financial power, particularly as regarding communications between and within the islands. But in general the Løgting remained what, ever since its revival it had been intended that it should be — a body proposing legislation to the Danish parliament rather than one with extensive authority in its own hands.

Probably the most considerable undertaking during this period was the construction of harbour works at Tórshavn. Despite its name (Thor's Harbour), the Faroese capital possesses only a poor natural harbour, inadequate for the protection of large vessels and dangerous even for small ones if there are strong winds from the south-east or north-east. The project of building a mole across the seaward side of the twin bays at Tórshavn was first discussed as early as 1903, but it was nearly a decade before positive measures were taken to put the plan into effect. A law of 1913 envisaged a main harbour in Tórshavn, a number of lesser harbour works elsewhere and a road network on Sandoy; and authorised the expenditure of 1½ million kroner on the project. The first world war delayed the fulfilment of the plan, but the harbour scheme was taken up again in 1921, with a budget of 2,200,000 kroner. The chief features of the scheme were a mole 200 metres long and a wharf 145 metres long, on the eastern side of the double bay. In 1929 the harbour was taken over by Tórshavn municipality.

So in spite of a good deal of general progress, the period 1906–28 was a bleak one for home rulers, the Samband usually occupying the positions of power or at least being able to block any manoeuvres of the Sjálvstýri aimed at enlarging Faroese autonomy. But the next age of Faroese politics, which began with the rise of the Social Democratic Party, was to curtail very severely the influence of both the Samband and the Sjálvstýri.

ECONOMIC PARTIES, 1928–1939

The first Social Democratic government in Denmark, with Thorvald Stauning as prime minister, took office in 1924.

The Faroe Islands Folketing member, Samuelsen, remained firmly attached to the Venstre, now in opposition. So the Social Democrats had to look elsewhere for Faroese allies. With a few cultural concessions, it seemed at first as though the Sjálvstýri were to be wooed; but the big-farmer outlook of *kongsbóndi* Jóannes Patursson sorted ill with Social Democracy, and in 1925 the Danish Social Democratic Party accordingly took steps to set up a Faroese branch. This was called *Javnaðarflokkurin* — the Equality Party. It was independent of the Danish Social Democratic Party, but received from it financial help for its newspaper *Føroya Social-Demokrat* and for its election campaigns. It achieved its first electoral success in the 1928 Løgting elections, when the new party won two of the twenty-three seats.

The most prominent member of the Faroese Social Democratic Party, from its foundation until the day of his death, was Peter Mohr Dam (1898–1968). He was born in Skopun on Sandoy, trained as a teacher and settling in the growing fishing port of Tvøroyri, represented that town in the Løgting from 1928 onwards. From 1934 until his death he was party chairman. Dam was a politician of burning zeal, second only in this quality to Jóannes Patursson himself — a zeal which he threw into building up the party, editing its newspaper and taking a prominent part in a number of co-operative enterprises.

The Social Democratic success in 1928 was only modest, but it enabled the party to hold the balance in the Løgting. The new party appeared to have gained its supporters largely at the expense of the Samband. The Unionists, from a poll of 2,917, won ten seats; the Sjálvstýri, with 2,680 votes more strategically distributed, won eleven; and the Social Democrats, with 671 votes, won Tórshavn and Tvøroyri. As a result of the Løgting elections, Jóannes Patursson was returned as Landsting member for Faroe. But the price of Social Democratic support in the Løgting's choice of a member for the Landsting, and of electoral alliance in the Folketing elections of the following year, was a soft-pedalling of Patursson's home-rule demands. The Social Democrats depended far too heavily on Danish government help to carry out their aims for them to countenance anything tending towards an independent Faroese state.

To combat growing unemployment, and incidentally to provide a financial basis for political power, the Faroese Social Democrats were active in sponsoring co-operative enterprises. The most ambitious of these were *Ísvirki*, a fresh fish co-operative, and the trawler-owning co-operative *Arbeiðaranna Trolaradrift*. Unfortunately, neither was a success.

Ísvirki was an attempt to move into the fresh fish market which had already been successfully entered by certain Danish firms, and which gave a much greater return than the traditional Faroese production of salt fish and klipfish. The entrepreneurial organisation was the Tvøroyri trade union, *Fylking*. Fylking had only a few thousand kroner, but with this money and the assurance of government assistance, the project was launched in 1928. In the autumn of 1929 refrigeration plant, bought in Germany, was installed in its building not far from the wharf at Tvøroyri.

The difficulty now was that the plant was too big for the boats that were to supply it, especially as at that time the inshore fishery was particularly poor. With the help of the Danish government, first one vessel and then another was purchased, until at last the co-operative was running nine fishing craft, nearly all of them expensive and modern, and one transport vessel for carrying fish to the market in Hull. The co-operative was grossly under-capitalised, and the economic blizzard of 1931 killed the whole undertaking.

Arbeiðaranna Trolaradrift was launched in 1936 to carry on the economic activity of a bankrupt Suðuroy firm on co-operative principles. A small amount of money was put up by Fylking and another Suðuroy trade union, and much more was raised in Denmark. The shore establishment of the bankrupt firm was taken over, and a twelve-year-old steam trawler was purchased. The outbreak of war and high fish prices ensured for Arbeiðaranna Trolaradrift a longer life than that enjoyed by its predecessor. But with the post-war recession it fell into difficulties. In 1952, the undertaking received 500,000 kroner in Danish government assistance, but in spite of this, the co-operative was forced into liquidation two years later.

In 1930, when the minimum age for electors was lowered from twenty-five to twenty-one, the Samband reaped the greatest benefit. Fresh from the economic fiasco of Ísvirki, the Social Democrats were lucky to retain their two seats. There were eleven Samband members in the new Løgting, and eight Sjálvstýri. The 1932 election was the last in which the Samband was to win an overall majority. From this time onwards, the continuing world economic depression, the Greenland dispute and the curtailment of the Italian and Spanish fish markets turned public attention away from national issues towards economic problems.

The 1936 Løgting elections were a disaster for the Samband. Instead of eleven seats out of twenty-one, the unionists retained only eight out of twenty-four. The Sjálvstýri held another eight, while Dam's Social Democrats won six. The remaining two seats were captured by a new party, *Vinnuflokkurin*, the Economic Party.

The Social Democratic victory suddenly gave P. M. Dam an unexpected importance in the affairs of the Danish realm as a whole. His party group held the balance in the Løgting. The Løgting now had to elect a new Landsting member. Proposals were afoot in Denmark at this time for the amendment of the constitution and the abolition of the Landsting. And it seemed possible that the member for Faroe might hold the balance in the Danish upper house. The Social Democratic Party conducted negotiations with both the Samband and the Sjálvstýri. In the end, they secured the return of the editor of *Dimmalætting*, the Samband member Poul Niclasen — with the droll condition that, although on economic questions he was a moderate conservative in Faroe, he should vote with the Social Democrats in Copenhagen. Against all expectation, Niclasen performed his dual role with great success, although it provided a rich vein of humour for the cartoonists of the Copenhagen newspapers.

The new political group in the Løgting, the Economic Party, belonged to the right and was opposed to social democracy. Its founders were the businessmen who in 1932 had founded the first purely Faroese bank, *Sjóvinnubankin*, and its leader was the bank's dynamic director, Thorstein Petersen (1899–1960). The Economic Party's aims were to build up Faroese prosperity by deploying the resources available within the islands to best advantage. The party opposed unproductive expenditure such as old age pensions for which the Social Democrats were pressing, making the capital development of the Faroese economy the top priority.

The rise of the Social Democrats had robbed the Unionists of some of their traditional supporters. The Economic Party made headway at the expense of the home rulers. Neither of the old parties was annihilated, but their power was severely curtailed.

The Sjálvstýri, the old home rule party, split on an issue of land reform. The land commission report of 1911 had been a valuable document, but it had thrown light on the Faroese agricultural position rather than proposing solutions for its complex problems. In the depressed state of the Faroese fishery, the proposal was now made for a wide extension of the allotment system, making landless fishermen a grant of enough land to keep body and soul together — at the expense of the uncultivated outfield of the crown tenancies. At the same time, an attempt was to be made to arrest the endless process of subdivision to which private land in the islands was subject on inheritance. These measures were warmly supported by the Samband, the Social Democrats, and most of the Sjálvstýri — but they were anathema to the largest crown tenant in the Faroe Islands, the old Sjálvstýri chieftain, Jóannes Patursson. He now left the party he had led for over thirty years, and in 1939 joined forces with Thorstein Petersen. The two men together launched the People's Party, *Fólka-flokkurin*, which incorporated the recently founded Economic

Party and, as the next elections showed, about half of the old Sjálvstýri. The People's Party favoured the home-rule side on national issues, and state-fostered capitalism in the economic field. Its great period of strength came during the second world war, though it never controlled the administration. In the Løgting elections of January 1940, it increased its representation from two seats to six. The Sjálvstýri was reduced from eight seats to four, and the other parties held their own. Wartime prosperity was to bring the People's Party a large measure of electoral support, especially when it was clear that *de facto* home rule was working well.

THE FAROESE LANGUAGE ISSUE

At the beginning of the twentieth century the Faroese language had no official status within the islands. As the use of Faroese as a written language spread in private life, opposition to its use in public affairs weakened and, by the eve of the second world war, it had won its way by degrees into acceptability for nearly all public purposes. It was perhaps inevitable that the language struggle should become a political issue — it was easy for the Samband to accuse the Sjálvstýri of using their language policy as a lever for advancing secret aims of political separation from Denmark; and it was equally easy for the Sjálvstýri to represent the Samband as traitors to their native language. The truth was less simple. The Samband feared the cultural impoverishment that would follow if the Faroese people ceased to be bilingual, while the Sjálvstýri saw it as an affront to Faroese nationhood that the official language should be other than the mother tongue.

Danish was used in church, in school, in administration and in the law-courts. By the time party political life began in Faroe, the vernacular had made only the most limited entry into the church, was used in schools only as an aid to the understanding of Danish, and in the law-courts was treated on the same footing as English, German or any other foreign language.

The Samband wanted to see the development and literary use of the Faroese language, although at the same time they believed that constant efforts must be made to preserve the fluency of the people in written and spoken Danish. And they were determined not to allow the Sjálvstýri to introduce Faroese everywhere merely on dogmatic grounds; and the two main objects of the Samband — the preservation of the constitutional link with Denmark, and the exercise of the utmost economy in public expenditure — had to be safeguarded. Thus the Samband had a certain ambiguity of approach to the language issue.

The attitude of the Sjálvstýri was more straightforward. A clause in their party programme favoured the free use of Faroese in all circumstances and its wide use as a medium of instruction in the schools. In their 1928 campaign, the Social Democrats ignored the issue, but a brief clause in their 1932 manifesto favoured general support for the Faroese language and culture.

The bitterest struggles were waged over the place of Faroese in the schools. The campaign lasted from 1908 until 1938, by which time national aspirations had been reasonably well satisfied. In 1908, the teachers at the *realskole* (high school) in Tórshavn requested permission to use Faroese as the medium of instruction. The school board replied that this was not admissible except when the Faroese language itself was being taught. At other times it might be used only "as a supplementary means towards clearer understanding". In 1909 a complaint was laid before the school board that one of the teaching staff, Jacob Dahl (later to become a priest), was nevertheless using Faroese for teaching. The case was referred to the Danish ministry of education, who in turn asked the opinion of the Løgting.

The Løgting was bitterly divided. The committee which had been set to consider the matter failed to agree, and in 1910 presented majority and minority reports. The Samband majority held that the position of Danish as the official language of Faroe, and as the chief cultural medium, necessitated Faroese children being enabled to acquire more than a mere facility in reading and writing it — in the oral instruction in other lessons they ought to have the opportunity of hearing and speaking Danish. According to the Sjálvstýri minority, it was a universal principle that pupils should be instructed in their mother tongue — as was the case in other parts of the Danish realm. Icelandic was employed in the schools of Iceland, Greenlandic in the schools of Greenland, and in the Danish West Indies, where English was spoken, English was the medium of instruction. However, in Faroe there existed two special difficulties. One was that Faroese circumstances demanded mastery of a second language, which must clearly be Danish. The other was that school textbooks in Faroese did not exist in quantity and would be expensive to provide. The Sjálvstýri recommended that every teacher should be free to choose the language in which he gave his instruction. The Løgting finally supported the majority proposals, recommending Faroese for the younger children, and as a supplementary aid to comprehension for the older ones, but Danish as the principal language of instruction for the seniors. This recommendation became paragraph 7 of the regulations for Faroese schools issued by the Danish government on 16 January, 1912. The amendment of paragraph 7 became one of the battle-cries of the home rulers.

From the very beginning, however, paragraph 7 proved unworkable. The Velbastaður teacher Louis Zachariasen openly defied the regulation, and resigned his post rather than submit to it — thus providing the Sjálvstýri with a useful martyr. Jacob Dahl became another hero to the home rulers, and his appointment as provost in 1917 exacerbated the political troubles of that time (see page 157). Yet it was clear to everyone that in practice a teacher could use as much Faroese as he liked if he did not advertise his action but pretended that he was using the vernacular only as a supplementary aid.

The point was raised in 1918 that written Faroese had not yet become a compulsory subject in the schools. It was maintained that the 1912 regulations had not provided for this because at that time many of the teachers were not themselves skilled in the art of writing their own language. Later, however, holiday courses had been available for teachers, so that even the older ones, who had been educated before the national movement had fully emerged, had the opportunity of deepening their knowledge of literary Faroese. A request on this point from the Løgting to the government was at once conceded, unlike the accompanying request for an amendment to paragraph 7. It proved very difficult to arrive at a formula that would at once allow the Faroese language as a medium of instruction, yet ensure that school-leavers had sufficient fluency in spoken Danish for their adult needs. A proposal from the Danish ministry of education in 1925 for Faroese to be the general language of instruction, but for Danish to be used for Danish history and geography lessons, proved to be unacceptable to the Samband, now once again the majority party in the Løgting. It was only after the 1936 election, when the Social Democrats had made their big gains at the expense of the Samband, that a convincing Løgting majority could be mustered for an amendment. The Social Democrats voted with the Sjálvstýri and Vinnuflokkurin for an amendment effectively giving the two languages equality in the schools. This was endorsed by the Danish government on 13 December, 1938.

The use of Faroese in church services was first permitted in 1903, to a limited degree and under stringent conditions: namely, at services other than the eucharist, and with the sanction of the minister, the provost, and the parochial council. In 1912, the minister was allowed to preach a certain proportion of his eucharistic sermons in the vernacular, if the parochial council and the bishop both agreed. Two factors in particular delayed the general introduction of Faroese into services: the conservatism of the Faroese, among whom the Danish language had come to be specially associated with solemn occasions, and the lack of a Faroese liturgy, hymn-book and Bible.

This question was repeatedly discussed by the Løgting between the wars. The Samband, as might be expected, took the cautious line about any change to the vernacular. They pointed out that polls in Tórshavn had shown a clear majority favouring the retention of Danish, and made the further relevant observation that the Faroese church was in part served by Danish ministers, and if each minister were allowed to choose for himself how much Faroese he used, some congregations might become so unfamiliar with the Danish ritual and scriptures that when a Danish priest succeeded to the living, no-one would be able to understand his services.

In the long run, the determining factor was the work of translation. Pastor Schrøter had made a Faroese version of St. Matthew's Gospel as early as 1823, and in 1908 A. C. Evensen translated St. John's Gospel. But it was Jacob Dahl who was the creator of the Faroese religious idiom. In 1921 appeared his translation of the Psalms, and the following years saw the publication of the books of the New Testament, which were issued in collected form in 1937. Dahl continued with the Old Testament, and after his death in 1944 the work was completed by Kristian Osvald Viderø (born 1906). The complete Bible, translated direct from the original tongues, appeared in 1961. A version made by Victor Danielsen (1894–1961), a missionary for the Plymouth Brethren, had already appeared in 1948. Between the wars this sect won a strong following in Faroe, and regularly used the vernacular in worship. However, Danielsen's translation had been made from various modern European languages. Dahl's Bible was authorised for public worship as soon as it appeared, as had been his translations of the service book (1930) and the general prayer book (1939). He also translated the catechism, a biblical history, and two books of sermons. The last-named was important because in Faroe a single minister may have six churches in his care, and on any Sunday, the service in five of them is conducted by the local deacon. The ancient Faroese custom is for the deacon to read the sermon from a printed collection.

General authority to use Faroese in church services was
given by an ordinance of 13 March, 1939. By this, the
individual minister was permitted to use whichever of the two
languages appeared natural to him. The sermon, moreover,
did not need to be in the same language as the liturgy. The
hymns might be in either Danish or Faroese, or both. A
Faroese hymn-book was published and authorised in 1956,
but there are still churches which employ the old Danish
hymn-book, which contains many hymns, for instance the
well-loved hymns of Kingo, considered part of the spiritual
heritage of the Faroese. At the present time, however, Faroese
church services are the rule, and opposition from congregations has completely disappeared. Moreover, the Faroese
church today is staffed almost completely by native Faroemen.

Discussions about raising the status of Faroese in the law-
courts began in 1920, as a result of a proposal to extend to
Faroe certain legal reforms already carried out in metropolitan Denmark. These reforms mainly concerned the much
greater use of the spoken word in law-courts, in place of the
traditional practice of relying largely on written submissions.
The Løgting deliberations on the matter were finally embodied in a law of 11 April, 1924, which confirmed Danish as
the language of the courts, but permitted a judge with a
command of the Faroese language to use it in the examination
of Faroese-speaking persons. Documents laid before the court
that were written in Faroese had to be accompanied by a
certified Danish translation if the court or the opposite party
demanded it.

From 1931, there were proposals for still further extending
the place of Faroese in the courts. These were opposed by the
Samband on the grounds that as long as the constitutional
link with Denmark subsisted, there must be a common legal
language. Court records, for instance, must be kept in Danish
in case of an appeal to the high court in Copenhagen. Partly
because of the opposition of the Samband, which held a
commanding position in the Løgting until 1936, and partly
because of the technical complexities of the matter, no final

decision had been reached by the outbreak of the second world war. Faroese finally came to be of equal standing with Danish in a rather unsatisfactory way — in a law of 4 January, 1944, under the emergency wartime constitution, and hence without the sanction, at the time, of the Danish government. After communication was restored between Faroe and Denmark, the decision was left in force. At the present time, Faroese is in principle on a par with Danish for all legal purposes, but in practice Danish is still widely used.

Between the first and second world wars, the Faroese language won its way to acceptability in a number of minor official fields. From 1920, the telephone directory appeared in Faroese. From 1925, the language became acceptable for postal and telegraphic purposes. From 1927 onwards, the deliberations of the Løgting were recorded in it — and so on.

By the outbreak of the second world war, the language issue had been largely determined in accordance with the aims of the Sjálvstýri. But success was achieved less because of votes in the Løgting than as a result of the simultaneous growth of Faroese as a literary language, which took place on a scale beyond the expectations of most observers. Perhaps the most decisive of the actions of the Løgting in the language question were those which commanded the support of all parties — the sponsorship of a whole series of literary and other works in Faroese, which allowed the language to reach maturity.

CHAPTER IX

WARTIME IN THE FAROE ISLANDS

BLOCKADE STRATEGY

The war between Britain and Germany during 1914–18 had affected Denmark profoundly, because of the British naval blockade of Germany and the submarine warfare by which Germany attempted to subdue Britain. British naval strategy in the war had been first to seal off the English Channel at both ends to protect the vital supply routes from Britain to the armies fighting on the Western Front; and then to prevent merchant vessels sailing to Germany by the northern route between Shetland and Norway, by means of minefields and naval patrols from Orkney to Shetland and extending as far as Norwegian territorial waters. In order to win their own exemption from blockade, the Danes had to agree to import only just sufficient for their own requirements and not to use their territory for the transit of contraband. The Germans, on the other hand, to protect the back door to their great naval base at Kiel, compelled the Danes to mine the entrances to the Baltic to prevent the passage of British naval units. This disposition of forces tended to cut off the Faroe Islands from Denmark, although the exigencies of that war did not lead either combatant to occupy Denmark or its Atlantic dependency.

In 1939 the strategic situation was basically the same, but with the significant difference that air power was now vital in both offensive and defensive operations. This time, the Germans mounted their daring attack on Denmark and Norway with the object of outflanking the British naval blockade, securing the safe passage of Swedish iron ore through the ice-free Norwegian port of Narvik, and obtaining a broad operational front for U-boat and air attacks against Great Britain. The British blockade line during the second world war was thus a far more difficult one running through Shetland, Faroe and Iceland, compared with the comparatively short Shetland to Bergen line of 1914–18.

Soon after the outbreak of war in 1939, a provincial import control board was established in Faroe. Its duty was to ensure that salt, fuel, and other products needed for the fishery were maintained in the islands in sufficient quantity, and that imported foodstuffs and footwear should not be allowed to run short. On 11 March, 1940, the board issued a proclamation advising the Faroese people to be as economical as possible with imported goods, and to grow the largest possible crops of potatoes and green and root vegetables. The public were further informed that imported coal would be scarce and dear, and that every household should cover its needs by cutting peat. Those with land were urged as a patriotic duty to make plots available at a reasonable rent to those with none.

Altogether, the Faroe Islands were reasonably well supplied when war came to the northern countries. Sugar was the only article of domestic consumption already subject to rationing. However, a number of Danish merchant vessels had been sunk in the early months of 1940 by German U-boats, and three Faroese seamen were among those lost. Postal connection with Denmark was very poor at this time, not only because of the disruption to shipping caused by the U-boat blockade, but because of the censorship efforts of the belligerent powers.

The last postal delivery from Denmark to Faroe, apart from the wartime Red Cross letters, arrived in Tórshavn in February 1940.

If there was little physical privation, there was an intense feeling of isolation; and as naval activity in the North Sea and in Scandinavian waters intensified in late March and early April, there was apprehension about what was to come.

OCCUPATION

In the early morning of Tuesday 9 April, telegraphic communication between Denmark and the Faroe Islands was abruptly cut off, and over the Danish radio came the shattering news of the sudden German invasion, the brief but fruitless resistance of a few Danish units, and the capitulation of the king and government early that morning. The isolation of Faroe was now absolute, and the sense of foreboding among the public was only increased by the utter peacefulness of both air and sea around the islands. A few Danish and Norwegian merchant vessels took refuge in Tórshavn, but otherwise there were no signs of the war that had engulfed Scandinavia and the 3,000 Faroemen then in Denmark, cut off from home and friends.

By the fortunate chance of a fishery dispute, the Løgting happened to be in session in Tórshavn. It was a new Løgting, elected on 30 January. There were eight members of the Samband, four of the old Sjálvstýri, six Social Democrats, and six members of the People's Party, which had gained four seats at the expense of the Sjálvstýri. It was thus possible for the *amtmand*, C. A. Hilbert, to consult at once with the elected representatives of the people about the course of action that should be followed in these harassing circumstances.

The first action, taken on 10 April, was a proclamation over Tórshavn radio by the *amtmand* to the people of Faroe. He announced that the capitulation of Denmark in no way applied to Faroe, but that the provincial administration would continue to govern the islands on behalf of the Danish government. The present difficulties, he said, could be overcome if the islands carried on calmly and the people conducted themselves with restraint and deliberation. To this proclamation, the chairman of the Løgting, Kristian Djurhuus, added an appeal for calm and loyalty. The Løgting would do everything possible to secure provisions for the people and enable the fishing fleet to carry on its work for the benefit of the Faroese people.

The *amtmand* now ordered that no Danish vessel was to leave the harbours of Faroe without his permission. It was hoped that the cargoes on board the vessels which chance had driven to Faroe might include things necessary for the wellbeing of the islands. Unfortunately, the supplies which it was possible to requisition from this source proved to be of limited value.

Later the same day (Wednesday 10 April), the authority of the *amtmand* was challenged by the People's Party. This party declared in the Løgting that Faroe had passed from Danish sovereignty, and that the Løgting should now be fully responsible for legislative and executive acts in the islands. This declaration was coupled with the threat that if secession from Denmark had not been accomplished by 6 o'clock that evening, its proposers would themselves take whatever steps were necessary. However, all the other parties in the Løgting rejected the declaration, and the challenge fell flat.

The next day, Thursday 11 April, the Faroese people heard accounts of the long speech made in the House of Commons on the Scandinavian fighting by Winston Churchill, then still first lord of the admiralty. At this stage, Churchill was still optimistic about the outcome of the campaign in Norway. Since the outbreak of war, a major difficulty in enforcing a blockade of Germany had been the corridor to the north afforded to German vessels by Norwegian territorial waters. Churchill rejoiced that the Germans had destroyed this neutral protection by their own act. As he said:

Hitler has effected his German lodgments at various points of the Norwegian coasts, and he has felled with a single hammer blow the inoffensive kingdom of Denmark, but we shall take all we want of this Norwegian coast now, with an enormous increase in the efficiency of our blockade. We are also at this moment occupying the Faroe Islands, which belong to Denmark and which are a strategical point of high importance, and whose people showed every disposition to receive us with warm regard. We shall shield the Faroe Islands from all the severities of war and establish ourselves there conveniently by sea and air until the moment comes when they will be handed back to the crown and people of a Denmark liberated from the foul thraldom into which they have been plunged by German aggression.

The only sign that day of Churchill's words being put into effect, however, was the appearance over Tórshavn of a British reconnaissance plane.

About midday on Friday 12 April two British destroyers, H32 and H57, steamed up through Nólsoyarfjørður and dropped anchor just outside the mole at Tórshavn. The two British commanders went ashore to visit the *amtmand*, who received them in the presence of the Løgting chairman. The officers requested that arrangements be made for the reception of a garrison of marines in Tórshavn and Skálafjørður. *Amtmand* Hilbert replied that the situation gave the provincial authorities no alternative but to comply with the British request. The next day, the Løgting made a formal protest to the British consul in Tórshavn against the occupation. This, however, was no more than a formality; throughout the islands there was much heartfelt relief that a British and not a German force was coming ashore. Censorship was now introduced over all telegraphic and radio messages, overseas postal services were temporarily suspended and blackout regulations came into force, first for Tórshavn, and after a few days for the whole of Faroe.

The first British forces came ashore in the afternoon of Saturday 13 April from two armed trawlers, which were escorted by the two destroyers and the 10,000-ton cruiser *Suffolk*. They were Royal Marines, not more than 200 in number, commanded by Lieut.-Col. T. B. W. Sandall. The following day a detachment was sent over to Eysturoy to secure the large and safe harbour of Skálafjørður, a natural naval base.

The prime purposes of the British occupation of the Faroe Islands were naval, and throughout the war the Faroe garrison was commanded by a naval officer. The headquarters was set up in the old fort of Skansin, on the east side of Tórshavn harbour. Powerful naval guns were installed on the headland there to command the approaches to the Faroese capital.

The Royal Marines were relieved on 25 May, 1940, by about 500 men of the Lovat Scouts, who arrived in the troopship *Ulster Prince*. The Lovats were to form part of the Faroe garrison during the whole war. At its largest, the British garrison consisted of some 8,000 men, distributed throughout the archipelago in larger or smaller detachments. From 1942 to 1944 the most strongly guarded part of Faroe was the island of Vágar. There a military aerodrome was established in one of the very few locations in the islands suitable for the purpose, a shallow valley east of Sørvágur. During this period the inhabitants of the islands were issued with special identity cards, and visits to the island from outside were allowed only to those with special security passes.

German operations against the British garrison in Faroe were limited to a few isolated air attacks, mostly against naval vessels in harbour or near the islands. The most serious incident was on 21 February, 1941, when two German bombers made a low-level attack on the shipping in Tórshavn harbour, and sank the armoured trawler *Lincoln City*. Eight British seamen lost their lives on this vessel, which sank within a few seconds. The rest of the crew were rescued by a multitude of Faroese small boats that put out as soon as the German bomb exploded under the hull of the unlucky trawler — despite machine-gun bullets raining down over the harbour area. One of the attacking aircraft was brought down by the anti-aircraft batteries guarding the naval base in Skálafjørður.

The garrisons in Faroe and Iceland had the twofold task of enforcing the blockade of German-controlled Europe, and combating the U-boat menace in the north Atlantic. By the early months of 1944, the Battle of the Atlantic had been largely won, and it was possible for most of the land forces in Faroe to be withdrawn for the invasion of Europe. Many left on the troopship *Empress of Russia* on 18 March, 1944. The defence of the islands was henceforth left largely to the naval units in Skálafjørður and a few planes remaining on the airfield at Sørvágur. Only 400 men remained in the islands for the victory parade through Tórshavn on Sunday 13 May, 1945.

Throughout the war, relations between the British forces and the Faroese population were excellent. The close ties between the Faroese and the Danes ensured that there would be a lively sympathy amongst the islanders for the allied cause, and the troops stationed in the Faroe Islands behaved extremely well. Nothing was taken without being duly paid for, and isolated incidents — of drunkenness and so on — were suitably dealt with, civil and military police being on the best of terms. The last forces were withdrawn from Faroe on 16 September, 1945. Some soldiers took Faroese wives home with them, and two or three who had married locally made permanent homes in the Faroe Islands.

WARTIME POLITICS

The Faroe Islands entered their long period of isolation from Denmark with a new Løgting, elected on 30 January, 1940. The result of this election had been a considerable advance in strength for the People's Party, and a decline in support for the old Sjálvstýri, with the Samband and the Social Democrats holding their own. The People's Party was winning the support of former adherents of the Sjálvstýri who favoured a right-wing economic policy of state-fostered capitalism but were losing confidence in the ability or willingness of the Danish state to help in the manner necessary. The prosperity which wartime fish prices brought to the islands, coupled with the break in communications with Denmark, worked politically in favour of the People's Party. In 1943 the party captured the Folketing seat, polling 3,542 votes against 2,308 for the Samband and 1,385 for the Social Democrats. The member so elected could not travel to Copenhagen to take his seat, but the figures showed how powerful the new party had become in a short time. In the Løgting elections of 1943,

the People's Party also did well, taking twelve of the twenty-
six seats. The old Sjálvstýri was left without any representation at all, and the Samband and the Social Democrats won
eight and six seats respectively. Thus, throughout the war
years, despite the public sympathy for Denmark, Faroe was
close to secession.

When communications between Denmark and Faroe were
broken off by the German occupation, the People's Party,
as we have seen, wanted to declare independence. They took
the view that the Danish state had ceased to exist, and that
Faroe should now set up its own government, legislature and
judiciary. This was opposed by the other three parties in the
Løgting, and on 9 May, 1940, agreement was reached on a
temporary form of administration for the islands.

Existing laws and regulations were to remain in force as far
as conditions permitted. Where the law demanded administrative action by a government minister, however, this would be
carried out by the *amtmand* in consultation with a committee of
the Løgting. New legislation applicable to the islands might
be proposed by either the *amtmand* or the Løgting, but to
come into force it had to be debated and voted by the Løgting
and confirmed and proclaimed by the *amtmand*. The Løgting
committee, which with the *amtmand* now constituted the
executive, consisted of three members. Measures were later
taken to provide Faroe with a substitute for the appeal courts
and other judicial bodies formerly functioning in Denmark.

The British military authorities interfered as little with the
running of the islands as possible, being content to leave
internal administration in the hands of *amtmand* and Løgting.
The military worked in co-operation with the temporary civil
power over such matters as security, provisioning and the
needs of the garrison.

Financial arrangements presented special difficulties
demanding early attention. Faroe clearly could not be
allowed to continue using the same currency as circulated
in German-controlled Denmark; some substitute also had to
be found for the facilities normally afforded by the Danish

treasury and the Danish national bank. A Faroese delegation travelled to London at the end of April 1940 to discuss these matters, and at once began talks with the Danish ambassador in London and with the British government. It was agreed that while the war lasted, Britain should give Faroe the aid normally forthcoming from Denmark, and that claims by individuals and firms in the islands on Danish debtors should be settled through a clearing account in Føroya Banki. A guaranteed minimum price was set for Faroese fish, and the British government declared itself willing to continue the support hitherto given to the Faroese fishing industry by the Danish government.

The possession of foreign currency other than sterling was now forbidden. The Danish banknotes circulating in Faroe were first overstamped, then by degrees withdrawn and a provisional note currency, printed in England, substituted. A rate of exchange of 22.40 kroner to the £ was fixed.[1]

In the early years of the war, the People's Party was in opposition to a coalition of Samband, Sjálvstýri and Social Democrats. In 1943, the People's Party gained representation on the Løgting's administrative committee, but the combined strength of the Samband and Social Democrats was just enough to prevent them from making any constitutional changes in line with their long-term aspirations towards a loosening of the ties with Denmark.

THE CIVIL POPULATION IN WARTIME

The supply situation in the Faroe Islands was reasonably good throughout the war period, and no hardship was felt by the civil population. Some imported foodstuffs — sugar, coffee, tea and margarine, for instance — were rationed but bread and flour never became subject to restriction. Supplies of fruit and green vegetables were in short supply, and the islands had to be more or less self-sufficient in potatoes.

---

[1] The war-time exchange rate between pounds and dollars was £1 = $4.03.

Nearly all the fish caught by the Faroese sloops and trawlers was sent to England, and the Faroese themselves consumed only what the village boats could catch. Meat was available in varying quantities. The supply of dried mutton, the islanders' favourite meat, did not suffice for the whole year round. It was supplemented by the meat of the caaing-whale, schools of which the Faroese hunted in the war with all their customary diligence and enthusiasm, with the garrison troops joining in to help. Sea-birds were hunted on a scale reminiscent of the days of the subsistence economy, and the occasional meat shortage had to be bridged with supplies of imported corned beef.

The clothing situation was better in Faroe than in Britain, since much Faroese clothing was still home-produced from local wool. Thus it was never necessary to ration clothes, although later in the war footwear became scarce and dear. Fuel was never short for those who cut their own peat, but both imported and Suðuroy coal was rationed. That petrol was rationed goes without saying.

Only a few Faroese lost their lives at home as a direct result of enemy activity. The occasional air attacks were mostly directed not against land targets but against naval vessels or fishing-boats, and although property was at times damaged, no lives were lost on shore from this cause. Far more serious was the problem of drifting mines and other explosive devices. Two or three hundred houses in Faroese villages suffered damage at different times from German mines being washed ashore and exploding. Five persons were killed in two incidents in 1941 when unknown objects found on the shore were tampered with. To combat this danger, warnings were issued by the *amtmand*, and marksmen in the villages received military rifles for destroying any mines seen drifting in: some 850 had been blown up in this way by the end of the war. To combat other dangers, the islands had a civil defence volunteer force, working principally in Tórshavn, from 1942.

Thus as long as he stayed ashore, the Faroe islander suffered little wartime hardship compared with his fellow-citizen in Denmark. But the Faroese are a nation of fisher-

men; and it was as fishermen that they made their contribution towards the defeat of Germany, and suffered casualties
on a scale comparable with those of most of the fighting powers.

THE FISHING FLEET, 1940–1945

In the first year of the British occupation of Faroe the fishing
fleet went as usual to Iceland and Greenland, and the catch
was sold either as salt fish or klipfish. But Britain's need for
fresh fish increased, and in 1941 a resultant change took place
in the Faroese fishing industry.

The Icelandic fishermen had refused to sail to Britain with
cargoes of fresh fish unless an air escort were provided, but
there were insufficient aircraft and pilots for such a duty. The
Faroese sloops and schooners therefore undertook the task of
ferrying fresh fish from Iceland to Aberdeen and other
Scottish ports; the trawlers continued fishing on their usual
grounds. Faroese fishing vessels were responsible for landing
more than a fifth of all the fish eaten in Britain during the five
and a half years of war.

Excellent prices were paid for the landings. The total
value of Faroese exports during the war — nearly all of fresh
fish — was as follows:

```
1940 — 13,207,000 kroner
1941 — 38,367,000
1942 — 44,123,000
1943 — 41,416,000
1944 — 49,294,000
1945 — 30,174,000
```

During the same period, Faroese sterling balances in Britain
rose from £248,000 in January 1941 to £2,792,000 in July
1945. Payments to crew members were of course on a correspondingly handsome scale. However, the transport of fish
employed far fewer crew members than the fishery had done,
so that some unemployment was caused among the fishing
community.

The cost was heavy. Four of the ten trawlers in the fishing

fleet and twenty-one other craft — fifteen sloops and six schooners — were lost. These losses were caused as follows:

	Sloops	Schooners	Trawlers
Air attack	4	2	1
Mined	2	2	1
U-boat attack	1	1	—
Unknown causes	8	1	2
	15	6	4

The total number of fishermen killed as a direct result of enemy action was 132, nearly 0.5 per cent of the total population. While this is not to be compared with the percentage loss suffered by Poland, Russia or Finland, it was still heavy, of the same order as any of the western allies was called upon to bear. Probably the heaviest single loss during the war was that of the steam trawler *Nýggjaberg* of Miðvagur, which vanished on or about 28 March, 1942 without trace while fishing off Iceland, with twenty-one men on board.

The early attacks by German aircraft on Faroese fishing vessels led to their being armed with light machine-guns. On 21 April, 1941, the *amtmand* announced to the Faroese fishery organisations that the British naval authorities were prepared to issue two light machine-guns and ammunition to every Faroese fishing vessel plying between Iceland, Faroe and Britain. The acceptance of armament was not obligatory, but the weapons would be issued to any vessel on application at any British port, provided that at least two members of the crew were given training in their use and maintenance. And once on every trip, either before departure or after return, the vessel had to report to Skansin for the weapons to be checked as in good working order.

The installation of machine-guns on Faroese boats was some deterrent to German bomber pilots, who were often unwilling to risk an expensive aircraft in the cause of destroying a small and old fishing-boat. And the Faroese fishermen scored up one success. Early in 1942, the skipper of a sloop from Sandavágur managed to destroy a Heinkel, and was in consequence awarded a British M.B.E.

REUNION

At 8.45 p.m. on Friday 4 May, 1945, Faroese listeners heard the news that the German forces in Denmark, Holland and north Germany had capitulated. The usually unemotional people of Tórshavn swarmed into the streets to celebrate the end of the five-year ordeal of their fellow-citizens, and the joyful circumstance that liberation had come to them without land fighting having taken place on Danish soil. The following day, services of thanksgiving were held in all the churches and a loyal telegram was sent to the aged King Christian X.

On Monday 7 May, full telegraphic communication with Denmark existed for the first time in five years. Only one fact now marred the general jubilation: the German forces in Norway had not yet capitulated, and there were signs that they might be preparing to resist to the last. The Faroese have never forgotten their ancient Norwegian origins, so that the possibility of another campaign in Norway, with the Germans adopting a scorched-earth policy as they had already done in Finmark and Troms to hinder a Russian advance from the north, was disheartening. Indeed, that very day a German plane from Norway unsuccessfully attacked a Faroese fishing vessel. The German surrender of all forces on 8 May relieved the general anxiety.

One of the first telegrams that passed from Copenhagen to Tórshavn at this hectic and jubilant time was one from the Danish government thanking *amtmand* Hilbert and his colleagues for their good work during the years of separation, and authorising a continuation of government by *amtmand* and Løgting for the time being. But a conference on future constitutional arrangements was obviously needed at an early date.

CHAPTER X

HOME RULE

THE CONSTITUTIONAL CRISIS

When the war ended in May 1945, the Faroe Islanders were relatively well off economically. They had plenty of experience of managing their affairs through their own legislative body, and were full of confidence for the future. There could be no automatic return to the political situation that had existed in 1939, when constitutionally Faroe was simply Denmark's most northerly province. The powerful position of Thorstein Petersen, the leader of the People's Party — which lacked only a single seat to have an absolute Løgting majority — plainly showed the urgent need for constitutional discussions with the Danish government. Meanwhile, the wartime constitution remained in force, though the *amtmand* was now in a position to communicate with his superiors in Copenhagen.

The first step, as in most countries straight after the war, was to hold fresh elections. These took place on 6 November, 1945, and produced a chamber of roughly the same composition as before. Of the twenty-three seats, the People's Party now held eleven — again, a single seat short of absolute majority. The Social Democrats and the Samband won six seats each, and the old Sjálvstýri once again failed to win any representation. On 13 December, the Løgting chose an all-party delegation to go to Copenhagen for constitutional discussions, and in January 1946 the talks began.

The Danish government expressed a warm wish for the old constitutional link between Faroe and Denmark to continue, but stated that they had no desire to force the Faroese into a resumption of the union if the plain will of the Faroese people were against it. The three Løgting parties,

however, were deeply divided. The Samband wished to
restore, in broad outline, the pre-war constitutional position,
making only a few concessions to national feeling in the light
of wartime experience. The People's Party, which during the
war had tended to be separatist, now aimed at a status for
Faroe somewhat similar to that of a British dominion, with
a loose link with Denmark, and with as much Faroese control
of Faroese economic life as possible. The Social Democrats
wanted the islands' economic life to develop along co-operative
lines, and in broad terms, favoured a continuation of the
wartime constitution.

Of the three parties, it seemed that only the Samband and
the Social Democrats were in a position to work together. So
the Danish government put forward proposals forming a
compromise between their views, since no other alliance
seemed able and willing to accept any conceivable proposal.
The constitutional union between Denmark and Faroe would
be restored, while the Løgting would have legislative power
over matters concerning the islands alone, and the right to
levy local taxes. It would have the right to pronounce on any
Danish laws other than constitutional laws, before they were
applied to the Faroe Islands. The office of *amtmand* was to be
abolished, and replaced by that of state commissioner, or
rigsombudsmand. The Danish government maintained that this
was the limit to which the Faroe Islands could go while still
remaining within the Danish constitution.

Neither the Samband nor the Social Democrats were happy
with these proposals. The former thought they went too far,
the latter that they did not go far enough. But if the alternative, as the Danish prime minister maintained, was Faroese
secession, they were prepared to sink their differences and
make the best of it. With their one-man majority in the
Løgting, the two parties believed themselves able to push the
proposal through against the opposition of the People's
Party, but because one of the Social Democrats in the
Løgting, Jákup í Jákupsstovu, refused to vote for the proposal,
their attempt miscarried.

The People's Party now suggested that the issue should be put to a referendum for the guidance of the negotiators. Thorstein Petersen advocated a choice of four possible votes on the ballot paper: (i) in favour of the Danish government proposal; (ii) in favour of a constitution nearer the pre-war provincial status than that of the Danish government proposal; (iii) in favour of a looser constitutional link than that of the Danish government proposal; and (iv) in favour of complete secession.

There can be little doubt that this four-fold choice on the ballot paper would have thrown the maximum possible light on the issue. But the Samband and the Social Democrats were suspicious of the plan. Alternative (ii) seemed designed to split the Samband vote, and alternative (iii) seemed designed to augment the People's Party vote from the more home-rule-minded Social Democrats. They reduced the alternatives to two only: the government proposals — or secession: the Danish prime minister made it clear that if the government proposals were rejected, secession would indeed follow. This manner of proceeding was favourable to the two allied parties, who calculated that the Faroese people would draw back from the prospect of complete separation and vote for the Danish government proposals. The referendum was fixed for 14 September, 1946.

It was in every way an unfortunate ballot. In the first place, the poll for so important an issue was low: only 66.4 per cent of the registered electors cast their votes. This was partly because many fishermen were still at sea, and partly because conservatives in favour of the pre-war provincial status of Faroe tended to stay at home. It was said, too, that many older voters abstained because they held that it was the younger ones who should decide the constitutional arrangements for the future. In the second place, Thorstein Petersen managed by an electoral trick to convert the two alternatives into three. The questions were: "Do you want the Danish government's proposal put into effect?" and "Do you want the Faroe Islands to secede from Denmark?", the electors being required to set a cross against the alternative they supported. Thorstein Petersen advised those who wished Faroe to have a dominion status short of complete separation to spoil their papers by writing the word "no" against both alternatives.

Only one established Faroese political leader declared himself whole-heartedly for secession. This was the 80-year-old Jóannes Patursson, who died on 2 August, six weeks before voting took place. But secession was also advocated by a cross-party group consisting chiefly of young people, who in May 1946 had formed themselves into an association with the emotive title *Føroyingafelag*. The People's Party leaders were generally in favour of the dominion solution excluded from consideration, but many of their regular electoral supporters were in favour of secession.

The result of the referendum was:

	votes	*per cent*
For the government proposal	5,499	(47.2)
For secession	5,660	(48.7)
Spoilt papers	481	(4.1)
	11,640	

This was a masterpiece of inconclusiveness. Unionists could interpret it as a narrow rejection of separatism, separatists as a narrow rejection of unionism. And since only two-thirds of the electorate had voted, there was not on any construction a clear majority in favour of anything. The Danish prime minister, Knud Kristensen, took the view that the spoilt papers must be ignored, and that the vote was thus a narrow one in favour of secession. He believed that measures for the separation of Faroe from the Danish state should now be put into effect. The Danish parliament, however, took the view that so narrow a majority, taken in conjunction with the invalid votes, was far from being an unequivocal expression of the popular view, and that the question was still open. As Knud Kristensen's government was a minority one, he was unwilling to press his individual view of the matter, and agreed to conduct further negotiations.

In Faroe, supporters of union with Denmark were appalled that the decision to secede might be determined by fewer than a third of the registered voters, and they raised a powerful protest against any such conclusion. They pointed out also that articles in the foreign press made it seem doubtful in any case whether the great powers would allow so strategic a position in the north Atlantic to remain unprotected. The Samband and the Social Democrats, who before the referendum had referred to "no" votes merely as spoilt papers, were now only too happy to use their impressive total to support a plea for further discussion of the constitutional issue.

The man of the moment was, of course, the People's Party leader, Thorstein Petersen. He had appealed to the electors either to vote for secession, or to vote "no". With the help of the dissident Social Democrat, Jákup í Jákupsstovu, Thorstein Petersen now had a majority of one in the Løgting. Taking the Danish prime minister's pre-referendum words at their face value, he now put through a resolution that, because sovereignty had passed into the hands of the Faroese people as a result of the referendum, a provisional administration chosen by the Løgting should take control, until new elections could be held and a fresh Løgting chosen to negotiate with Denmark on future constitutional arrangements between the two countries. This resolution was widely misunderstood in Denmark as a coup d'état, and some Danish editorials said that in any other country Thorstein Petersen would have been put behind bars. Petersen was not, however, heading a revolt but attempting to secure an orderly continuation of the administration and an early resumption of constitutional discussions.

The uncertainty lasted only a few days. Then on 25 September the king, on the advice of the Danish government, dissolved the Løgting. This action, although unprecedented, was perfectly legal. The Danish corvette *Thetis* was sent to

Tórshavn, nominally so that its modern radiotelephonic equipment could provide a better channel of communication between Faroe and Copenhagen, but no doubt also as a deterrent to any popular disorder which might arise.

The view of the People's Party was that since the referendum had transferred sovereignty to the Faroese people, the king's dissolution of the Løgting had no legal force. However, after verbal protest, the party acquiesced in the dissolution. Only Jákup í Jákupsstovu (who had been expelled from the Social Democratic Party as soon as he had voted for Thorstein Petersen's post-referendum resolution) turned up at the chamber on the next day when a Løgting meeting would normally have been held.

The new Løgting elections were held on 8 November, 1946. In order to prevent the waste of any anti-secessionist votes, the Social Democrats made an electoral alliance with the old Sjálvstýri, which still had a following, although the party had been unrepresented in the Løgting since 1943. The result amounted to a defeat for the People's Party. Of the twenty seats, Thorstein Petersen's followers won only eight. The Samband had six, the Social Democrats four and the Sjálvstyri two. Jákup í Jákupsstovu did not contest this election. Though the People's Party remained the largest group on the new Løgting, it had polled only 5,396 votes against the 7,488 cast for its opponents. Ironically enough, this election showed plainly what Thorstein Petersen had all along maintained — that while the Faroese wanted a larger measure of home rule than the Danes had hitherto been willing to offer them, they did *not* want complete secession from Denmark.

The crisis was now over, although much detailed work remained to be done. In March 1947 the Løgting voted unanimously in favour of a request to the Danish government to grant legislative power to the Løgting, but on the basis of Faroe continuing to form part of the Danish kingdom. The result was the negotiation, over the next twelve months, of the Faroese Home Rule Act. This was approved by both the Danish parliament and the Faroese Løgting. It received the

royal signature on 23 March, 1948, and came into force on
1 April the same year. The only opposition to the ordinance
came from Thorstein Peterson and the People's Party, but
this was not because they were opposed to its measures in
principle, but because they believed the new constitution to
be unworkable in practice, since it would demand the co-
operation of three parties with widely differing aims.

THE HOME RULE ORDINANCE, 1948

The Act of 23 March, 1948, defined the Faroe Islands as
"within the framework of the law, a self-governing community
within the Danish kingdom". Provision was made for matters
of internal administration to pass into the hands of the
Løgting as the popularly elected body, and the Faroese local
government (in Faroese termed *Landsstýrið*, in Danish
Landsstyret). Matters affecting the defence or the foreign relations of the islands would remain in the hands of the Danish
government. If there were doubt over whether a particular
matter came within the competence of the Faroese or the
Danish government, the question was to be referred to a
commission made up of two members appointed by the
Danish government, two appointed by the Faroese government, and three high court judges. If, after deliberation, the
four government members were in agreement, the matter
would be thereby settled; if they disagreed, the judicial
members would decide the case. Up to the time of writing
(1972), the commission has never been called upon to sit.

The Act contains two schedules, called List A and List B.
List A consists of affairs which are unequivocally local, like
education, public health, harbours, highways, power supplies
and cultural institutions. List B consists of matters with both
a local and a joint aspect, like church affairs, police, radio and
air transport. Responsibility for affairs on List A might be
transferred from the Danish government to the Faroese as
soon as either the Faroese Løgting or the Danish government
requested it. The responsibility for affairs on List B might be

transferred to the Faroese local administration, but only following negotiation.

In those fields of administration in which it assumes competence, the Faroese government has to pay all expenses. For matters over which the Danish government retains control, statute in the Danish parliament determines how the expenses shall be shared between the Danish and the Faroese exchequers. The Faroese must be represented in the Danish parliament by at least two members in the lower chamber (the Folketing) and, until it was abolished in 1953, by a member in the upper chamber (the Landsting). The home rule act laid down, moreover, that any law applying exclusively to Faroe must be considered by the Løgting before passing to the Danish parliament. All laws common to Denmark and Faroe, on the other hand, were to be submitted to the Faroese government before they could be promulgated within the Faroe Islands. (Since 1896, promulgation of laws has been by publication in *Dimmalætting,* the officially appointed gazette.)

Foreign affairs are a Danish government responsibility. But the home rule act gives the Faroese certain rights in this field, especially when international negotiations on trade or fisheries are being carried on. The Faroese government may attach its nominees to the Danish foreign ministry or to Danish embassies abroad to advise on matters of special Faroese interest. There has hitherto been only one Faroese diplomat outside the Danish kingdom so appointed — a commercial attaché to the Danish Embassy in London, with an office in Aberdeen. The post was only recently abolished.

Finally, the home rule act made certain symbolic concessions to Faroese national pride. The chief Danish administrative officer in the islands was no longer to be the *amtmand,* or provincial governor, but the *rigsombudsmand,* or state commissioner. Faroese was recognised as the official language of the islands, although Danish was to be well and thoroughly taught in the schools, and might continue in use for all official purposes on an equal footing with Faroese. The

Faroese flag received official recognition and blessing. Upon the passports of Faroese citizens, the words "Faroe Islands" and "Faroese" would henceforth appear in addition to "Denmark" and "Danish". The home rule act did not provide for a special Faroese currency, but in the following year a way was found of permitting Faroese banknotes to circulate without upsetting the status of the islands within the Danish currency area. These banknotes were put into circulation within the islands, while a corresponding sum in Danish notes stood to Faroese credit in a special account in the Danish national bank in Copenhagen. These notes were printed by the Danish national bank to designs by Faroese artists. The coinage used in Faroe, however, remained the same as in the rest of the kingdom, and since the Faroese government has not elected to take over the postal services, there has not hitherto been any separate issue of Faroese postage stamps.

THE FAROESE FLAG

In the Scandinavian countries, flags have greater ceremonial and emotional significance than they do in Britain, although the Scandinavian attitude perhaps lacks that solemn reverence so commonly found in the United States. But it was natural and fitting that Faroese home rule should receive a visible expression in the form of international recognition for her national flag.

The most ancient symbol for the Faroese community was the ram, representing the chief source of wealth of the Faroe Islands in former times. From the middle ages onwards, this symbol was used on the lawman's official seal and it is to be found amongst the scenes depicted on the fine medieval carved pew-ends formerly in the village church at Kirkjubøur, and now preserved in the national museum in Copenhagen. In the latter part of the nineteenth century, the ram symbol was sometimes used as a Faroese flag, a white ram being set on a blue background with a red border.

As the national movement gained momentum, Faroe acquired another national symbol, the cheeky little red-beaked bird, the *tjaldur* or oyster-catcher. The use of this symbol was, of course, a reference to the *Ballad of the Birds* written early in the nineteenth century by Poul Nolsøe, who was now regarded as a national hero and as a forerunner of the national movement. This symbol too was displayed against a blue background with a red border.

Banners displaying the ram and the *tjaldur* were much used at the great open-air meetings that were an important feature of the early years of the Faroese national movement. These assemblies were usually held out in the country on public holidays. Faroese national songs would be sung, some of them especially written for the occasion, and well-known Faroemen would deliver speeches. Sometimes there would be a religious service. These were at once social and cultural events; they were enjoyed by the participants, and were an excellent advertisement for the strength of the national movement. The first such open-air meeting was held on Whit Monday, 1894, on Sandoy, and attended by people from every village in that island, by visitors from Tórshavn and many other places on Streymoy, and even — as was thought remarkable — by the crown tenant of Stóra Dímun, the smallest inhabited island in Faroe.[1] The success of these assemblies led to their imitation by religious and teetotal organisations and, after 1906, by political organisations.

As a symbol on banners for use at such open-air meetings the ram and the *tjaldur* were as good as anything. At international cultural meetings, it could be tolerated only as long as it was not the only one its kind. Until the Icelanders became independent in 1918, they used as their national symbol a falcon on a blue background, but in that year they too adopted a cross flag of the Scandinavian pattern. So too, in the same year, did the newly-independent Finns.

---

[1] Stóra Dímun contains only one large farm, and getting to or from the island is a difficult operation except in very good weather.

The Faroese *tjaldur* now began to look like a poor relation.

The first to put their minds to the problem of designing a flag for Faroe that would stand comparison with the other flags of Scandinavia, were a group of three Faroese students at Copenhagen University. One spring day in 1919, they sat down and sketched the existing Scandinavian flags, and then experimented with other possible colour combinations. Red, white and blue were selected as the colours for the new flag, probably because of their use in the Norwegian and Icelandic flags. The design eventually agreed on as the most effective was a blue-bordered red cross on a white background. A flag of this pattern was ordered from a manufacturer, and was first used at a meeting in Copenhagen that year. In 1920, the new flag was adopted by a young men's organisation in Tórshavn, and in the following years it made slow headway in the islands, mainly among home-rule groups.

The designer of the Faroese flag is officially listed as Jens Oliver Lisberg, born in 1896 in Fámjin on Suðuroy. After his education at Tórshavn Realskole and Sorø Academy, Lisberg entered Copenhagen University in 1917 to study law, but he fell a victim to the Spanish influenza epidemic in the summer of 1920. Lisberg is buried in Fámjin churchyard, and in the church itself is preserved the first Faroese flag ever to be made. Equally responsible for the design, however, was Emil Joensen, then a theological student, now a retired Copenhagen clergyman, and perhaps others.

The new flag first became known outside purely Faroese circles in the spring of 1930, when it flew from Lerwick Town Hall during the visit to Shetland of a Faroese football team. Next, also in 1930, it was taken to the millenary celebrations of the Icelandic Althing. On that occasion it was hoisted while Edward Mitens, then chairman of the Faroese Løgting, delivered his speech of congratulation to the Icelanders on behalf of his fellow-countrymen. However, the use of the flag was highly displeasing to the Danish delegation, which considered that for it to fly side by side with the flags of independent nations was inadmissible. They persuaded the Icelanders not to allow any Faroese flags to fly from official mast heads during the celebrations. Mitens himself was reprimanded, despite his protest that no disrespect was intended towards either Denmark or her 700-year-old flag, the Dannebrog.

When the story got back to Tórshavn, there was resentment among those who cherished the new flag; the latter now resolved on a counter-move. That year, on St. Olaf's Day (29 July, 1930), Tórshavn was commemorating the 900th anniversary of the death of the saint at the battle of Stiklestad. The intention had probably been simply to haul down the Dannebrog flying from the Løgting building; but the demonstrator who was carrying out this task found the rope impossible to loosen, and he cut it. A policeman disturbed him as he was so engaged, and the flag dropped abruptly from its mast at the height of the solemnities. The *amtmand* and several other prominent persons present left the assembly in protest at what they regarded as a deliberate insult.

In the 1930s, the Sjálvstýri made several attempts to get the flag accepted as a provincial symbol, but the Samband opposed its introduction, regarding it as a partisan emblem, and either opposing any provincial flag or conceding, at the most, the Dannebrog with a ram in the centre. Not until the second world war did the Faroese flag come into its own.

At the outbreak of war in 1939, *amtmand* Hilbert ordered all Faroese ships sailing outside territorial waters to fly the Dannebrog, and to have the national colours and the word "Denmark" painted on the ship's sides. The seizure of Denmark by the Germans in April 1940 complicated matters, making it necessary to distinguish between Danish ships under German control and Faroese ships with a friendly neutral status. On the day of the German attack, the sloop *Eysturoy* sailed from Klaksvík for Aberdeen with a cargo of frozen fish. It was halted the next day by a British naval vessel, whose commander ordered the Dannebrog to be struck, and after enquiring what other flags the ship possessed, ordered the Faroese flag to be hoisted in its place. In Aberdeen were several other Faroese vessels. After the arrival of the *Eysturoy* these all hoisted the Faroese flag, and painted the word "Faroes" on their sides. The first of these ships arrived back in Tórshavn on 21 April. *Amtmand* Hilbert tried to have the "rebel" Faroe flag replaced by a green signal flag, but this led to serious demonstrations in Tórshavn, and the *amtmand* decided to bow to the popular will. On 25 April, the British naval authorities ordered that for the duration of the war, Faroese ships should use the Faroese flag, and the B.B.C. broadcast an announcement to this effect. On 27 April, *amtmand* Hilbert signed the order authorising its use at sea. On land, the Danish flag continued to be used.

The action of the British authorities in forbidding the Danish flag at sea and ordering the use of the Faroese flag has been pointed out as the only occasion during the whole war when Britain interfered with the internal administration of the islands. The British action seems to have arisen initially from ignorance; nevertheless, since the war, 25 April, the anniversary of the British official recognition of the Faroese flag, has become Flag Day, an official public holiday in the islands.

The home rule act authorised the continued use of the Faroese flag on ships registered in Faroese ports; the act also authorised its use on land. Danish government institutions continue to use the Dannebrog, which may also be used by private persons at their discretion. Since its general introduction, the Faroese flag has ceased to be an expression of Faroese party feeling, and has become as natural to the younger generation as the Danish flag was to their grandparents.

HOME RULE IN ACTION

The home rule act officially came into force on 1 April, 1948, at the beginning of a new financial year. Early in May,

the Løgting met to begin its legislative business and to elect
the country's first home-rule government.

On 5 May, it approved a set of standing orders. These
provide for the scrutiny of credentials of newly-elected
members, the election of a chairman and vice-chairman, the
publication of order papers, the appointment of Løgting
committees, the manner of proposing legislation, the permitted length of speeches, and so on. For a motion to be passed,
more than half the Løgting's members must be present and
in favour. However, a substitute may take the seat of any
member who is sick or absent on other lawful excuse. The
Løgting's business is normally to be held in public, but on the
proposal of the chairman or of any four members, it may elect
to go into secret session.

On 13 May, 1948, the Løgting settled the form of this
relationship with the Faroese government. The Løgting first
elects a prime minister, to be known by the historic title of
lawman (in Faroese *løgmaður*, in Danish *lagmand*), and at least
two other ministers. As with all other Løgting resolutions,
these appointments must be made by at least half the assembly
present and voting in favour. By this law, the Faroese government is placed in charge of all affairs on lists A and B taken
over from the Danish government. It is normally the government that proposes legislation, and each measure must be
discussed three times by the Løgting. When a law has passed
the Løgting, it must be signed by the lawman and one other
minister, and then published.

The lawman has no power on his own initiative to dissolve
the Løgting. This can only be done when its four-year term
has expired, or when the Løgting itself resolves on dissolution.
The new Løgting must meet within a month of its election.

Certain features of the Faroese constitution thus differ
considerably from British constitutional practice. One difference is that government ministers need not be members of the
legislative chamber. Another is that since at least half the
Løgting must be present and vote for a new government,
minority administrations are impossible. However, the rejec-

tion of legislation proposed by a Faroese government is not
followed by the automatic resignation of the ministry or the
calling of fresh elections.

In order to propose legislation, or to answer questions, the
members of the government may address the Løgting, but
they may not vote unless they are elected members. The
Danish state commissioner has a similar right to address the
chamber and to propose legislation on matters within his
special competence.

Commentators have noted that these rules make a Faroese
government especially powerful at the beginning of its term of
office, since the Løgting can turn the government out of
office only by dissolving, which it is rarely willing to do soon
after election, but as the date for automatic dissolution
approaches, the power of the Løgting over the government
increases.

On the same day as these constitutional rules were approved, the Løgting also agreed to take over the following affairs
from the A list:

1. Local constitutional arrangements.
2. Municipal and parish council affairs.
3. Housing regulations and fire brigades.
4. Pharmacy.
5. Labour, employment, and apprenticeship regulations.
6. Direct and indirect taxation.
7. Løgting income other than from taxation.
8. Harbour dues.
9. Archives, libraries, and museums.
10. Preservation of buildings and of the countryside.
11. Communications, including the telephone system, but
excluding the post and telegraph systems; and the electrical
supply.
12. Agricultural affairs; fishing within territorial waters.
13. Licensing of theatres and cinemas, entertainments;
public subscriptions; wreck; lost property; poisons, explos-
ives, weapons.
14. Regulations concerning food supplies, price control,

rationing; regulations concerning intoxicants; trade regulations; registration of ships; insurance; and various miscellaneous trade functions.

15. Public trustee's office; publication of laws; tourism; regulations concerning printed matter; regulations concerning local time; rights of equality between men and women; the folk high school; the school of navigation.

From the B list, the Løgting, with the subsequent sanction of the Danish government, took over broadcasting in Faroe, and import and export control. More important items on the A list that remained joint affairs, were social insurance, the health service and education (other than the navigation and folk high schools).

The following day, the Løgting fixed salaries for the ministers who were to become responsible for Faroese government business. A minister is not allowed to carry on any other employment during his term of office without special sanction.

The first Faroese administration under the new home rule constitution was a coalition of Samband, Social Democrats, and Sjálvstýri. With an irony typical of Faroese politics, the first lawman was the seventy-five-year-old Samband leader, Andreas Samuelsen, who had spent a long political life in support of the unionist cause. Also in the government were Kristian Djurhuus (Samband), J. P. Davidsen (Social Democrat), and Louis Zachariasen (Sjálvstýri). Louis Zachariasen had been the young teacher who in 1912 brought official wrath down on himself by using the Faroese language in school and boasting about it. He later trained as a civil engineer in Denmark, and in his spare time worked away at the study of Faroese history. After Jóannes Patursson had left the Sjálvstýri to ally himself with Thorstein Petersen, he and Edward Mitens had kept the remnants of the party together through the dark days. By a further irony of events, the Sjálvstýri now found their small party an essential factor in almost every coalition over the next twenty years, enjoying far more continuous power than they had ever done in the days of their strength. The reason lay in the twofold political spectrum in the Faroe Islands, parties differing left and right on economic issues, and unionist or separatist on national issues. The Sjálvstýri, occupying an almost central position in both problem areas, have been in constant requisition as a makeweight in coalitions formed now on national, now on economic alliances.

The position of state commissioner for the Faroe Islands demanded an incumbent with much administrative ability, and diplomatic skill. The last *amtmand* and first state commissioner for the islands was C.A. Vagn-Hansen, an open-minded Danish official of the modern school, who occupied this difficult post from 1945 until 1954 with resilience and a sure hand.

The first home-rule government had two years to run before the next Løgting elections. Among its most important measures were the introduction, through laws passed through the Danish parliament on 31 March 1949, of greatly improved old age and retirement pensions. From this time on, however, a rift developed between the Samband and the Social Democrats. In February 1950 the two parties found themselves in disagreement over the budget, which the Samband finally pushed through with the help of the opposition People's Party. With the national issue for the time being settled, the Samband and the Social Democrats found the original basis for their alliance wholly eroded, while those old enemies the Samband and the People's Party began to find more and more policy issues on which their thinking was similar. At the same time, a new Faroese political party was appearing on the scene.

The initiators of the new party were a group holding left-wing economic views combined with a separatist outlook — men such as Jákup í Jákupsstova. Most of its members had advocated secession in 1946, and in June 1947 they founded a newspaper called *14. september,* a title intended to keep fresh in the public mind the date of the referendum that in the view of its publishers ought to have brought Faroese independence.

In May 1948, whilst the Løgting was taking its first steps
towards shaping the institutions of home rule, the fifth
Faroese political party was formally established. It was called
Tjóðveldisflokkurin, or the Republican Party. The most promi-
nent of its founders was a son of Jóannes Patursson, Erlendur
Patursson (born 1912). After graduating in economics,
Erlendur Patursson had followed an academic career in
Denmark until the end of the war. Like many of the Faroese
stranded in Denmark during the German occupation,
Patursson became a fervent separatist — while his economic
outlook was left-wing, although not communist in any
accepted sense of the term.

The Republican Party made a good start because of Denmark's adherence in 1949 to the North Atlantic Treaty
Alliance. Although the Danish and Faroese authorities had
established a good system of co-operation in joint affairs such
as education and hospital administration, the Danish parliament failed to consult the Løgting before joining NATO.
A Tórshavn naval district came into being, and the Republicans, in opposing (on national grounds) the stationing of
Danish forces in the islands, were able to divert some latent
resentment into their own political channels.

In the elections of 1950, the new party secured two seats
out of the twenty-five. The Samband won seven, the Social
Democrats six, the Sjálvstýri two, and the People's Party
eight. Arithmetically, a continuation of the coalition between
Samband and Social Democrats was a possibility, but
differences on economic issues were now so great as to rule it
out as practical politics. Instead, the Samband formed an
alliance which at the time was considered in the highest
degree surprising — with their deadly wartime opponents, the
People's Party.

The explanation of this coalition was to be found in the
worsening economic state of the country. The post-war boom
was over, and the fishing fleet had begun to experience hard
times. All parties felt that for the time being, no alteration in
the relationship between Faroe and Denmark was likely, and

that a shared economic outlook was the best basis for coalition. The two right-of-centre parties were able to raise fifteen out of the twenty-five seats, so the Social Democrats, the Sjálvstýri, and the new Republican Party were left in opposition.

The second home-rule prime minister was Kristian Djurhuus, who had served as minister in the previous administration. Born in 1895, he had followed an official career, and had first become a Løgting member in 1932. He represented a more modern and progressive style of unionism than that of the old Samband leader Andreas Samuelsen. The other two ministers in the new government were representatives of the People's Party—Thorstein Petersen, the bank director, and Rikard Long, a teacher at the Tórshavn high school and the teachers' training college. Long, a poet and for many years the editor of *Varðin*, the leading Faroese literary review, had entered politics during the war, and now represented the cultural aspirations of the People's Party, as Thorstein Petersen represented its economic aims. Thorstein Petersen, however, had to retire from the three-man government after the continuing financial difficulties of the fishing fleet had brought about the collapse of the Sjóvinnubankin in 1951 (see pages 209-10). His place was taken by a party colleague, the chairman of the Løgting, Hákun Djurhuus.

The 1954 elections were marked by a notable advance by the Republican Party — a development also consequent on the economic state of the country. Of the twenty-seven seats, the Republicans took six. The Social Democrat representation slipped from six to five, and that of the People's Party from eight to six. The Samband and Sjálvstýri strengths stood unchanged at seven and two seats respectively, and one seat went to an independent. Thus the right-wing coalition was now one seat short of majority. They were able to continue in office, however, by accommodating the Sjálvstýri within their alliance. For the next four years, the Faroese government consisted of a Samband prime minister, Kristian Djurhuus, and one minister from each of the other two coalition parties. The Sjálvstýri provided the veteran Edward

Mitens, while the People's Party minister was at first Hákun Djurhuus as before, and when in 1957 he was elected as Folketing member, Ole Jacob Jensen took his place.

The independent Løgting member, Kjartan Mohr, in 1956 launched yet another Faroese political party, bringing the tally up to six rival groups pursuing some 15,000 votes. Mohr's party was distinctly conservative in economic affairs, standing to the right of the People's Party. But in national aspirations it was nearly as extreme separatist as the Republican Party. It took the name of *Framburðsflokkurin*, or the Progress Party.

The political spectrum in Faroe since 1956 can best be understood if the position is summarised as follows:

ECONOMIC ISSUES

Left wing

Republican Party
Social Democratic Party
Sjálvstýri
Samband
People's Party
Progress Party

Right wing

NATIONAL ISSUES

Separatist wing

Republican Party
Progress Party
People's Party
Sjálvstýri
Social Democratic Party
Samband

Unionist wing

A successful coalition thus demands that a group of parties shall sink their differences in one problem area in order to pursue common aims in the other. To date (1972) there have been alliances on both wings over national issues, and on the right wing on economic issues. A left-wing coalition has not yet been practicable.

The trying first decade of Faroese home rule was more successful than many observers had dared to expect. The 1950s were an era of both political and economic difficulty, but the new institutions, and the politicians in Tórshavn who worked within them, were equal to the demands made upon them — despite the extraordinary complexity of the Faroese political structure which had grown up.

CHAPTER XI

THE FAROESE ECONOMY SINCE THE WAR

THE POST-WAR CRISIS

The Faroese emerged from the second world war with a much reduced fishing fleet, but with very respectable sterling balances. It seemed that if only ships could be bought in sufficient numbers, the wartime prosperity of the islands could be made permanent. The British were full of goodwill towards the Faroese because of their contribution to victory, and seemed unlikely to discriminate against Faroese fish in favour of their own producers.[1]

The Faroese were anxious to seize this opportunity of buying vessels of types that would emancipate them from the monotonous and exhausting thraldom of the old wooden sloops. "No return to the hand-line!" was the slogan, and the vessels purchased immediately following the war accordingly included over fifty seine-net vessels of 30–60 gross registered tons, and some thirty trawlers. By 1948 Faroe had the largest trawler fleet in Scandinavia — no fewer than thirty-seven vessels with a total tonnage of 12,769 g.r.t. Every village of any pretensions felt it a point of honour to possess a trawler of its own, and many new ship-owning firms started in business, often assisted by the Løgting's industrial loan fund, *Vinnuláns-grunnurin*, which was itself derived from the Løgting's wartime budget surpluses.

This impulse to invest was healthy, but the choice of vessel

---

[1] The Faroese have not, however, derived much practical advantage from British goodwill since the war, although the restrictive measures against Faroese fish have not been the result of general economic policy, but arose from the dispute over fishery limits that started during the 1950s.

made by the new and inexperienced firms was often unwise: a large proportion of the Faroese fishing fleet acquired soon after the war consisted of old and sometimes worn-out steam trawlers bought from Britain and Iceland, sometimes even bought without proper inspection. Two or three years of prosperity were enjoyed until the post-war boom was ended, and the day of reckoning came.

The terms of trade turned sharply against the Faroese fishing industry from 1950 onwards. The reasons were external. In September 1949, Sir Stafford Cripps drastically devalued the pound sterling in relation to the American dollar, leading to a correspondingly steep rise in the cost of dollar purchases for the Faroese shipowners. In July 1950 the outbreak of the Korean war forced up the operating costs of all shipping firms. Because of their small size and limited range, combined with the increased operating and repair costs, the old trawlers proved uncompetitive. Many of the new firms were undercapitalised and unable to face the changed conditions. It is said that the seasons of 1950 and 1951 involved nearly every firm in a loss of between 2 and 20 per cent of operating costs. Trawler after trawler was laid up, and hulks lay rusting away in harbours throughout the islands until they could be sold outside for breaking up. Only firms which had been particularly far-sighted in their choice of ship managed to remain solvent; and the insolvency of many of the weaker Faroese businesses led in turn to a crisis for the Sjóvinnubankin.

The Sjóvinnubankin (fishery industries' bank) had done well in the war. There had, admittedly, been some difficulty of a politico-economic character immediately after the war. This resulted from the differing exchange rates of the Danish and the Faroese krone. During the war, the provincial authority in Faroe had stabilised the exchange rate at 22.40 kroner to the pound, its pre-war parity. There was general expectation that because of German demands on the Danish economy, the Danish krone would have fallen steeply by the end of the war. For this reason the Sjóvinnubankin kept its funds as far as possible in sterling. By 1945, however, the Danish krone had depreciated rather less than sterling, and when exchange dealings were re-opened, the rate was fixed at 19.34 kroner to the pound. When the time came for the Faroese currency to be reassimilated to that of Denmark, Thorstein Petersen asked the *amtmand* to exchange £190,000 at the old rates first. *Amtmand* Hilbert refused, on the grounds that the Danish government had neither the duty nor the authority to make good the speculative losses of a private company. This was a perfectly tenable moral and legal position, but in the political circumstances of the time, many Faroe islanders interpreted the decision as an attempt by the *amtmand* to damage a political opponent financially. Thorstein Petersen took Sjóvinnubankin's case to the high court in Denmark, and had the good fortune to win his appeal.

Prosperous years followed, and the Sjóvinnubankin shared the prosperity. By 1951, however, export prices for fish and fish products were stable or declining, while import prices continued to rise. The bank had invested no less than 28,700,000 kroner in the post-war development of the Faroese economy, principally in the trawler fleet. The bankruptcies started. By July 1951, the Sjóvinnubankin was experiencing its first grave crisis, during which practically the whole of its share capital was lost. The following month the bank was temporarily saved by the subscription of fresh shares and a loan of 2,000,000 kroner from the Danish government.

However, the help thus afforded by the Danish government and the Faroese public proved inadequate. Large loans tied up in stores of unsold klipfish and unemployed salt continued to hamper the liquidity of the bank. On 1 February, 1952, Sjóvinnubankin had to suspend payments: the entire share capital, old and new, was lost. So that it might resume business, 500,000 kroner in fresh share capital was subscribed; the Danish government on its own account advanced 1,600,000 kroner, and on behalf of the Løgting and with its guarantee, a further 1,350,000 kroner; and a further 5,000,000 kroner were subscribed by the Danish national bank, likewise subject to

Løgting guarantee. With this assistance, the bank was able once again to open its doors on 27 February.

Naturally, there was an official commission of investigation into the Sjóvinnubankin collapse. Its report (published on 25 February, 1953), in recounting the history of the bank's difficulties, pointed to various alleged breaches of Danish banking laws. From the moment it appeared, the report was hotly contested. Certainly, the unpopularity in Denmark of the People's Party was at this time so marked that an unprejudiced assessment of businessmen so closely associated with it would have been a difficult task for any Dane; and there are features about the report which lend colour to allegations of political prejudice by the commissioners. After nearly two decades, it is still a political hot potato.

Thorstein Petersen faced a long-drawn-out and highly technical series of court proceedings, which removed him from the political scene for the rest of his life. However, he was acquitted on all charges of fraud and other grave breaches of law. For certain technical banking offences he served a total of forty days' imprisonment in 1955. He died in 1960, before he had had time to shake off the controversy.

In December 1951, the Løgting appointed a committee to make recommendations on the reconstruction of the fishing fleet. This committee spent the whole of 1952 examining the balance-sheets of every kind of fishing vessel, to see which was the most profitable for the Faroese to run. In their report, published in March 1953, they recommended three types of craft. For distant-water fishing, the best results could be expected from either steel-built long-line vessels of 200 to 230 g.r.t., incorporating a small freezing plant, or large diesel trawlers of 165 to 200 feet in length (i.e. 500–800 g.r.t.). For fishing off Faroe and Iceland, the best craft were small wooden long-line vessels of 30 to 60 gross registered tons.

But the purchase of such ships would not be a small matter. A long-line vessel of the kind suitable for distant-water fishing might well cost over 1,000,000 kroner, and a trawler four times as much. The smaller wooden long-line vessels would cost about 100,000 kroner each. It was plain that special credit facilities would be needed before the Faroese fishing fleet could be reconstructed along the desired lines. The key to this reconstruction lay ultimately in Marshall Aid.

At the same time as it was confronted with its reconstruction problem, the Faroese fishing industry had to face labour troubles. The seasons of 1952, 1953 and 1954 were all marked by serious strikes, all largely successful. The economic victory of the fishermen's union also had important political effects, since the chairman of Føroya Fiskimannafelag, Erlendur Patursson, was also the leader of the Republican Party, with its programme of both socialism and separatism. Many fishermen cast their 1954 votes for the party of their triumphant union leader, and Republican representation in the Løgting rose from two to six. The right-wing coalition of Samband and People's Party had to take in the small Sjálvstýri in order to retain control of the situation.

During the 1954 election campaign, Erlendur Patursson was in prison, serving a forty-day sentence for his part in violently preventing the departure of a strike-breaking trawler from Tórshavn that spring — a martyrdom that *14. september*, the republican newspaper, used to good effect in advertising his cause. Although the attack on the trawler had gone far beyond the bounds of peaceful picketing, and there could be no question of the sentence being other than correct in law, especially since the strike was itself an illegal one, the republicans could represent their leader as a generous-hearted man who was not afraid to go to prison in the interests of justice for the fisherman. The economic outcome of this series of strikes was indeed a considerable improvement in the pay and conditions of the fisherman, including a guaranteed minimum wage. If a ship's earnings now fell short of the legal minimum, the fishermen's wages were made up from an equalisation fund financed by a 1 per cent levy on all fish exports.

The post-war troubles of the Faroese fishing industry were thus considerable, but their prompt solution was of vital importance to the future of the nation. During the crisis years, many Faroese fishermen were finding work at tempting rates on Icelandic, Norwegian, German or British fishing vessels — in competition with the Faroese fishing fleet. Besides this, there was a danger of migration. As experience in the 1930s showed, it was very easy for unemployed Faroemen to forsake their native islands, migrate to Copenhagen, and become merged within the population of metropolitan Denmark, and a prolonged slump would tend to rob the islands of some of their ablest and best-educated inhabitants, the very ones whose help was most needed to hasten the return of better times. The loss of its young and able members in times of crisis is a danger to which every small nation is subject. With the help of the Danish government, the Faroese fortunately faced their troubles and overcame them.

RECONSTRUCTION AND PROGRESS

The key agency in the renewal and reconstruction of the Faroese fishing fleet was *Færøernes Realkreditinstitut,* the Faroe Islands mortgage finance corporation, founded in accordance with a Løgting law of 12 March, 1955, and starting work on 29 July of that year. In essentials, the corporation operates like a building society, granting loans on mortgage security and being repaid over a term of years, together with interest. The repayments, plus their accrued interest, are placed out on further loans. The original capital of the mortgage finance corporation was Marshall Aid to the extent of 10,000,000 kroner, to which the Danish national bank added an interest-free loan of 2,000,000 kroner for a period of ten years. The corporation was also authorised to issue stock, through which its work might be further extended.

The mortgage finance corporation devotes itself exclusively to first mortgages on fishing vessels of approved types, up to 50 per cent of their appraised value. Until 1958, a firm wishing to purchase such a ship might get in addition a Danish state loan of 15 per cent and a Løgting loan of 15 per

cent, thus having to provide 20 per cent of the purchase price
from its own resources. A law of 6 March, 1958, raised the
permitted level of both state and Løgting loans to 20 per cent,
thus making it possible for the owner to find no more than
10 per cent of the value of the ship himself. The banks,
however, no longer undertake mortgage business, but concentrate instead on providing working capital on the security
of ship's stores or catch.

A further institution designed to speed up the renewal of
the Faroese fishing fleet is a kind of shipowners' co-operative
society, called *Ognarfelagið*, the ownership society. This
society purchases fishing vessels with public help as outlined
above, and then leases them out to member-companies on
contract. The society does not itself operate vessels — it is
concerned only with ownership and making leases with the
option of purchase.

The reconstruction of the Faroese fishing fleet took place
chiefly between 1956 and 1964, after which the pace of ship
purchase has slowed down. The dramatic change in this period
may best be seen by comparing the composition of the fleet in
November 1955, before the mortgage finance corporation's
work had begun to have an effect, and August 1964, when it was
generally agreed that the reconstruction work was complete:

Composition of the Faroese fishing fleet

November 1955		Tonnage in gross registered tons	
		Total	Average
18	steam trawlers	4,951	275
11	motor trawlers	1,838	167
12	schooners	2,335	195
142	sloops and other smaller craft	10,129	71
3	seine-net vessels	134	45
186	vessels totalling	19,387 g.r.t.	

Note: The steam trawlers were nearly all old vessels built between the wars.
The schooners were built mainly during the early 1920s, and the sloops were
older still — over fifty of them dating from between 1874 and 1900, although
in each case more or less rebuilt.

August 1964			Tonnage in gross registered tons		*Average age in years*
			Total	*Average*	
8	steam trawlers		6,247	781	14
6	motor trawlers		4,147	691	13
58	steel long-line vessels		16,549	285	2.5
43	wooden long-line vessels, 20–70 g.r.t.		1,736	40	22
14	wooden long-line vessels, over 70 g.r.t.		1,495	106	27
9	schooners		1,550	172	42
37	sloops		3,720	100	72
175	vessels	totalling	35,444 g.r.t.		

Note: Within the next three years, five of these steam trawlers had gone, leaving only three of the very largest (average tonnage over 1,000 g.r.t.). The sloops and schooners, though still officially part of the fleet, were not in more than occasional service.

The most dramatic feature of the reconstruction programme was the speed with which steel long-line vessels were acquired for the fleet. These were found to be suitable for distant-water fishing in all the traditional Faroese fishing grounds and also some new ones; and at the same time they were not too large for the smaller Faroese companies to maintain and operate successfully.

*Steel long-line vessels in the Faroese
fishing fleet*

	Number	*Average tonnage*	*Average age in years*
1960	10	240 g.r.t.	1.5
1961	23	249	2
1962	30	251	1.9
1963	48	260	2
1964	58	285	2.5
1967	54	286	5

As the Faroese fishing fleet was re-equipped with more efficient and versatile ships, and as industrialisation progressed ashore, there was a widening of the operational area and a diversification in both the type of catch and its use. Before 1939 Faroese exports were almost exclusively of cod, in the form of either salt fish or klipfish. By the 1960s, fresh fish, quick-frozen fillets, salt herring, herring oil and herring meal had all become important. And among the fishing grounds, Iceland had ceased to be of any prominence, largely because Iceland extended its fishery limits to twelve miles in 1958, although negotiations with the Icelanders resulted in a few concessions within territorial waters for Faroese fishermen from 1961 onwards. The Barents Sea, important as long as the old steam trawlers were in the fleet, ceased to be important after 1958 and was abandoned completely after 1963. However, the Newfoundland Banks have assumed an important place in Faroese fishing, particularly for the new steel long-liners, which can operate in almost any weather. The fishery around the Faroe Islands themselves has increased to about a fifth of the total catch, following the introduction of vessels better able to work during the winter months, and with the growth of fillet factories ashore, which require fish in absolutely fresh condition. The Greenland fishery has kept its importance, and Faroese production of fish fillets on shore in Greenland began in 1959.

The reconstruction of the fishing fleet has meant that not only have catches increased, but they can be disposed of far more profitably than before. Detailed statistics of Faroese fishing from 1953 to 1968 are given in Appendix B (page 266), but some of the leading features will be summarised in this chapter.

The total catch nearly doubled between 1953 and 1968. The catch in each of the years 1953 and 1954 was slightly under 90,000 metric tons, but the catches for each of the three years 1966–8 exceeded 165,000 metric tons. Of this the herring catch was 17,000 tons in 1953 and 27,600 tons in 1954 (a good year), but in each of the three years 1966–8 the landings were over 60,000 tons. Of demersal species, only 8,000 tons were caught in the waters around Faroe in 1953 and 9,000 tons in 1954, but over 18,000 tons were caught there in 1966 and 1967, and nearly 28,000 tons in 1968.

The development of the herring fishery was spectacular. It was in 1951 that herrings were first observed in large numbers in the water north of Faroe. The following season, a few of the sloops made a trial at drift-netting herring, and nearly 4,000 tons were taken in the course of the year. In succeeding years, the sloops increased herring production to 10,000—20,000 tons per summer. From 1963, the sloops were joined by some of the new steel long-line vessels, specially adapted for the herring fishery, and catches now began to increase dramatically. Ten such ships took part in the 1965 herring fishery, catching in all over 20,000 metric tons. In 1966, fourteen modern vessels took part, catching a total of around 50,000 metric tons. In 1967 and 1968, drift - netting failed almost completely, and almost the entire output was due to the modern vessels.

The modern herring-fishing technique is to locate the shoals by echo-sounder, and then scoop them up with a purse seine operated by a power block. Broadly speaking, the trick is to run a net about 600 yards in length and 200 yards in depth right around the shoal. A motor-winch pulls in the draw-ropes at the bottom, so that the net is pursed together underneath the shoal. The net is then hauled aboard from one end, stage by stage, until a mass of what may be as much as 300 tons of herring is surging about in a confined space by the ship's side. The fish may now be pumped aboard, or dipped out with a sort of ladle-net operated from a derrick. When first introduced into the fishing industry, the purse seine had to be hauled in by hand, a difficult and exhausting task for the crew, their only mechanical help being a light winch. To create slack in the net for the crew to haul in, a motor-boat had to tug at the seine from a point twenty or thirty yards away. In addition, the seine-net vessel had to be helped by a second ship, which maintained tension on the opposite side of the ship to that on which the net had been cast, to prevent the first ship dragging itself over its own net. However, the process of seine-netting has now been completely streamlined by the introduction of the power-block, invented during the middle 1950s and first used by the Norwegians and the Icelanders. This looks something like an ordinary pulley-block, but it is capable of hauling aboard the heavy seine-net, and enables an unaided ship to make huge catches of herring. Besides using this very sophisticated equipment, purse-seine vessels are large enough and sturdy enough to operate all the year round, whereas the sloops could fish only during the summer months. There is even talk today in Faroe of buying a helicopter to assist the location of shoals of herring, large quantities of which can now be processed for industrial purposes.

The markets for Faroese fish and fish products have become far more diverse since the reconstruction of the fishing fleet. In 1953, the principal markets were Italy, Greece and Norway for salt fish, and Spain and Brazil for klipfish. By 1968, Spain was declining as a customer for klipfish, but exports to Brazil were being maintained, and Italy, previously a small buyer, was taking larger quantities. Salt fish was mainly going to Spain, Italy, Greece, Norway and Portugal, with smaller consignments to Britain and France. The principal customers for frozen fillets were Britain and the United States, some also going to Czechoslovakia, Sweden, and France. Fresh fish on ice was being landed principally in Britain, though Denmark was taking a good deal of fresh herring caught in the North Sea. Salt herring was being sold to Sweden, Denmark, East Germany and the Soviet Union.

Sales of Faroese fish are now organised through several agencies. The pre-war syndicate Føroya Fiskaexport, which had a monopoly of the export of salt fish and klipfish, was revived in 1948 under the name of Føroya Fiskasøla. This company had an export monopoly until 1952. In 1953, a separate company was formed for the export of salt and pickled herring, Føroya Sildasøla, and it handled nearly all of these products. Two other export firms for fish have been founded since, one in 1954 by a fishermen's co-operative, the other in 1964 by a consortium of small-scale shipowners. Føroya Fiskasøla is, however, still the principal exporter.

Fresh fish and frozen fillets are exported by the individual producers.

The power base for the growing Faroese fish-serving industries has been electricity. Of the power stations in the islands, by far the largest is the S.E.V. hydro-electric plant near Vestmanna in north Streymoy. The first of its turbines was set in motion in December 1953, and during the period 1956 to 1963 the station has been much extended, by the tapping of further water supplies and the installation of more turbines. S.E.V. stands for Streymoy, Eysturoy and Vágar, for it was the local communes of these islands that were responsible for planning and carrying out the ambitious scheme. The finance came partly from the communes themselves, partly from the Løgting, and with the help of some very large loans from the Danish government as well as others floated publicly in Denmark.

S.E.V. supplies electric power from the Vestmanna installations to the whole of Streymoy, Eysturoy and Vágar, the two latter islands being reached by overhead lines spanning the straits between them and Streymoy. In 1956, the important and fast-growing town of Klaksvík was linked to S.E.V. by a cable spanning the mile-wide channel between Eysturoy and Borðoy, providing Klaksvík with a supplement to the power produced by the municipal station. The S.E.V. undertaking now manages nearly all the local oil-driven and other power plants throughout the Faroe Islands, as well as the big Vestmanna hydro-electric station. Since the 1950s, electrification has become universal, and very few homes in Faroe are today without an electric supply. Peat-cutting, indeed, has become almost a thing of the past.

Faroese industry, which S.E.V. was designed to stimulate, is concerned primarily with servicing the fishing industry or working up its products. Thus we find eight shipyards, six rope and net manufacturers, twenty-one freezing plants, twenty-four klipfish drying plants, a cannery and four fish-meal factories. The outstanding feature of Faroese industry in recent years has been the increase in the size of the enterprises : among the larger to be founded are Skála Skipasmiðja, a shipyard on Skálafjørður employing over 300 persons and building steel ships for the Faroese fishing fleet. Sometimes it supplies overseas buyers, as for example a Danish customer who in 1966 took delivery of a merchant vessel for which he paid 2,600,000 kroner. In Klaksvík there is a modern fish fillet factory employing seventy-five persons and capable of turning out 30 tons of fillets a day. A new herring oil and meal factory in Fuglafjørður is capable of processing 500 tons of raw material per day. It is supplied by Danish and Icelandic fishing vessels as well as Faroese ones. Amongst the many expanding Tórshavn firms may be mentioned in particular the Bacalao company, founded in 1953, which maintains cold stores, klipfish-drying plant and a fillet factory on the western side of Tórshavn harbour. The firm also has a mink farm in Hoydalur (fed from reject material from the fillet factory), and a small fish meal factory in Velbastaður. The employees of Bacalao now number about 200.

The reconstruction of the Faroese fishing fleet has thus been accompanied by such a diversification of shore-based industry as makes it unlikely that Faroe could in the future experience crises as severe as those of the 1930s and early 1950s. But the growth of industry has led to changes in the settlement pattern within the islands — not as yet on an alarming scale, but sufficient to require the attention of those concerned with planning and investment problems.

AGRICULTURE

Although agriculture was the traditional staple of the Faroese economy during the Monopoly period, and although, even during the second world war, the Faroe Islands were to an important degree agriculturally self-supplying, the rise of an industrialised deep-sea fishery has brought about a corresponding decline in the importance of agriculture.

Agriculture today accounts for less than 5 per cent of the

gross national product, and much of the agricultural produce consumed in Faroe is imported. Indeed, the much-loved *skerpikjøt* has become something of a luxury, and a great quantity of mutton is now imported from Iceland, Greenland and New Zealand.

Of the three types of Faroese land tenure, only the crown lease is of real economic significance today. Privately owned land is now divided into such small holdings that few villagers possess as much as a whole mark, and infield cultivation is typically an occupation for an older couple to carry on while their sons are at sea. The allotment system is still in operation and has a continued value for inshore fishermen, but the value of smallholdings today is generally becoming a matter of sentiment rather than of serious household economics. People like to retain land in their hands because it gives them a stake in the agriculture of the village and a voice in joint village affairs.

In 1937, a series of agricultural reforms was carried out. Among the many provisions was one under which the administration of crown land was taken over by a Faroese agricultural council, which devoted the income from leases, and any sums accruing from the alienation of land from the leases for building sites or further allotments, to the development of agriculture in Faroe. The administration of the land fund passed to the home rule government in 1948. The fund can, for example, assist in the provision of operating capital, or finance the purchase of agricultural machinery. (Mechanisation has not proceeded very far hitherto, but during the past fifteen years, miniature tractors have appeared in the islands). In addition to the proceeds of crown land, the fund receives an annual subsidy from the Løgting.

Since 1920, an agricultural research station has been in operations at Hoyvík, a few miles north of Tórshavn. It has concerned itself chiefly with the improvement of growing crops, both by securing better strains of seed, and by finding out which manures best suit the local conditions.

The land registry office (*Matrikulstovan*) in Tórshavn is

undertaking the very difficult task of rationalising the infield
ownership position in Faroe. The process of inheritance has
led to the infield becoming subdivided into plots that are not
only uneconomic, but sometimes downright ridiculous. A
Nólsoy infield holding of 5 gylden which the author of this
book investigated in 1954 consisted of eighteen different
plots, one of them only five yards square. The villagers did
not regard this smallholding as in any way exceptional. The
process of rationalisation (*útskifting*), by which holdings are
consolidated into a smaller number of larger plots, can
obviously make village agriculture more productive and less
laborious. And it is worth carrying out even if the economic
gain is small, because the Faroese village community has
human values which are well worth preserving, and which
are a link with the islands' past. Too sudden an urbanisation,
in particular, would leave the islands much poorer in human
terms.

SHIFTS IN POPULATION

The economic changes now proceeding in Faroe are beginning
to have a very noticeable effect on where young people are
living. The modernisation of the fishing fleet and the development of fishery-related industry are inevitably leading to a
measure of urbanisation. The total population of Faroe
continues to increase at a high rate[1] and the towns and larger
villages are in a state of rapid expansion. The smaller villages
hold their own as long as they have reasonable access to the
larger population centres. It is only the outlying villages on
the more remote islands that have ageing and declining
populations, although even here there are no signs as
yet of the wholesale rural depopulation characteristic of
Shetland.

As long as the Faroese fishing fleet consisted principally of
the old wooden sloops and schooners, there were no special

---

[1] At the census of 16 November, 1970, there was a total population of 38,610

advantages for a fisherman if he moved from village to town. As he was going to spend four or five months at home during the winter, a day or two spent in getting from home to ship in spring and back again in autumn was of no significance. Living in a village had positive advantages for a sloop fisherman: many owned small plots of land, and before 1939 it was common practice for the sloops to return for a week in May to enable crew to go home and plant their potatoes.

On the other hand, all-the-year-round fishing with shorter returns to port between trips, demands settlement of a more concentrated pattern. A fisherman working on a Tórshavn-based distant-water fishing vessel will find it best of all to live in Tórshavn, convenient enough to live on Nólsoy or in Kollafjørður, but out of the question to make his home on Fugloy or Mykines. When the prospect of factory or shop employment for the women and other non-fishing members of the family is considered, the attraction of living in or near town becomes very obvious. Young married couples are as always especially mobile, and the towns, Klaksvík in particular, are very youthful in population — just as the population of the remoter villages tends to be an ageing one.

The development of the Faroese population by districts in 1950—66 was as follows:

	1950	1955	1960	1966	Increase 1950–66	per cent
Northern Isles	4,448	4,804	5,086	5,322	880	19.8
Eysturoy	6,988	6,954	7,382	7,714	719	9.3
Streymoy	9,728	10,152	11,692	14,078	4,272	43.9
Vágar	2,637	2,645	2,655	2,590	—48	—1.8
Sandoy	1,712	1,710	1,736	1,684	—28	—1.1
Suðuroy	6,268	6,182	6,045	5,734	—547	—8.7
Faroe Islands	31,781	32,456	34,596	37,122	5,248	16.5

The reason for the rapid expansion in the population of Streymoy lies in the 73.0 per cent growth in the population of Tórshavn over this period. The advance in the population of the Northern Islands is likewise due to the 38.2 per cent growth of Klaksvík's; and the growth of the Eysturoy population is concentrated largely around the excellent harbour of Skálafjørður.

A breakdown of the population changes parish by parish from 1960 to 1966 illustrates this trend in more detail:

NORTHERN ISLANDS		1960	1966
Viðareiði		202	202
Hvannasund		291	294
Fugloy		140	113
Svínoy		146	117
Klaksvík		3,894	4,257
Kunoy		151	144
Mikladalur		122	96
Húsar		140	99
	Total	5,086	5,322

EYSTUROY	1960	1966	VÁGAR	1960	1966
Nes	2,017	2,231	Miðvágur	820	842
Sjógv	783	849	Sandavágur	704	663
Skáli	461	560	Sørvágur	928	928
Eiði	620	587	Bøur	82	65
Sund	284	274	Mykines	121	92
Funningur	147	149	Total	2,655	2,590
Gjógv	146	138			
Fuglafjørður	1,271	1,278			
Leirvík	618	621			
Gøta	667	688			
Oyndarfjørður	225	202			
Elduvík	143	137	SANDOY		
Total	7,382	7,714	Sandur	578	570
			Skopun	568	543
			Skálavík	246	234
			Húsavík	201	198
			Skúvoy	143	139
			Total	1,736	1,684

STREYMOY			*SUDUROY*		
Tórshavn	7,447	9,738	Hvalbøur	829	751
Tórshavn rural	595	796	Fróðbøur	2,042	2,033
Kaldbak	165	124	Fámjin	185	164
Kirkjubøur	100	100	Porkeri	408	359
Hestur	87	86	Hov	183	182
Nólsoy	352	345	Vágur	1,747	1,642
Kvívík	430	407	Sumbøur	651	603
Kollafjørður	497	508	Total	6,045	5,734
Kvalvík	289	267			
Hósvík	170	163			
Haldársvík	352	325			
Saksun	34	33			
Vestmanna	1,174	1,186			
Total	11,692	14,078			

The population loss on Suðuroy is general, and is no doubt due to the better industrial opportunities opened up in the more northerly islands by power from S.E.V. The population loss is least from the Fróðbøur parish, which includes the important fishing port of Tvøroyri. With the recent completion of a road network on Suðuroy, population loss from the island may slow down or even halt in the next decade.

Rapid population loss is being suffered by the more remote islands, particularly those where landing facilities are poor. These islands are Mykines off Vágar, and Kalsoy, Svínoy and Fugloy in the Northern Islands. Kunoy had already suffered a considerable population loss before 1960, and so had less to lose between 1960 and 1966. The populations of Viðareiði and Hvannasund hold their own by virtue of a road system stretching from Klaksvík to Viðareiði, through two road tunnels on Borðoy and over a narrow ferry crossing at Hvannasund. Thus the two parishes are in the process of becoming suburbs of Klaksvík.

On the large islands of Streymoy and Eysturoy, the fate of a village depends largely on layout of the road system. On Eysturoy, the parishes surrounding Skálafjørður — Nes, Sjógv and Skáli — are growing dramatically. Most other parishes are holding their own, but the remoter villages —

especially those like Oyndafjørður, which the road system has
not yet reached — show a tendency to lose population.

The intensive expansion of the road system began in the
middle 1950s as part of the general development plan. North
of Skopunarfjørður, travel has already become largely a
landward affair, by car or bus with short ferry connections.
The number of motor vehicles in Faroe has, indeed, increased
rapidly in recent years, with opportunities for their more
extensive use.

1955	1960	1965	1966	1967
582	1,023	2,052	2,560	2,804

1968	1969	1971
3,001	3,270	4,258

The next generation may well see the consequent growth of
dormitory villages serving Tórshavn and Klaksvík, in which
the wealthier Faroese will choose to live as town life loses its
novelty and some of its attraction.

CHAPTER XII

THE NATIONAL CULTURE

EDUCATION

In the present century, Faroese education has steadily increased in quality, quantity and diversity until at the present time it will bear comparison with education in Denmark. For children of seven to fourteen instruction is compulsory, and between these ages most attend the *fólkaskúli*. Despite the scattered population of Faroe, of the 5,849 children attending *fólkaskuli* in 1968, only ninety-four were in attendance at schools with fewer than ten pupils, and thus so small as to need to share a teacher with the school of another village. Over 4,000 attended schools with 120 or more pupils, many of which had a teacher for every year-group. The chief difficulties for Faroese schools outside the towns have been over making adequate provision for handicrafts, building up school libraries and providing audio-visual aids.

About 60 per cent of the children continue their schooling beyond the minimum school-leaving age. For them there are high schools in Tórshavn, Klaksvík, Tvøroyri and Vágur, and continuation classes elsewhere. Today Tórshavn also has a flourishing *studentaskúli* (in Danish, *gymnasium*), situated pleasantly among some of Faroe's rare trees in the shallow valley of Hoydalur, a short distance to the north of the town. The *studentaskúli* corresponds roughly to an English sixth-form college, and since it serves the whole of Faroe, it is partly residential. Also in Tórshavn are a navigation school, a teachers' training college, a folk high school and a school of nursing.

Higher education for a Faroese student almost invariably means travelling out of the islands. In the early months of

1967, there were 162 Faroese students in institutions of higher learning. In Copenhagen there were 135, twenty were in Århus, three in Norway, one in Sweden, and three in Faroe. The subjects being studied were theology (6), medicine (40), dentistry (9), pharmacy (4), psychology (2), law (13), politics and economics (11), actuarial studies (1), humanities (25), natural science (14), engineering (11), architecture (2), music (1), commerce (17), agriculture (3) and Faroese studies in Faroe (3). This is an impressive number of students, although clearly many of them will be lost to the islands after graduation: it is in the nature of things that Faroe can neither expect to have every professional post filled by a Faroeman, nor to retain every professionally-trained Faroeman within the islands.

In general, it may be accounted healthy for Faroese students to attend seats of learning in Denmark or elsewhere, where there is a larger and more varied academic society than could be brought together in Faroe. But the study of Faroese language and literature (in particular the rich oral literature) now properly takes place in the islands themselves under the leadership of a Faroese philologist, Professor Christian Matras, late of Copenhagen University. By a law of 20 May 1965, the Løgting established an institution of higher learning in Tórshavn, *Fróðskaparsetur Føroya* (Academia Faeroensis).

Fróðskaparsetur Føroya undertakes research and higher education of the university type. The research is mainly directed to the study of the language and the oral and modern literature of the islands. The higher education work consists partly of year-long full-time enrichment courses for teachers, and partly of university extension classes conducted in the winter evenings. Enrichment courses are offered in Faroese language and literature or in natural history. The subjects for the extension classes are multifarious: in the winter of 1967—68, they were European church history, the laws of marriage and maritime law. Fróðskaparsetur Føroya has its own purpose-built premises near the central library of the

Faroe Islands. Besides its classrooms, library, and so on, it has four bed-sitting rooms for the accommodation of students from overseas. The building also houses the Faroese marine biology laboratory and the laboratory of fishery economics, which are loosely associated with the academy.

The academy's linguistic and literary work includes the further collection of oral literature in summer forays round the villages, and the compilation of a supplementary volume to the second edition of the Faroese-Danish dictionary compiled by Professor Matras and published in 1961. (The first edition, by M. A. Jacobsen and Christian Matras, was issued in 1928.) In these two fields of research, help is sought from the layman as well as the specialist.

More modest evening schools exist both in Tórshavn and in the villages. Their high-point before the war was in the middle 1930s when economic conditions were bad and there was some unemployment. The total number of pupils was then about 1,600. The numbers dropped considerably during and immediately after the war, but have now climbed back to about the same level.

The folk high school is an important institution in Faroese national culture. It has a staff of two full-time and about eight part-time teachers. Like the Danish institutions (such as Askov) on which it was modelled, it aims to give an education in the practical and liberal arts to the population as a whole, but particularly to those in rural areas. The purpose is to strengthen and enrich the national life by widely disseminating the national values and the national cultural heritage. The Faroese folk high school does not carry on this work in any narrow, parochial spirit, but includes Danish language and cultural history, and sometimes English, in its syllabus. As well as running courses for adults, the school acts as a continuation school for pupils of fifteen to eighteen. For this purpose there were until recently three-month summer courses for girls, and five-month winter courses for boys. The latest development is to have simultaneous courses for both sexes, since the pattern of employment is no longer so highly seasonal. Of late years, enrolment has been from forty to fifty girls, or from thirty to forty boys to each course.

Thus the Faroese educational system, although it operates under special difficulties because of the small and scattered population, is nevertheless coping well with its dual task of equipping the young for their eventual daily work and of giving young and old alike a sense of participation in the culture of their nation and of the world.

CULTURAL INSTITUTIONS

The Faroe Islands library was founded in 1828, on the initiative of *amtmand* C. L. Tillisch and his assistant, the provincial auditor Jens Davidsen (1803–78), helped by the Danish antiquarian Professor C. C. Rafn. The library acquired its own building in 1830, and from that time until his death Jens Davidsen acted as honorary librarian, working there in his spare time. The library grew rapidly, largely through gifts, and by the 1850s had a collection of more than 5,000 volumes.

From 1878 until 1905, the library went through a lean period, sometimes being closed altogether, but in 1905 the Løgting granted the library financial support, and regular loans of books began again in the following year. It entered a period of rapid growth in 1921, under M. A. Jacobsen, who had then newly returned from two years' study of librarianship in Denmark. In 1931 the library was moved to its present premises, which seemed adequate at the time, but were bursting at the seams ten years later.

The main purposes of the Faroe Islands library were defined in 1923 as (i) to collect the whole of Faroese literature and as much as possible of the literature about the Faroe Islands; (ii) as a central library, to work for the spread of knowledge and enlightenment throughout the country, by providing technical literature, fiction, and other literature appropriate to general education; (iii) to assemble a collection of scientific and learned literature. M. A. Jacobsen (1891–

1944) made it his life's work to forward these aims, in spite of having to run a national library on the limited funds which the Løgting could allow him. In the war, it became impossible to replace books in the Scandinavian languages, and the condition of the library stock became very poor. By his early death M. A. Jacobsen was denied the opportunity of carrying through the post-war reconstruction with increased resources.

Since home rule in 1948, the library has had a large increase in Løgting grant and had entered a second period of rapid expansion. Twelve branch libraries now exist in Faroe, and there is a system of lending out boxes of books to the smaller villages and to Faroese ships. Books lists and information bulletins now aid these outlying borrowers. In 1952 a Løgting law was passed requiring all printers in the Faroe Islands to send a copy of everything printed to the library. The library now collects, as a matter of course, everything written by a Faroeman in Faroese or any other language, every Faroese work translated into another language, and everything written by others about Faroese conditions.

The Faroe Islands National Library, as it has been officially named since 1948, is a key institution in the culture of the islands, and fulfils its difficult tasks with diligence. But as well as having outgrown its premises, it suffers from a shortage of staff, so that, for example, much of the manuscript collection remains without being properly catalogued.

In the same building as the library are the record office, the historical museum, the natural history museum, and the maritime museum. The record office was founded in 1932, and since 1952 has been the repository of all official documents in the islands, other than Danish state documents, once they are out of current use. The first archivist was Anton Degn (1871–1950), who was trained in the state archives in Copenhagen. Degn wrote a number of valuable books on various technical aspects of Faroese history from the sixteenth to the nineteenth century. The present (1972) archivist, Páll J. Nolsøe, has published a comprehensive maritime history of Faroe, which is already in its seventh volume, with more to come.

The natural history museum was founded in 1955 by a Løgting law, with the aim of collecting and exhibiting objects of scientific interest, especially those casting light on Faroese natural history. The museum is in three main sections, devoted respectively to geological, zoological and botanical collections. The zoological collection has been built on the magnificent collections presented by the author Hans Andreas Djurhuus, the Nólsoy ornithologist Niels á Botni and others. The botanical collection was likewise founded on the collection made and presented by the scientist, novelist and folk high school principal, Rasmus Rasmussen (1871-1962).

The historical museum, founded by private initiative in 1895, contains an excellent collection of exhibits illustrating Faroese daily work and domestic life in the seventeenth, eighteenth and nineteenth centuries. There is a smaller amount of archaeological material, including artefacts from graves of the Viking period excavated by the Faroese archaeologist, Sverri Dahl. The museum's premises are, however, pitifully inadequate, with consequent crowding of the exhibits. The maritime museum, accomodated in an adjacent building, houses a collection of every possible type of Faroese boat and seafarers' equipment. In at least two villages, Miðvágur and Saksun, are folk museums in old houses; the mediaeval farmstead of Kirkjubøur, once the bishop's palace, contains a wealth of Faroese relics of past times, which are protected by law. A society in Klaksvík which owns many old implements and clothes has acquired as its museum the now abandoned hamlet of Fossá.

A key institution for Faroese scientific and learned life is Føroya Fróðskaparfelag, the Faroese scientific society, founded in 1952 with the object of promoting co-operation in all fields of learning, collecting scientific literature, and publishing the results of research on or carried out in Faroe. The society is concerned with philology and history as well as the natural sciences. A yearly periodical, *Fróðskaparrit,* is published

in Faroese with summaries in English; books on Faroese
studies of various kinds, such as original medical research or
previously unpublished historical source documents, are also
published. It was through the work of the society that the
academy, Fróðskaparsetur Føroya, came to be founded.
Føroya Foroskaparfelag has been a great stimulus to profession-
ally qualified Faroemen and foreign residents in or visitors
to the islands to undertake research of various kinds.

Faroese interest in the fine arts has likewise been on a
considerable scale, and the islands have a wide range of
institutions for their cultivation and encouragement. As a
small nation remote from any neighbours, the Faroese have
understandably been more successful in literature and the
visual arts, which call mainly for individual performers, than
in drama and music, which require numbers to work together.
In Britain it requires a population of about 250,000 adequa-
tely to support a professional theatre and about 1,000,000 to
support even a small symphony orchestra. The Faroese are
never likely to possess either in any world that we can imagine
today. Drama and music must remain arts practised by the
amateur.

Traditionally, Faroese music was entirely vocal, the *kvæði*
never having any instrumental accompaniment. In every past
age there must naturally have been musically gifted individuals
who played instruments of one kind or another, either self-
taught or having learned their skill abroad. Jens Christian
Svabo, for instance, was an excellent violinist. The Nolsøes
have always been a musical family, and when in 1831 the
Monopoly presented an organ to Tórshavn church, it was
Napoleon Nolsøe, the son of Jacob Nolsøe and later the first
Faroe-born doctor to work in the islands, who played it at
church services. The present musical tradition in Faroe stems,
however, from a remarkable man who came to Tórshavn soon
after the abolition of the Monopoly. This was Georg Caspar
Hansen (1844–1924), a baker by trade, but a musician by incli-
nation. His special instrument was the violin, but he also played
the viola, cello, double bass, flute, clarinet, piccolo, trumpet,

horn and bassoon. He taught the youth of Tórshavn all these instruments, and finally gave up his baking to devote himself entirely to music. There are old men still alive who recount in glowing terms the brightness and life which baker Hansen brought to the little town. He started choral and instrumental groups, the latter including string quartets, small mixed ensembles and a good brass band. Musical life in Faroe today is largely in the hands of his pupils, one of whom in 1940 founded the Tórshavn school of music, the only establishment in Faroe where it is possible to learn to play instruments. The school sponsors concerts, and occasionally receives visits from foreign professional musicians.

The amateur theatrical movement started in the days of the Føringafelag under Rasmus Effersøe, but only a short time before the second world war did it gain any stature. The Tórshavn theatre society opened the first theatre building, *Sjónleikarhúsið*, in 1926. For over a decade the plays performed were seldom of any literary or dramatic quality, but since the war a professional actor has been employed as artistic director, and he instructs young people in stagecraft. A modern theatre, with seating for 500, will soon be completed, and perhaps a Faroese dramatic art will have a chance to develop. In recent years some demanding foreign plays have been staged in the old theatre, and public interest is developing, both in the capital and in the villages.

Since 1941, there has been a Faroe Islands art society, consisting of artists and friends of the visual arts. This society arranges exhibitions, and with the aid of funds from the Løgting is building up a worthy collection of works by Faroese artists. The principal exhibition in the society's year is that held at the St. Olaf's festival period, when Tórshavn is crowded with visitors. The society's first gallery, near the plantation just north of the town, was opened for the St. Olaf exhibition of 1970. The artistic tradition in the islands is a development only of the present century, but today a dozen or more artists of high ability are at work, two or three of them of international calibre.

The encouragement of Faroese literature has been the work of a succession of Faroese societies, and in addition much public money has been spent in this cause. When a sale of 2,000 copies constitutes the best of best-sellers, publishing cannot be left to unaided private enterprise, otherwise there would be little or no vernacular literature.

Publishing began in the Faroe Islands when the bookseller, H. N. Jacobsen started business in a small way in 1870. Early in the twentieth century, other publishing enterprises were founded, many of them on a non-profit-distributing basis, with the object of putting out literary and other works of merit. One of these, the society *Varðin* (the Cairn), founded in 1912, specialised in literature for young people, but after 1919, it became a general literary society, and is today the counterpart in the arts of Fróðskaparfelag. Its journal *Varðin*, published since 1921, is the leading literary review in the islands, and has published work by every Faroese writer of any standing. Perhaps eight or ten other publishers operate today from time to time, and a large amount of work is published by authors themselves.

Official subsidy may come from *Mentunargrunnurin Føroya Løgtings* (the cultural fund of the Faroese Løgting) or *Føroya Skúlabókagrunnurin* (the school book fund of the Faroe Islands). Most grants of the cultural fund support the publication of Faroese books, but they also aid the arts and sciences.

The position of the Faroese language as a cultural medium has been further strengthened by the introduction in 1957 of a Faroese-language broadcasting service, *Útvarp Føroya*. Television has not so far been considered in Faroe and with so small a population base, there are obvious difficulties. A Faroese-language service would be expensive and probably of indifferent quality; but the extensive use of foreign material would present long-term cultural dangers.

Cultural institutions in Faroe are thus of many kinds, and are well supported by private and public money. Faroese arts and sciences will never, in absolute terms, be able to rival those of the great nations, but since the total population of

Faroe amounts only to that of a small market town in other countries, they may be considered to be flourishing. It is doubtful whether any population of similar size would spend as much or work as hard in these fields without the stimulus of being a nation with a distinct language and culture.

FAROESE WRITERS AND ARTISTS

As in most literatures, so in that of Faroe, the development of poetry preceded that of prose. Indeed, in Faroe the age of lyric verse still flourishes.

It is important to remember that the poetry of the oral tradition overlaps the poetry of the modern lyric tradition and influences it deeply. In the first half of the nineteenth century, the farmer Jens Christian Djurhuus (1773–1853) was writing *kvæði* of the old heroic kind, based on themes like those found in Snorri Sturluson's *Heimskringla*. His son Jens Hendrik Djurhuus (1799–1892) also composed ballads in the ancient tradition, to which the Faroese still sometimes dance. Indeed, it is far from certain that the ballad tradition is yet dead, since Jóannes Patursson, Mikkjal Dánjalsson á Ryggi (1879–1956), and Poul F. Joensen (1898–1970) have all written *kvæði* with something of the ancient spirit about them during the present century.

However, the modern Faroese poet is typically a writer of short lyrics. The pioneering work of Frederik Petersen (1853–1917), Rasmus Effersøe (1857–1916) and Jóannes Patursson was mentioned in Chapter VI: other important lyric poets of the earlier period were Símun av Skarði (1872–1942), the first principal of the folk high school, and author of the present Faroese national anthem, *Tú alfagra land mítt* (Thou, my most beautiful land), and Jóan Petur Gregoriussen (1845–1901), a smallholder and craftsman of Kvívík, who frequently contributed to *Føringatíðindi*. Gregoriussen (also known as Jóan Petur uppi í Trøð) was a remarkable man, self-educated, but with a knowledge of five or six languages, and with outstanding poetic gifts. His enthusiasm for writing in his native

language was aroused through making the acquaintance of
V. U. Hammershaimb, and his support for the Faroese
national cause long antedated the national movement: it
began when, in his youth, he attended a church service at
Bessastaðir in Iceland, at which Icelandic was used. The
lowly status of Faroese at once became dramatically apparent
to him.

The first Faroese writer of genius was the poet Jens Hendrik Oliver Djurhuus (1881–1948) a descendant of Jens Christian Djurhuus. J.H.O. Djurhuus, or 'Janus', told how his
"poetic baptism", as he called it, came when, as a pupil at the
Tórshavn *realskúli*, he heard Jacob Dahl (then a student on
the teacher training course) recite Jóannes Patursson's poem
Nú er tann stundin komin til handa. But J.H.O. Djurhuus was
not destined to become any mere inward-looking nationalist.
He was a lawyer. During his education he imbibed a deep
love of the ancient and modern classics, especially the literature of ancient Greece. It is told how one day a Greek
merchant vessel arrived in Tórshavn harbour: Janus went
aboard, and asked the ship's boy to fetch the captain on deck.
When the captain arrived, Janus began to recite the *Odyssey*,
from memory, in ancient Greek. The captain, himself a well-
educated man, listened for a time in astonishment — and
then joined in.

Although J.H.O. Djurhuus made an immense contribution to Faroese literature, he spent most of his life outside the
islands. He remained in Copenhagen after graduating from
the university, and practised as a lawyer, only returning to
Faroe in the late 1930s. But during his Copenhagen years he
maintained touch with his native land through contact with
the Faroese students in Copenhagen. Thus many Faroemen
came to know him well, although few intimately enough to
share his inner thoughts and feelings.

Linguistically, Djurhuus developed his idiom from modern
Faroese, from the Faroese ballad tradition, and from the
ancient and modern poetry of the other Scandinavian
countries. For his poetic rhythms, he was as ready to seek

inspiration in ancient Greek or modern German poetry. His subject matter shows a restless quest for ideals of beauty, purity and peace. Temperamentally he was a romantic and a nationalist, yet in his work the reader constantly meets at one and the same time a fascination with a poetic vision, an idealisation of the Faroe Islands, and something of a revulsion from their reality.

Djurhuus was of immense importance to Faroese literature not only as an original poet (with five collections of verse published in his lifetime), but also as a translator of a high order. He produced Faroese versions of poetic works by Frøding, Heine, Goethe, Dante, Sappho and many others. In prose, he made sensitive renderings of some of Plato's dialogues, but his crowning achievement was a translation of the entire *Iliad* into Faroese hexameters. This was published posthumously.

Hans Andreas Djurhuus (1883–1951), the younger brother of Janus, was also a poet but, unlike his brother, was a poet of the simple and the familiar. J.H.O. Djurhuus is respected by his countrymen, whereas H.A. Djurhuus is loved. Among his gifts were a rare understanding of the mental and emotional life of children, and his children's verse has become part of the national heritage. His patriotism was of a simple, passionate and uncomplicated kind, and he never experienced the deep emotional split that runs right through his brother's attitude to his native country.

H. A. Djurhuus, like most young Faroemen of his time, had a spell at sea on one of the sloops — during which he composed a series of sea songs. He later attended the Faroe folk high school, then in its early days. This was followed by a course in Tórshavn to qualify him as a teacher, and from 1905 onwards he occupied a succession of posts in private and maintained schools. From 1909 to 1916 he was teacher in Sandavágur, from 1916 to 1919 in Tvøroyri; and in 1919 he was appointed to the staff of the *realskúli* in Tórshavn. Besides his poetry, H. A. Djurhuus wrote many prose works, including a novel, several plays, many short stories, and some school books. His complete works fill seven substantial volumes.

Mikkjal Dánjalsson á Ryggi (1879–1956), like the younger Djurhuus, is a poet with a broad, popular appeal. He was born in Miðvágur and trained as a teacher in Tórshavn. His earliest works appeared at the time when the national movement started to become political, and were written to promote the cause of home rule. He later found his true poetic vocation in the life of the Faroese peasant by sea and land. Some of his poems are work-songs, written to specific tunes and designed to be sung on given occasions in the daily round of the Faroese peasant. Mikkjal á Ryggi also wrote some fine hymns.

Out of his large miscellaneous prose output, one work is of great importance. This is his history of the village of Miðvágur, *Miðvinga søga*, first published in 1940. It is a collection of orally-transmitted stories about the inhabitants of the different old houses of Miðvágur, and forms a fascinating link with the village story-tellers of a previous age. At the suggestion and with the help of the archivist Anton Degn, Mikkjal á Ryggi added a series of notes to each chapter, linking the traditional stories to the court records and other surviving documentation about the people concerned. The village history has now become a well-established prose genre, although few approach *Miðvinga søga* in literary quality.

Two other poets born before the turn of the century are Rikard Long (born 1889) and Poul F. Joensen (1898–1970), In his youth, Long wrote a series of fine and fresh love lyrics. In later years his output became sporadic, but new poems are still occasionally to be seen from his pen. Long is also important as a leading critic of Faroese literature, and for many years as editor of the literary review *Varðin*. Poul F. Joensen, too, has been known to write love poems, but his speciality is satire. Joensen was a native of Sumbøur, the southernmost village of Suðuroy, where a strong village poetic tradition persists. Joensen is a scourge to the pretentious or the self-righteous. One of his poems, which has become a great favourite in Danish translation, describes a preposterous burial procession in which the mourners, having refreshed themselves too liberally on their way across the mountains with the coffin, finally lay their dead comrade in his grave to the accompaniment of heroic ballads about pagan warriors instead of suitably pious Christian hymns.

Christian Matras (born 1900), the philological professor who now directs Fróðskaparsetur Føroya, is also a lyric poet of importance, but besides his writings, Matras has translated some of the best-loved works in the Danish hymnal (those of Kingo and Brorson), and many of the poems of Robert Burns. His version of "Auld Lang Syne" beautifully catches the rhythm and spirit of the original.

Of the generation that grew up between the wars, the outstanding names are Karsten Hoydal (born 1912) and Regin Dahl (born 1918). Karsten Hoydal is a marine biologist, who has also been a member of the Faroese government. His lyrics display a deep love of nature, and although his language is sometimes difficult, his lines are never discordant. Regin Dahl is a distinct modernist, with a vein of satire, often self-directed, running through his work. He is probably to be rated highest amongst Faroese poets writing today; some Faroese esteem him nearly as highly as J.H.O. Djurhuus. Younger than Dahl and Hoydal is Thomas Napoleon Djurhuus (1928–71), whose work has been compared with that of his relative Hans Andreas Djurhuus.

In Faroe today there are some eight poets under the age of forty, whose work has appeared already in book form. Some observers suggest that the poetic tide in the islands is on the ebb, others that better is to come than has yet been seen. Only one thing is certain: with so many Faroese students in Copenhagen, the islands are no longer culturally isolated, and new ideas and new verse-forms used in other literatures are likely to be rapidly adopted by the younger Faroese poets.

The pioneers in Faroese prose writing were Sverre Patursson (1871–1960), Regin í Líð (1871–1962) and Hans Marius Eidesgaard (1887–1966). Sverre Patursson, a younger brother of Jóannes Patursson, was the earliest to achieve ease and limpidity in Faroese prose writing, although he wrote no major works. From 1898 to 1902, he published and edited his own fortnightly newspaper, *Fuglaframi*. Here and elsewhere he wrote wonderful descriptions of Faroese bird life, on which he was an authority. He also wrote some short stories, sketches, essays, and a superb translation of *Robinson Crusoe*.

Regin í Líð was the pseudonym adopted for literary purposes by the botanist and folk high school principal, Rasmus Rasmussen. Influenced by Galsworthy, some of whose works he translated into Faroese, Regin í Líð wrote the first Faroese novel, *Bábelstornið* (The Tower of Babel), published in 1909. This novel traces the fortunes of a family through three generations, bringing out the conflict in ideals between the young and old that so signalised that period, in Faroe as in England. Regin í Líð wrote no other novels — indeed, it was a long time before anyone else did — but he produced a collection of short stories, and in 1949 a series of recollections of his youth in Miðvágur in *Sær er siður á landi* (Every Country has its own Customs).

Hans Eidesgaard was born in Oyndarfjørður, and spent most of his adult life there as a teacher. His works include two collections of short stories, a play and two novels. The first novel to appear was *Hitt ævinliga gonguverkið* (The Perpetual Motion Machine), published in 1951 though written much earlier. The second was *Ein stjørna er tendrað* (A Star is Kindled), published in 1960. Eidesgaard is skilful in dialogue and description and his situations are life-like, but his plots are episodic and consequently tend to be unsatisfying to the reader.

Born just after the turn of the century were Martin Joensen (1902–66) and Heðin Brú (born 1901). Martin Joensen, a teacher by profession, was a novelist of social realism, skilfully and confidently depicting the harsh life of the sloop fishermen in two novels, *Fiskimenn* (Fishermen), published in 1946, and *Tað lýsir á landi* (The Land is Bright), published in 1952. He also wrote many short stories.

Heðin Brú is the pseudonym used by Hans Jacob Jacobsen, who grew up in the out of the way village of Skálavík on

Sandoy. As a young man he spent two seasons on the sloops, but afterwards he worked on a farm in Denmark, went on to agricultural college, and after graduation returned to Faroe as government agricultural consultant. His first novel, *Lognbrá* (Mirage), published in 1930, is an account of a boy's development in a Faroese village. Its sequel, *Fastatøkur* (Firm Grip), which appeared five years later, recounts the experiences of the hero as a young man on one of the sloops. *Feðgar á ferð* (Father and Son on the Move), published in 1940, wittily contrasts the life and associated moral values of the old-fashioned Faroeman, living by a subsistence economy, with the ways of the younger generation tied to the money economy of the deep-sea fishery. *Leikum fagurt* (Play Prettily), published in 1963, is a satire on Faroese politics between the wars; and in 1970 yet another novel was published, *Tó lær lívið* (And Still Life Laughs), set in a Faroese village about 1800. Amongst Heðin Brú's other works are three collections of short stories and translations of *The Tempest* and *Hamlet*.

Heðin Brú is the most considerable Faroese prose author of the older generation. His style has the freshness, irony and pithiness of the born storyteller. He has long since won international recognition. His novels have appeared in Danish, Swedish, Norwegian, Icelandic, German, Dutch, Spanish, Polish, Greenlandic and English translation. *Feðgar á ferð*, published in New York in 1970 under the name *The Old Man and his Sons,* a version made by the present author, is the only Faroese novel hitherto available in English.

Of the younger Faroese prose writers, Jens Pauli Heinesen (born 1932) is a skillful, witty and prolific author. He has published two collections of short stories and three novels, one of them a trilogy, *Tú upphavsins heimur* (World of my boyhood), published 1962–6. The last-named is a fast-moving and subtle social satire.

Some Faroese novelists have elected to write in Danish rather than Faroese, and three of these have had novels translated into English. Jørgen-Frantz Jacobsen (1900–38) was a talented historian and journalist, but died young from tuberculosis. In the last four years of his life, he wrote a wonderful novel of Faroese life in the eighteenth century, a love story of great sensitivity, *Barbara*. It was published in Danish in 1939 and in English translation in 1948. Richard B. Thomsen (1888–1970) has written a number of novels in Danish, and one of them, *De stærke viljer*, was translated into English as *The Tyrants*, and published in 1955.

The work of William Heinesen (born 1900) includes at least nine important novels, the author being a figure of some stature in the Danish literary scene. Most of these have been translated into German and other languages, but only one of his earliest, *Noatun*, published in Denmark in 1938, has been translated into English as *Niels Peter* (1939). Heinesen has also written poetry in Danish, and is a competent painter. One of his paintings, which treats a theme from the *Sjurðar-kvæði* (the Sigurd ballad cycle), was commissioned for the main assembly hall of Tórshavn's new municipal school.

The rapidity with which the visual arts have developed in Faroe is surprising, since there was no tradition for artists to build upon, such as the old stories and ballads provided for the Faroese author. The impulse to paint was sparked off in a number of places by the example of foreign artists, mostly amateurs, who happened to visit the islands in the late nineteenth century. But the dramatic scenery and the wealth of colourful motives in the folk life of the islands provide a wealth of potential inspiration to the artist. Not surprisingly, the first Faroese artists were landscape painters, all more or less self-taught. The pioneers were Niels Kruse (1871–1951), Christian Holm Isaksen (1877–1935) and J. Waagstein (1879–1949). Others followed, and by the 1920s seven or eight talented amateurs were at work.

The first dedicated professional artist to emerge in Faroe was Sámal Joensen Mikines, who was born in 1906 on the island of that name, the most remote and inaccessible but possibly the most beautiful of the Faroes. He received his first instruction in painting from a Swedish bird artist who visited his native island. After five years of painting at home and a

successful exhibition in Tórshavn, he was granted a state
bursary to study at the Academy of Art in Copenhagen. He has
ever since been unquestionably the leading artist in Faroe,
and his work is of international importance. Amongst the
best-loved works in his native islands are pictures of the
communal whale-killings, sometimes depicted with dynamic
figure compositions, sometimes treated abstractly. Mikines
has suffered much from ill-health, and a pessimistic streak is
often visible in his work.

Ruth Smith (1913–58) was born in Vágur on Suðuroy,
and loved to draw and paint even as a child. At the age of
seventeen, as her family were badly off, she went to Copenhagen to work as a housemaid. Here her talent was discovered,
and she was sent to the Academy, where she stayed for eight
years, 1936–44. A prolific painter, her best work was in
portraiture. She very often painted self-portraits — not
through self-absorption, but because she was a shy
woman, finding self-expression easiest alone in front of a
mirror. Among her finest works are her pencil drawings of
children.

Another Faroese painter of well-established reputation is
Ingálvur av Reyni (born 1920), also a pupil of the Copenhagen Academy of Art in 1943–6. He has also made study
tours abroad, especially in France, which have been influential
in his development. He has produced many sensitive pencil
portraits, and oil paintings that are often strong and savage in
their colouring. His later oil paintings have turned much
towards the abstract.

At least a dozen other artists have been at work in Faroe
in recent years, four or five of whom have had formal training
in Copenhagen or England. These include Elinborg Lützen
(born 1919), whose book illustrations show a rich vein of
fantasy; Hans Hansen (1920–70), who studied fresco-
painting in Copenhagen and mosaic work in Ravenna; and
Barður Jacobsen (born 1942), son of the novelist Heðin Brú,
whose work shows that he has inherited his father's fine sense
of humour. Of the self-taught artists, perhaps the most inter-

esting is Stefan Danielsen (born 1928), a native of Nólsoy, who paints stark landscapes of great power.

There are two sculptors now at work in Faroe, both formerly pupils of the Copenhagen Academy of Art. Janus Kamban (born 1913), who lives in Tórshavn, has produced expressive work in both clay and Faroese basalt; his favoured subjects are men at their daily work. He carves both in the round and in relief, and has had many important public commissions in the islands. In Klaksvík there is Frithjof Joensen, who also makes a living from his art.

The work of both writers and visual artists is appreciated in Faroe: as in Iceland, one finds a devotion to literature and the visual arts quite out of the ordinary for such a small population. Further achievement may be expected as long as the Faroese continue to be true to themselves, without being self-sufficient.

RELIGIOUS AND PHILANTHROPIC MOVEMENTS

For three centuries after the introduction of the reformed faith into Faroe, the religion of the country was as stable as the social order. Luther's catechism, Kingo's hymns and Brochmand's homilies were the staple spiritual food for an orthodoxy that went largely untouched by movements elsewhere in Europe. With the growth of population, there was from 1833 onwards an intensive programme of church building, and today the islands possess fifty-seven churches to serve the hundred or so villages. From 1913, the number of ecclesiastical parishes has steadily increased from the original seven, until today there are eleven parishes served by sixteen ministers. Since 1963, the chief minister in the islands has held the title of vice-bishop instead of provost. Churches continue to be well attended, in contrast to the situation in modern Denmark.

The Danish Inner Mission, an evangelical movement within the Danish Lutheran Church, began work in the islands in 1904. It has since opened twenty-five mission houses, runs Sunday schools, works among fishermen in Iceland and Greenland, and carries on a certain amount of social work. At times it has operated amongst Faroese fishermen in Aberdeen.

Religious bodies other than the Danish Church were, until the present century, very inconsiderable, but today they are numerous and their adherents total some 12 per cent of the Faroese population. Their gain in strength has resulted partly from the break-up of the old peasant community, and urbanisation has given them a further stimulus. The religious bodies that have won an appreciable footing are the Roman Catholics, the Salvation Army, the Seventh Day Adventists, the Pentecostalists and the Plymouth Brethren. Missionaries from several other sects, such as the Mormons and the Jehovah's Witnesses, have been seen in Faroe from time to time, but they have not so far achieved much success.

The Roman Catholics started work in Tórshavn in 1857, but after a brisk start Catholicism languished and was almost extinct for the first two decades of the present century. Since then a small congregation has been built up in Tórshavn, which maintains a church, a school and a small convent in the town.

Protestant sects with a fundamentalist bias and stressing the need for a conviction of sinfulness and for subsequent personal conversion, have found Tórshavn a fruitful field. The religious situation there is not unlike that in the smaller fishing ports of eastern Scotland. The strongest religious group today, both in numbers and financial resources, is the Plymouth Brethren. The Faroe congregation of the Plymouth Brethren was founded by a Scottish missionary, W. B. Sloan, in 1865. By the turn of the century, the community numbered no more than thirty, but then, as a result of the work of the energetic Victor Danielsen (1894–1961), they rapidly gained ground, and today probably number at least 3,000, among whom it is said are some of the wealthiest citizens of the islands. Danielsen was a talented organiser, and in addition a diligent translator of hymns and religious literature into Faroese. He made the first Faroese version of the Bible, although not from the original languages. The Plymouth Brethren used the vernacular for worship long before the Danish Church. The community refer to themselves simply as The Brethren (although they are commonly known in Faroe as the Baptists) and they diverge from the Danish Church principally in their informal but highly democratic church organisation, their rejection of infant baptism, and the prominence they give to the expectation of an early return of Christ to this earth. Their Tórshavn meeting-house, Ebenezer, built in 1962, is one of the architectural sights of Tórshavn, a fine modern building, with its largest assembly room capable of accommodating well over a thousand people.

Amongst the philanthropic organisations of Faroe, the temperance movement deserves attention. Societies opposing the use of strong liquors were founded in Faroe as early as 1846, but it was in 1878 that the important total abstinence society Thorshavns Afholdsforening began its work. Rasmus Effersøe and some other early nationalists were keen advocates of the temperance cause, although Jóannes Patursson viewed the movement with disfavour. From 1894 to 1928 the society published a periodical, *Dúgvan* (the Dove). The excessive drinking of cheap spirits was indeed a serious social evil between the introduction of free trade and the end of the century, and after a referendum on the subject on 1907, the sale of intoxicants was forbidden. In the Faroe Islands today, apart from a very light and innocuous locally-brewed beer, all alcoholic liquors have to be individually ordered from Denmark. There is a quarterly allowance for each adult citizen, and purchasers have to produce evidence that they are not in arrears with their tax payments before the customs will release their bottles. It is doubtful whether a return to a free sale of intoxicants would be of service to the islands; and total abstinence still has its powerful advocates.

CHAPTER XIII

THE FAROE ISLANDS TODAY

FAROESE POLITICS, 1954—1971

The Faroe government of 1954–8, a coalition of the Samband, the Sjálvstýri, and the People's Party, must take the credit for the very far-sighted economic plans that were laid during this period. The coalition probably had more difficult problems to solve than any of the other seven governments that have been in power in Faroe since 1948. Besides the reconstruction of the fishing fleet there were renewed labour troubles, problems of developing communications within the islands, and, at the beginning, some serious rioting at Klaksvík.

The Klaksvík troubles arose when an attempt was made to replace the temporary doctor-in-charge at the small Klaksvík hospital with another doctor appointed on a permanent basis. This appointment was made, not by a local hospital management board, but by a Tórshavn-based board managing all the hospitals in Faroe, and local dignity felt itself affronted by what it felt to be a clear flouting of the local wish that the temporary man should be put on a permanent footing. The board took the view that, because this temporary doctor, Olaf Halvorsen, although Danish, was not a member of the Danish Medical Association, he could not hold any permanent official appointment. Labour troubles in the town had led to a certain impatience with constituted authority, and the townsmen resisted the replacement of Dr. Halvorsen by force. With an irony that seems to have become characteristic of Faroese politics, the Klaksvík citizens, noted for their separatist tendencies in politics, were now supporting a Danish doctor against a Faroese replacement.

The Faroese government was not, strictly speaking, responsible for either the hospital service, which was in question, or the police, who were responsible for enforcing a lawful decision. However, the Danish government did not care to get involved with an issue so closely interwoven with island politics and rivalry between Tórshavn and Klaksvík. So it was left to the Faroese government and the Danish state commissioner to do what they could. But eventually they found themselves unable to enforce their will against the violent resistance of the Klaksvík people, and order was only restored with the help of 100 extra policemen brought in from Denmark. The affair seems laughable in retrospect, but at the time it was serious enough and to a certain degree it has affected politics, especially in Klaksvík, ever since. The police had been sent by the Danish government, then Social Democratic; and the Social Democrats, who had previously been gaining strength in Klaksvík, have ever since had poor results in the town, the lost votes being now cast for the Republicans.

However, the 1958 Løgting elections turned out otherwise to be a great victory for the Social Democrats, who increased their representation from five to eight. The Samband held its seven seats, the Sjálvstýri its two, and the Progress Party its one. The People's Party slipped back from six to five, and the Republicans advanced from six to seven seats. The Social Democrats were bound now to be the senior partners in the new government, since the only alliance with a hope of stopping them would have had to be based on the improbable co-operation of the Samband and the Republicans. The upshot was a revival of the old alliance of 1946–50 between the Social Democrats, the Samband, and the Sjálvstýri, with P. M. Dam as lawman. The other members of the government were Kristian Djurhuus of the Samband and Niels Winther Poulsen of the Sjálvstýri.

The issue which had given the Social Democrats the victory in 1958 was that of the old age pension. Legislation for this and other social security measures was a first priority for the new administration. Although all parties in the Løgting voted in favour of the old age pension law when it was introduced, there was, all the same, widespread fear that the cost involved would lead either to higher taxation within Faroe, or to an increased dependence on Danish subsidy, with a consequent increase in the islands of political influence centred on Copenhagen. Even among convinced unionists, there was uneasiness at the prospect of too great a dependence on decisions made in Copenhagen.

However, the election of 1962 led to only minor changes in party representation. The Samband and the Republicans each lost a seat, and the People's Party gained one. With sixteen seats out of twenty-nine, the coalition could have continued in office, but the diminished strength of the Samband now opened up a completely new possibility — that of a coalition of all the nationalist parties. The Sjálvstýri held the balance, and elected to work this time with the other home-rulers and separatists. Hákun Djurhuus of the People's Party became lawman; also in the government were two Republicans, Erlendur Patursson and Karsten Hoydal, and the Sjálvstýri minister from the previous government, Niels Winther Poulsen. The Progress Party supported the coalition, but was not represented in the ministry.

The nationalist coalition did not attempt to loosen the bonds between Faroe and Denmark and, indeed, it did not even take over any more functions from lists A and B. The government busied itself chiefly with building up the Faroese economy. An important part of its work was negotiating the extension of the Faroese fishery limits.

The Faroese and Icelanders had been discontented with the 1901 convention between Denmark and Britain setting a three-mile limit to territorial waters from the very day it was signed. In 1952, the Icelandic government unilaterally extended fishery limits to four miles, calculated from baselines drawn from headland to headland. As a reprisal, the British fishing industry placed an embargo on the landing of Icelandic-caught fresh fish in British ports, forcing the Icelanders to seek less profitable markets. This dispute was settled in November 1956 when an agreement was reached between the trawler-fishing industries of the two countries broadly accepting the Icelandic government action, although the British government still refused to concede the principle of a four-mile limit. On 1 June, 1958, the Icelandic government announced a further extension of fishery limits to twelve miles, to come into force on 1 September 1958. This led to the confrontation during the autumn of that year of Icelandic fishery protection vessels and British naval units, often called the "Cod War", in which there was fortunately no bloodshed. Icelandic fresh fish was again refused entry to Britain for some months, but by January 1959 it was once more being handled. The Icelanders were in such a strong position — in default of any hard-hitting reprisal the British could make — that it took two years for the British government even to bring the Icelandic government to the conference table. Eventually, on 27 February, 1961, the British government conceded the Icelandic claim to a twelve-mile limit in exchange for rights for British vessels to fish in the greater part of the zone between the six-mile limit and the twelve-mile limit at certain seasons of the year for a period of three years only.

The problem of Faroese extension of fishery limits followed directly on the Icelandic action. The Faroese were naturally anxious to reserve for themselves as much of the fishing around their islands as possible, but they were also anxious to retain rights over their traditional fishing-grounds off Iceland, which provided something like a quarter of the total Faroese catch. The Faroese were thus facing two ways over the problem, but the success of the unilateral Icelandic action, and the growth of facilities for the processing of fish caught near the islands, eventually led to the Faroese following the same rules as the Icelanders.

The first breach in the pure three-mile limit came in 1955, when an exchange of notes between Denmark (which handles Faroese international affairs) and Britain extended the closed area in order to protect vital spawning grounds, especially to the west of the Faroe Islands. This agreement had been intended to run for ten years, but the Icelandic action of June

1958 at once brought the Faroese position into prominence again. The Faroese pressed the Danes to announce at once a twelve-mile limit from straight base-lines. Early in 1959, however, the Danes secured agreement extending the fishery limits to twelve miles from low-water-mark, although the British had fishing rights up to the six-mile limit until 1963. Three areas between the six-mile and twelve-mile limits were reserved at certain times of the year for line-fishing only — trawling being forbidden to Faroese and foreign trawlers alike.

This provisional agreement came to an end on 24 April, 1963, when the Danish government passed a law extending the Faroese fishery limits to twelve miles from straight base-lines, the new limits to take effect from 12 March, 1964. The imposition of landing quotas by the British led only to the opening of other markets for fresh fish, and an increase in the manufacture of frozen fillets. The Faroe Islands now have such a diversity of production that it is difficult for any single customer to bite very hard by way of boycott or embargo.

Despite the Faroese government's success in persuading the Danish government to extend the fishery limits, the 1966 elections produced no great enthusiasm for the nationalist coalition, and it failed by a single seat to retain a Løgting majority. One commentator said that the coalition had frightened the conservative voters by radical pronouncements, and disappointed radical voters by conservative actions.

Of the twenty-six seats in the 1966 Løgting, the Social Democrats won seven, the Samband six, the Sjálvstýri one, the People's Party six, the Republicans five, and the Progress Party one. The opposition parties of the previous Løgting were thus precisely equal to the government parties. Almost the only possible way out of this deadlock was that which was eventually followed: the Sjálvstýri resumed its old alliance with the Samband and the Social Democrats. P. M. Dam once again became lawman, and as colleagues he had Kristian Djurhuus of the Samband and Sámal Petersen of the Sjálvstýri.

P. M. Dam died on 8 November, 1968, thus ending his busy public career at the summit of Faroese political life. He was succeeded as lawman by Kristian Djurhuus, who thereby took office for the third time, while Dam's leading place in the government was compensated by the accession to the government of two of his party colleagues. These were J. Lindenskov and V. Sørensen. The latter also died in January 1970, whereupon the Løgting chose in his place the thirty-seven-year-old son of P. M. Dam, Attli Dam.

Faroese elections took place once again in November 1970. There was little change in representation. The Republican Party gained one seat at the expense of the People's Party, while the other parties held their ground. Attli Dam has succeeded to the position of lawman, and has shown himself to be a politician of some talent. He has four ministerial colleagues: P.F. Christiansen and E. Nolsøe (Samband), J. Lindenskov (Social Democrat) and S. Petersen (Sjálvstýri).

At the Folketing elections held on 5 October, 1971, representation was unchanged, the Faroe Islands seats being held by Johan Nielsen (Social Democrat) and Hákun Djurhuus (People's Party).

Despite the multiplicity of parties, the Faroese political scene today seems relatively stable. The wielding of power has had a steadying effect on all the Faroese political groups. The People's Party, once deriving its chief impetus from separatism, is today broadly satisfied with the degree of autonomy allowed by the home rule ordinance. The Republicans, doubly the most radical party in Faroe, seem also to have come to terms with the realities of power. Of course, there are still problems which the government of Faroe will have to face, some of which have a familiar ring to observers in Britain: rising prices, an increasing tendency to labour troubles, a brain drain, and growing dependence on foreign capital. None of these is susceptible to a partisan solution; at the same time, none seems great enough in scale to threaten a crisis of any kind in the near future.

THE COMMON MARKET

The year 1971 saw the very lengthy negotiations for the entry of Britain, the Republic of Ireland, Norway and Denmark into the Common Market. The position of the Faroe Islands was one of the most difficult of the problems facing the Danish delegation, and the Faroese lawman, Attli Dam, was in Brussels for protracted periods to present his country's case.

Entry is very much in the Faroese interest provided their existing fishing limits are safeguarded. The Common Market countries consume far more fish than they produce, and the German market for frozen fillets, with a removal of the existing import duties, would bring great wealth to the islanders. If the Faroe Islands were outside the Market, and Norway became a member, on the other hand, the existing sales would undoubtedly drop, and the Norwegian fishermen would capture the German market.

Amongst the Faroese public, however, there is little enthusiasm for entry. The Republicans are opposed to Faroese membership, and their feeling is shared by a considerable minority of the people at large. The majority are probably even now undecided.

But the maintenance of the twelve-mile limit is an absolute prerequisite for Faroese membership. The Faroese simply cannot risk the fishing-out of their stocks by Common Market trawlers. If the Danes attempted to force the Faroese into the Market without defending the limits in full, the secession of Faroe from Denmark would be the rapid consequence.

The obstinacy of the Six over fishery limits made the Danish negotiations in Brussels very long-drawn. It was finally necessary to leave the question of Faroese fishing limits unsettled. The Islanders have until 1975 to decide whether to remain in the Community. The difficulty for the Faroese will be that if they stay out to defend their twelve-mile limit, their trade with Denmark will become subject to the Common Market tariffs. This might lead to a political estrangement. The Common Market question is undoubtedly the most difficult that the Faroe Islands have had to face since home rule.

THE ECONOMIC OUTLOOK

It was during the period from 1856 until the outbreak of the second world war that the traditional Faroese subsistence economy gave place to a market economy dependent on the export of fish. In the period since the war, the fish export has become diversified, with the emphasis shifting from sole reliance upon the two traditional cod products, wet salt fish and klipfish, to a variety of processed fish products, many now herring-based instead of cod-based. Other fish are also beginning to appear in the export statistics. At the same time, the total catch, and with it the total value of the export trade of the Faroe Islands, is increasing rapidly. (See Appendix B, page 265, for a table showing export tendencies between 1938 and 1968).

Between 1938 and 1968, exported values increased twenty-fold. Part of this gain is, of course, due to the depreciated value of the Danish krone, but even so, the increase is very impressive indeed. Between 1955 and 1965 the total value of exports doubled due to the reconstruction of the fishing fleet. The figure for 1971 amounts to a total export of over 7,000 kroner for every man, woman and child in the islands.

Salt fish is at present retaining its importance in the economy, but klipfish is declining both relatively and absolutely.[1] Iced fish is also declining, because the part of the catch which was previously sold on ice can now largely be profitably turned into frozen fillets, the total export value of which is increasing dramatically. Frozen fillets are now being made on four new factory trawlers as well as in factories ashore. The long-term prospect of this side of the industry is that the trade in wet salt fish may in time follow that of klipfish into unimportance, while the profitable frozen fillet becomes the staple.

In the herring trade it is more difficult to separate the long-term tendencies from the short-term fluctuations. Production

---

[1] By 1971, indeed, the trade had practically vanished, and will probably never be revived.

is likely to continue to grow and salt herring, spiced herring, herring meal and herring oil are all likely to maintain their importance in the export market. The explosive increase in Faroese income from fresh herring in recent years has been due to good sales and high prices in Denmark, which may not be permanent.

Salmon, halibut and porbeagle are fished by specially-equipped steel vessels of the long-line type. The halibut are sent frozen to Britain, West Germany or Czechoslovakia, or else used for the manufacture of frozen fillets. The salmon goes almost entirely to Denmark. Successful fishing for these species demands refrigeration plant on board, so that the catch may be marketed in top quality condition. Production of luxury fish may well prove to be one of the future lines of development for the Faroese. There has already been talk of equipping ships to operate off the African coast, and by the end of the century Faroese ships may well be ranging the north and south Atlantic for fish in the same way as the Japanese fishing fleet already operates over the Pacific.

But the continuation of a successful Faroese economy demands a high rate of both public and private investment. The scale of investment undertaken during the reconstruction years may readily be grasped from the bare fact that in 1959 the total insured value of the fishing fleet was 67,094,000 kroner, whereas in 1969 it was 228,979,000 kroner, an average annual increase of over 16,000,000 kroner. This investment resulted in a doubling of the income from the export of fish. Over a shorter period, the factory trawlers being currently purchased in Faroe are also making heavy capital demands. During the 1970s, the investment necessary to keep the fishing fleet at an efficient operating level will, it is estimated, stabilise itself at about 15,000,000 kroner annually. However, the processing factories on shore still have a good deal of unused capacity, and investment in this field is not likely to grow significantly in the near future, especially as much of the increased catch of the fleet will be due to the factory trawlers which process their fish afloat.

Other types of investment are likely to grow. House-building will have to increase considerably as urbanisation continues. There are no council house schemes in Faroe, and a householder normally has to negotiate for a bank mortgage, available for up to 80 per cent of the cost of the house or 80,000 kroner, whichever is the less. There is a proposal to ease house-building credit by turning over to this purpose some of the funds previously used for financing the fishing fleet. If credit is not eased in some way, shortage of labour may place serious obstacles in the way of important public investment plans.

Investment carried out 1967-68
and predicted for 1969-75
(million kroner)

	1967	1968	1969	1970	1971	1972	1973	1974	1975
Fishing fleet	4.0	23.3	57.1	30.0	20.0	15.0	15.0	15.0	15.0
Fishing industry	6.0	1.5	3.5	3.5	3.5	3.5	4.0	4.0	4.0
Freight and passenger ships	—7.4	3.9	1.0	9.8	4.5	10.7	3.5	4.5	4.5
Other industrial investment	15.8	17.0	18.0	19.2	21.2	20.5	21.5	23.0	24.0
House-building	21.5	22.0	22.0	22.0	25.0	25.0	27.0	28.0	30.0
Total private investment	39.9	67.7	101.6	84.5	74.2	74.7	71.0	74.5	77.5

Geography dictates that for a modern industrial society to exist in the Faroe Islands, there must be heavy public investment in roads, schools, hospitals and harbour works, and in radio, telephone and power installations. During the period 1962–8, indeed, public investment was at a high level, as the following table shows:

Public investment, 1962-68
(million kroner)

	1962	1963	1964	1965	1966	1967	1968
Roads, harbours, airfields, etc	11.5	11.3	9.7	13.3	17.0	24.2	25.8
Telephone, post, electricity, etc	7.3	9.1	12.5	10.9	7.8	6.3	7.1
Education	3.4	4.1	3.7	7.2	8.9	8.2	9.3
Health Service	4.1	5.8	7.6	8.6	9.8	10.5	10.6
Other public investments	1.6	4.7	8.4	4.1	4.5	5.3	4.8
Total	27.9	35.0	41.9	44.1	48.0	54.5	57.6

In the period 1969–75, public investment is expected to develop as follows:

Forecast of public investment, 1969-75
(million kroner)

	1969	1970	1971	1972	1973	1974	1975
Roads, harbours, airfields, etc.	23.7	27.1	30.1	33.1	35.8	35.9	35.4
Telephone, post, electricity, etc.	8.3	11.9	12.2	12.0	10.5	10.0	9.5
Education	7.5	12.8	15.2	15.7	14.7	15.2	15.2
Health Service	12.3	11.6	11.2	7.4	5.5	5.9	5.1
Other public investments	7.2	15.7	18.1	19.4	15.0	13.6	13.4
Total	59.0	79.1	86.8	87.6	81.5	80.6	78.6

The development of the road network is important for the economic future of the islands. The surfaces of the existing roads need improvement in order to carry more and heavier traffic; and in the foreseeable future bridges will have to be constructed linking Stremoy to Eysturoy and Borðoy to Viðoy and Kunoy. Perhaps eventually Streymoy may even be linked to Vágar by bridge. A second airfield is to be built during the 1970s, to improve contact between the main commercial centres of the Faroe Islands and the outside world. The telephone system needs to be converted to automatic operation, at least within the larger islands. School building is likely to be another high investment sector; it is intended to raise the school-leaving age and to increase the scope of technical education. A further expenditure area, listed here under "other public investments", is the provision of kindergartens, nursing homes and old people's homes. Hitherto, these have been unnecessary, but with the progress of urbanisation, the old Faroese village and family pattern will change, and Faroe will experience the same needs as Denmark or Britain.

The chief difficulty in carrying out this investment programme is that despite the efficiency and prosperity of the present-day fishing industry of the Faroe Islands, there is a heavy adverse balance of trade. This is at present met largely by the considerable net subsidy that Faroe receives from the Danish government. The remaining balance is met by long- and short-term loans originating in Denmark and, for certain shipbuilding items, in Norway.

The Faroese balance of payments, 1962-68
(million kroner)

	1962	1963	1964	1965	1966	1967	1968
Import	135.7	138.4	161.8	182.3	195.2	186.3	211.4
Export	120.8	129.7	130.1	167.8	143.9	177.5	154.1
Adverse balance (visible trade)	14.9	8.7	31.7	14.5	51.3	8.8	57.3
Net invisible import	21.8	34.5	30.8	34.3	22.2	25.9	30.0
Total adverse balance	36.7	43.2	62.5	48.8	73.5	34.7	87.3
Gross national product	259.9	311.4	354.8	400.3	444.8	460.7	488.9
TOTAL	296.6	354.6	417.3	449.1	518.3	495.4	576.2
of which Consumed	209.4	254.8	284.2	325.3	360.3	384.9	411.5
Invested	87.2	99.8	133.1	123.8	158.0	110.5	164.7
From the Danish Government	26.2	33.8	38.3	45.0	53.6	61.7	68.8

The Danish subsidy is not given by way of block grant; it arises because of the Danish government contribution to the expenses of jointly-administered governmental functions. The Faroese pay no direct taxes to the Danish government; and as the high-spending functions of health, education, and social security have not been claimed by the Faroese government from lists A and B, there is a considerable annual flow of money from the Danish taxpayer for the benefit of his semi-independent fellow-subjects. The picture can be seen in detail from the figures for the financial years 1965-6 and 1966-7:

Danish and Faroese government expenditure, financial years 1965-6 and 1966-7
(1,000 kroner)

	1965-6			1966-7		
	Danish Treasury	Faroese Treasury	Total	Danish Treasury	Faroese Treasury	Total
Administration	1,347	4,607	5,954	1,584	4,993	6,577
Health Service	11,640	4,962	16,602	14,006	5,190	19,196
Transport	2,514	10,508	13,022	2,147	13,866	16,013
Education	9,575	7,653	17,228	12,707	8,673	21,380
Fishery and Navigation	6,994	7,549	14,543	7,400	8,933	16,333
Agriculture	—	1,626	1,626	—	1,868	1,868
Social security	11,288	7,303	18,591	12,372	7,814	20,186
Police and Judiciary	2,815	—	2,815	3,205	—	3,205
Church	912	160	1,072	1,046	300	1,346
Interest, etc.	—	4,808	4,808	—	4,393	4,393
Other expenses	2,251	4,359	6,610	2,446	6,726	9,172
Totals	49,336	53,535	102,871	56,913	62,756	119,669

The principal item of health expenditure is the hospital service. Here the costs are divided equally between the Danish Farand oese governments for running expenses; but the building of new hospitals is met largely by the Danish government alone.

The communication network is, in general, a charge on the Faroese, but the Danes contribute to harbour works and airfields. The cost of roads is shared between the Faroese government and the communes.

In the education service, the chief item of expenditure is the payment of the teaching staff. The Danes pay 55 per cent of staff salaries and 80 per cent of staff pensions. The remaining school expenses are met by the communes. Some schools, such as the navigation school, have been completely taken over by the Faroese government. The cost of building a new *fólkaskúli* is met by the commune, helped by a 20 per cent subsidy from the Faroese government and an equal sum from the Danish government.

The Danish and Faroese contributions to social security expenses occur chiefly through payments into the old age pension and disablement pension funds. In church affairs, the Danes pay the priests and the Faroese maintain the churches. The chief item in "other expenses" is the loss on the post office.

Of the many forms of investment from Denmark that reach projects in the Faroe Islands, one ought to be mentioned: the co-ordinating fund for public investment, officially called *Investeringsfonden for Færøerne* (the Investment Fund for the Faroe Islands), but in the islands themselves, generally known as "the sixty-million-kroner fund". Its initial operation was from the financial year 1964–5 to the financial year 1969–70, with an allocation of 10,000,000 kroner each year. Its object was to channel public loan funds into such large-scale undertakings as roads, power stations, harbour works and so on, avoiding overlapping and making an allocation of priorities. The success of the fund makes it likely that the system will be continued.

With so much outside investment capital coming in, one might in one sense regard the Faroe Islands as an under-developed country, which the Danes, for reasons of history and sentiment, feel bound to aid. In another sense, especially in their ability and willingness to co-operate in running a modern industrial society, the Faroese are already a developed country. Danish aid will, however, need to continue for many years before the Faroe Islands can constitute a self-financing community. Indeed, investment continues on so large a scale that there are politicians in Faroe who question what it will cost the islands in the long run in financial and political freedom: this is a problem which many developing countries have to face.

The 1968 subsidy from the Danish government in aid of joint services amounted to about £3,500,000 ($8,500,000) for which the Danes got no financial return. The Danish tax-payer might well ask why he should continue to be bothered with the Faroe Islands. But the choice for the Danes lies between spending money to maintain an enterprising and nearly self-sufficient community in the islands, or neglecting them as Shetland and the Hebrides have for so long been neglected by Britain. The familiar pattern of the decaying province would then be seen once again — the young, the enterprising and the ambitious would emigrate to Denmark and, within a generation or two, only an ageing and dispirited community would remain, costing as much to the Danish treasury in social security benefits as would have sufficed to keep a vigorous community working and happy.

The world has an interest in an economically efficient Faroese population contributing the political stability of a strategically vital point in the north Atlantic; it thus has an interest in the Danes maintaining their help to the Faroese. There is no very large military presence in Faroe — a small Danish naval headquarters at Tórshavn, and an important radar station above Kollafjørður; but to have these installa-tions in the hands of a small state like Denmark rather than a great power is a guarantee of their non-aggressive intention.

The cultural consideration is an even more important one. A young Danish engineer working on the S.E.V. project at Vestmannahavn is said to have calculated that instead of building power stations, harbour works, roads, bridges and tunnels in order to maintain an acceptable standard of life in the Faroe Islands, it would pay handsomely to build a new suburb to Esbjerg, and settle the entire Faroese population where amenities of all kinds already existed. The only answer to this argument is an aesthetic one: that what exists is worth keeping and worth building on for its own sake.

In the great modern nation-states, the sheer anonymity of human life is a strong inhibitor of creativity. In the Faroe Islands there is far more stimulus to human achievement than there could ever be in a new suburb of Esbjerg — stimulus, for example, to the potential writer or artist. Over the past century the cultural achievements of the islanders have been impressive, especially in literature and the visual arts. From the study of conditions under which the arts flourish in such small communities, the world has much to learn, and the Faroese contribution to world civilisation is in itself anything but negligible.

The political arrangements by which Faroe is now linked to Denmark seem to be broadly satisfactory to national feeling within the islands at the present time; Danes and Faroese seem to have hit upon a happy and flexible home-rule system. When Faroe stands completely on her own feet economically, the remaining functions of government on lists A and B will no doubt be claimed, and the Faroese will then have become as nearly self-governing as any community so small and so strategically placed can in the nature of things ever hope to become.

With economic necessity leading to ever larger human units, it is good for the world to have a few examples of the contrasting values inherent in the small, self-conscious community, the community that can command the personal loyalty of its members, and in which its members are aware of the part their community is playing in the affairs of the world.

APPENDICES

A

GLOSSARY

Note. The Scandinavian letters in the following words are given their Scandinavian alphabetic positions, i. e. ð follows d; and after z follow respectively æ, ø, and å.

althing (Icelandic) Parliament and high court.

amtmand, pl. *amtmænd* (Dan.) Chief civil officer of a province; governor or lord-lieutenant. Faroese *amtmaður.*

fleygistong (Far.) A fowling net. Also spelt *fleygastong.*

Fólkaflokkurin (Far.) The People's Party. Danish *Folkepartiet.*

fólkaskúli (Far.) Junior school (7—14). Danish *folkeskole.*

Folketing (Dan.) Lower house (since 1953 the only chamber) of the Danish parliament. Faroese *Fólkating.*

folkeviser (Dan.) Danish folk ballads.

Framburðsflokkurin (Far.) The Progress Party. Danish *Fremskridtspartiet.*

Fróðskaparfelag (Far.) Scientific Society.

Fróðskaparrit (Far.) Scientific journal.

Fróðskaparsetur (Far.) University college.

Fylking (Far.) Rallying (name of a trade union).

Føringafelag (Far.) Faroese Union (name of a cultural movement). Two other organisations of this name have been called *Føroyingafelag.*

Føringatiðindi (Far.) Faroese News (name of a newspaper).

Føroyingafelag (Far.) See *Føringafelag.*

gylden (Dan.) A unit of account used by the Monopoly; also a unit of land reckoning. Faroese *gyllin.*

gymnasium (Dan.) A school approximating to an English sixth-form college. Faroese *studentaskúli.*

huspostil (Dan.) Book of sermons, for use in the home.

Højre (Dan.) The Right (name of a Danish political party).

Javnaðarflokkurin (Far.) The Equality Party, i. e. Social Democratic Party. Danish *Socialdemokratisk Parti.*

klipfisk (Dan.) Klipfish, split dried salt cod. Faroese *klippfiskur.*

kongsbóndi (Far.), pl. *kongsbøndur.* Crown tenant. Danish *kongsbonde,* pl. *kongsbønder.*

kongsskat (Dan.) A tax paid to the king. Faroese *kongsskattur.*

krone (Dan.) pl. *kroner*. The modern unit of Danish currency, the crown (equivalent to slightly more than a shilling.)

kvæði (Far.) Heroic ballad. Danish *kvad*.

lagmand (Dan.) Lawman, chief judge; since 1948, prime minister. Faroese *løgmaður*.

lagting (Dan.) Faroese provincial assembly and in earlier times, court. Faroese *løgting*.

landsmaal (Norw.) A Norwegian literary language derived from west Norwegian and valley dialect usage.

landsstyret (Dan.) The provincial government of Faroe. Faroese *landsstýrið*.

Landsting (Dan.) The upper house of the Danish parliament (abolished in 1953). Faroese *landsting*. Also the name for certain provincial assemblies in Scandinavia, e. g. on Bornholm.

Ljómur (Far.) Light; name of an Icelandic religious poem preserved in Faroe by oral tradition.

logmaður (Far.) See *lagmand*.

løgting (Far.) See *lagting*.

mark (Dan.) Name of a land unit. Faroese *mørk*, pl. *merkur*.

matrikelskat (Dan.) Defence rate.

Mentunargrunnurin (Far.) Cultural fund.

realskole (Dan.) Lower grammar school. Faroese *realskúli*.

realskúli (Far.) See *realskole*.

rigsbankdaler (Dan.) Unit of currency issued by the Danish government after the inflation during the Napoleonic War.

rigsdaler (Dan.) Rixdollar; former Danish currency unit.

rigsombudsmand (Dan.) State commissioner. Faroese *ríkisumboðsmaður*.

sagn, pl. *sagnir* (Far.) Traditional stories, especially those purporting to be true.

Sambandsflokkurin (Far.) The unionist party. Danish *Sambandspartiet*.

Seyðabrævið (Far.) The Sheep Latter, a law of 1298 regulating joint pasturage and other matters.

Sjálvstýrisflokkurin (Far.) The home rule party. Danish *Selvstyrepartiet*.

Sjónleikarhúsið (Far.) The Theatre.

Sjóvinnubankin (Far.) The Fishery Industries Bank.

skerpikjøt (Far.) Wind-dried raw mutton. Danish *skærpekød*.

skilling (Dan.) Unit of currency ($= \frac{1}{96}$ of a rigsdaler).

skind (Dan.) A skin, a unit of account used by the Monopoly; also a unit of land reckoning. Faroese *skinn*.

Skúlabókagrunnurin (Far.) School book subsidy fund.

skyds (Dan.) Requisitioned travel, especially by boat. Faroese *skjútsur*.

skydsskaffer (Dan.) Village organiser for *skyds*. Faroese *skjútsskaffari*.

sorenskriver (Norw.) Originally judge's clerk; later judge in court of first instance. Faroese *sorinskrivari*.

sparekasse (Dan.) Savings bank. Faroese *sparikassi*.

studentaskúli (Far.) A school approximating to a sixth-form college in England. Danish *gymnasium*.

syssel (Dan.) pl. *sysler*. Administrative district. Faroese *sýslu*.

sysselmand (Dan.) District sheriff. Faroese *sýslumaður*.

táttur, pl. *tættir* or *táttur* (Far.) Satirical ballad.

tingakrossur (Far.) A bidding-stick summoning people to the law-sessions. Later, the name of a newspaper.

tjaldur (Far.) Oyster-catcher (Hæmatopus ostralegus). Danish *strandskade*.

Tjóðveldisflokkurin (Far.) The republican party. Danish *Det Republikanske Parti*.

tróð, pl. *traðir* (Far.) Allotment. Danish *trø*.

útskifting (Far.) Rationalisation of land-holdings. Danish *udskifining*.

útvarp (Far.) Radio.

vaðsteinur (Far.) Oval grooved stone about the size of a man's fist, used as a sinker for a fishing-line.

Varðin (Far.) The Cairn. Name of a literary society and its magazine.

Venstre (Dan.) The Left. Name of a Danish political party.

Vinnuflokkurin (Far.) The Economic Party. Danish *Erhvervspartiet*.

Vinnulánsgrunnurin (Far.) Industrial loan fund.

ævintýr (Far.) Orally-transmitted stories of fabulous content.

B

FISHERY AND TRADE STATISTICS

TOTAL CATCH,
1953—1971
(metric tons)

Year	Catch
1953	88,756
1954	89,434
1955	105,619
1956	116,316
1957	105,584
1958	106,740
1959	87,200
1960	109,428
1961	120,078
1962	143,520
1963	137,071
1964	139,140
1965	**144,870**
1966	165,449
1967	173,293
1968	166,271
1969	196,300
1970	207,800
1971*	210,100

* *All 1971 figures are provisional.*

CATCH OF HERRING BY FISHING-GROUNDS, 1953–1968
(metric tons)

Year	Faroe grounds	Norwegian Sea	Spitz-bergen	North Sea	Iceland grounds	Total
1953	220	16,152	—	690	—	17,062
1954	182	27,424	—	—	—	27,606
1955	175	12,940	—	—	—	13,115
1956	703	22,966	—	—	—	23,669
1957	788	16,246	—	—	—	17,034
1958	1,917	15,771	—	—	—	17,688
1959	690	13,005	—	—	—	13,695
1960	445	10,972	—	—	—	11,417
1961	10	16,875	—	—	—	16,885
1962	175	9,680	—	—	—	9,865
1963	18	12,855	—	—	—	12,873
1964	—	18,289	—	973	—	19,262
1965	—	31,007	—	3,612	—	34,619
1966	6,424	44,080	—	1,492	9,608	61,604
1967	17,214	17,007	658	35,993	—	70,872
1968	3,926	16,058	—	49,955	—	69,939
1969						67,641
1970						109,159
1971*						116,939

* *All 1971 figures are provisional.*

CATCH OF DEMERSAL SPECIES BY FISHING-GROUNDS, 1953-1968

(metric tons, with percentages)

Year	Faroe grounds	per cent	Iceland grounds	per cent	North Sea	per cent	Barents Sea	per cent	Greenland	per cent	New-foundland	per cent	Total
1953	7,856	11.0	17,874	24.9	—	0.0	18,380	25.6	27,584	38.5	—	0.0	71,694
1954	8,950	14.5	17,075	27.6	—	0.0	9,621	15.6	26,182	42.3	—	0.0	61,828
1955	13,535	14.6	20,006	21.6	41	0.1	22,939	24.8	35,982	38.9	—	0.0	92,503
1956	13,704	14.8	18,161	19.6	—	0.0	28,875	31.2	31,807	34.3	101	0.1	92,648
1957	13,836	15.6	24,960	28.2	23	0.0	13,889	15.7	32,886	37.2	2,956	3.3	88,550
1958	15,768	17.7	21,691	24.4	27	0.0	4,072	4.6	43,572	48.9	3,939	4.4	89,069
1959	13,097	17.8	9,594	13.1	5	0.0	4,819	6.5	38,371	52.2	7,619	10.4	73,505
1960	19,684	20.1	14,397	14.7	45	0.0	3,509	3.6	50,698	51.7	9,678	9.9	98,011
1961	21,420	20.8	12,959	12.5	—	0.0	4,290	4.1	58,998	57.2	5,526	5.4	103,193
1962	19,211	14.4	11,933	8.9	—	0.0	3,228	2.4	93,361	69.9	5,932	4.4	133,665
1963	19,140	15.4	11,132	9.0	—	0.0	777	0.6	78,335	63.1	14,815	11.9	124,199
1964	20,848	17.4	9,577	8.0	—	0.0	—	0.0	65,931	55.0	23,523	19.6	119,879
1965	20,224	18.3	8,438	7.7	—	0.0	—	0.0	66,082	59.9	15,507	14.1	110,251
1966	18,317	17.6	5,004	4.8	—	0.0	—	0.0	64,874	62.5	15,650	15.1	103,845
1967	18,508	18.1	3,782	3.7	—	0.0	—	0.0	64,003	62.5	16,128	15.7	102,421
1968	27,761	28.8	4,779	5.0	—	0.0	—	0.0	46,000	47.8	17,792	18.4	96,332
1969													108,700
1970													98,600
1971*													93,200

* 1971 figure is provisional

DISPOSITION OF CATCH, 1953–1968

(metric tons, with percentages)

Year	Total landings	Marketed fresh	per cent	Sold for freezing	per cent	Sold for curing	per cent	Sold for canning	per cent	Sold for reduction (meal & oil)	per cent	Offal (for meal and oil)
1953	88,756	5,504	6.2	147	0.2	82,047	92.4	263	0.3	795	0.9	—
1954	89,434	6,788	7.6	759	0.8	81,523	91.2	364	0.4	—	0.0	255
1955	105,619	7,481	7.1	2,095	2.0	95,926	90.8	42	0.0	75	0.1	1,550
1956	116,316	5,861	5.0	2,445	2.1	107,320	92.3	90	0.1	600	0.5	2,448
1957	105,584	7,726	7.3	1,492	1.4	95,428	90.4	135	0.1	803	0.8	2,177
1958	106,740	13,044	12.2	2,789	2.6	90,182	84.5	25	0.0	700	0.7	2,013
1959	87,200	15,182	17.4	2,197	2.5	69,064	79.2	157	0.2	600	0.7	1,125
1960	109,428	24,264	22.2	4,909	4.5	79,678	72.8	132	0.1	445	0.4	2,961
1961	120,078	24,598	20.5	5,749	4.8	89,626	74.6	80	0.1	25	0.0	4,920
1962	143,520	23,407	16.3	10,733	7.5	109,120	76.0	85	0.1	175	0.1	10,165
1963	137,071	18,365	13.4	13,805	10.1	104,713	76.3	89	0.1	99	0.1	8,654
1964	139,140	15,489	11.1	15,773	11.4	107,034	76.9	51	0.0	793	0.6	4,632
1965	144,870	11,907	8.2	20,644	14.2	95,004	65.6	89	0.1	17,226	11.9	6,905
1966	165,449	18,804	11.3	24,619	14.9	88,795	53.7	151	0.1	33,080	20.0	7,175
1967	173,293	6,318	3.7	23,220	13.4	81,132	46.8	130	0.1	62,493	36.0	5,722
1968	166,271	15,392	9.3	25,822	15.5	72,587	43.6	100	0.1	52,370	31.5	7,701

ANNUAL OUTPUT OF PROCESSED COMMODITIES, 1953–1968 (metric tons)

Year	Frozen fillets	Wet-salted fish	Klipfish	Salted herring	Canned fish	Herring meal	Meal from demersal fish	Cod liver oil	Herring oil
1953	115	16,519	7,028	12,874	42	159	45	681	—
1954	51	9,196	9,306	20,045	47	—	124	687	—
1955	410	14,006	12,290	9,614	36	16	310	1,264	28
1956	404	10,036	15,092	15,541	74	108	490	1,499	73
1957	239	12,025	13,018	12,628	90	100	435	1,203	42
1958	465	12,367	11,565	12,007	25	153	403	1,458	71
1959	571	11,557	7,524	9,489	40	276	342	881	386
1960	1,223	18,302	5,253	7,804	110	61	734	757	19
1961	1,585	20,490	6,060	10,800	61	82	984	781	118
1962	2,724	21,954	10,872	6,365	85	21	2,033	1,046	14
1963	4,141	27,930	7,128	8,124	59	20	1,707	733	—
1964	3,727	25,290	6,042	11,478	46	30	1,226	760	104
1965	5,361	27,052	3,671	9,815	84	2,184	1,381	543	1,580
1966	7,307	26,335	2,635	10,837	120	6,057	1,435	391	3,891
1967	6,129	27,631	2,455	4,885	100	10,239	1,091	383	5,596
1968	7,125	24,681	3,763	5,161	100	14,304	605	403	7,049

FAROESE EXPORTS, 1939–69, BY VALUE

	1938		1955		1960		1965		1969		1971*
	1,000 Kr.	per cent	1,000 Kr.	per cent	1,000 Kr.	per cent	1,000 Kr.	per cent	1,000 Kr.	per cent	1,000 Kr.
Fresh fish on ice	44	0.5	6,159	7.9	25,530	26.5	12,925	7.3	2,862	1.6	1,100
Frozen fish fillets	—	—	843	1.1	3,427	3.6	20,561	11.6	43,723	23.6	70,000
Salt fish	2,313	26.9	16,863	21.7	29,873	31.1	77,665	43.7	69,947	38.0	88,800
Klipfish	5,511	64.1	34,609	44.5	20,598	21.4	21,204	11.9	6,661	3.7	Nil
Salt or spiced herring	118	1.4	13,237	17.0	12,409	12.9	17,907	10.1	9,328	5.2	10,400
Tinned fish	—	—	15	0.0	124	0.1	75	0.0	?		—
Frozen and salted roe	—	—	—	—	3	0.0	162	0.0	?		—
Cod liver oil	49	0.6	141	0.2	942	1.0	778	0.4	?		—
Herring oil	—	—	1,677	2.2	17	0.0	1,825	1.0	2,524	1.4	8,500
Fish and herring meal	15	0.2 93.7	28	0.0	514	0.5 97.1	4,134	2.3	16,475	9.0	23,800
Porbeagle	—	—	269	0.3 94.9	—	—	6,700	3.8	?		—
Fresh herring	—	—	—	—	—	—	2,800	1.6	15,327	8.3	43,700
Salmon	—	—	—	—	—	—	627	0.4	3,502	1.9	4,000
Black halibut	—	—	—	—	—	—	—	94.2	2,688	1.5	—
Whale meat	103	1.2	150	0.2	—	—	—	—	?		—
Whale meal	33	0.4	212	0.3	—	—	—	—	?		—
Whale oil	295	3.4 5.0	1,203	1.5 2.0	11	0.0	232	0.1 0.1	?		—
Sheep's offal	19	0.2	9	0.0	—	—	—	—	?		—
Sheepskins	16	0.2	267	0.3	299	0.3	195	0.1	694	0.4	—
Wool and cloth	34	0.4	171	0.2	174	0.2	47	0.0	?		—
Woollen yarn and knitted goods	24	0.3 1.1	197	0.3 0.8	450	0.5	561	0.3	679	0.4	2,400
Other goods	17	0.2	1,739	2.2	1,822	1.9 2.9	9,422	5.3 5.7	467	0.3	—
	8,591	100.0	77,789	100.0	96,193	100.0	177,820	100.0	182,154	100.0	278,400

* *Provisional figures*

C

ELECTION RESULTS IN THE FAROE ISLANDS SINCE 1906

LANDSTING (DANISH UPPER HOUSE)

From 1866, the Faroe Islands Landsting member was chosen by vote of the Løgting. The Landsting was abolished on 21 September, 1953.

1906—14	Frederik Petersen (Samband)
1914—15	Oliver Effersøe (Samband)
1915—17	Frederik Petersen (Samband)
1917—18	Andreas Samuelsen (Samband)
1918—20	Jóannes Patursson (Sjálvstýri)
1920—8	Oliver Effersøe (Samband)
1928—36	Jóannes Patursson (Sjálvstýri)
1936—53	Poul Niclasen (Samband)
1953	Hans Iversen (Samband)

FOLKETING (DANISH LOWER HOUSE)

The Faroe Islands Folketing members are chosen by direct popular vote. Since 1948, the Faroese have elected two members to this chamber. The Republican Party, on principle, has never contested these elections. The Samband members have always voted with the Danish Venstre; the Social Democratic members with the Danish Social Democratic Party; and the People's Party members have always refrained from participating in matters of purely internal Danish politics.

1901—6	Jóannes Patursson (Venstre)
1906—13	Oliver Effersøe (Samband)
1913—15	Andreas Samuelsen (Samband)
1915—18	Edward Mortensen (Independent)[1]
1918—39	Andreas Samuelsen (Samband)
1939—43	Johan Poulsen (Samband)
1943—8	Thorstein Petersen (People's Party)
1948—50	Thorstein Petersen (People's Party)
	Peter Mohr Dam (Social Democrat)

---

[1] Elected as an Independent, but soon afterwards joined the Sjávstýri in Faroe, and voted with the Radical Left in Denmark.

1950—7	Johan Poulsen (Samband)
	Peter Mohr Dam (Social Democrat)
1957—60	Thorstein Petersen (People's Party)[1]
	Peter Mohr Dam (Social Democrat)
1960—4	Johan Poulsen (Samband)
	Johan Nielsen (Social Democrat)
1964—6	Peter Mohr Dam (Social Democrat)
	Poul Adrian Andreasen (People's Party)
1966—8	Peter Mohr Dam (Social Democrat)[2]
	Poul Adrian Andreasen (People's Party)
1968—71	Peter Mohr Dam (Social Democrat)
	Hákun Djurhuus (People's Party)
1971—	Johan Nielsen (Social Democrat)
	Hákun Djurhuus (People's Party)

LØGTING (FAROE ISLANDS PROVINCIAL ASSEMBLY)

Løgting members are in general elected by popular vote in constituencies. Until the 1924 election, there were in addition to the elected members, two voting ex-officio members, the amtmand and the provost. Before 1918, moreover, only half the Løgting was chosen each election. Thus in the elections of 1908, 1912 and 1916, polling took place only in South Streymoy, Sandoy and Suðuroy; and in 1910 and 1914 only in Vágar, North Streymoy, Eysturoy and the Northern Islands.

From the 1924 election, there were eighteen constituency members and up to five supplementary members. The election rules have been changed several times, and there are today twenty constituency members and up to ten supplementary members. The supplementary seats are awarded according to rules devised to compensate parties with scattered support insufficient to win an equitable number of constituency seats.

---

[1] Because of the court proceedings against him, was declared incapable of election, and was replaced by Hákun Djurhuus.

[2] When Dam took office as Lawman (November 1966), he was replaced by Johan Nielsen for the remainder of his term. Johan Nielsen also took his place after his election in 1968. Dam died 8 November 1968.

Election Date	Semband	Sjálvstýri	Social D'crat	People's Party	Total
18 July, 1906	12	8	—	—	20
2 February, 1908	12	8		—	20
12 February, 1910	13	7	—	—	20
2 February, 1912	13	7	—	—	20
2 February, 1914	12	8	—	—	20
28 February, 1916	10	10	—	—	20
24 April, 1918	9	11	—	—	20
10 November, 1920	10	10	—	—	20
22 January, 1924	13	10	—	—	23
23 January, 1928	10	11	2	—	23
19 January, 1932	11	8	2	—	21
28 January, 1936	8	8	6	2[1]	24
30 January, 1940	8	4	6	6	24
24 August, 1943	8	—	6	12	26
6 November, 1945	6	—	6	11	23
8 November, 1946	6	2	4	8	20

The elections that have given rise to home-rule governments are as follows. A figure in italics indicates that the party in question was a supporter of a governing coalition.

Election Date	Sambd.	Sjál.	Soc. Dem.	Peop. Pty.	Repub. Party	Progress Party	Total
8 November, 1946	*6*	*2*	*4*	8	—	—	20
8 November, 1950	7	2	6	*8*	2	—	25
8 November, 1954	7	2	5	*6*	6	1[2]	27
8 November, 1958	7	2	*8*	5	7	1	30
8 November, 1962	6	2	8	*6*	*6*	*1*	29
8 November, 1966	*6*	*1*	7	6	5	1	26
7 November, 1970	*6*	*1*	7	5	6	1	26

---

[1] This figure applies to the Economic Party, which merged with the newly-founded People's Party in 1939.

[2] In this election elected as an independent; he founded the party two years later.

REFERENDUM, 14 SEPTEMBER, 1946

The referendum concerned an offer of limited home rule for the Faroe Islands, made by the Danish government in 1946, after constitutional talks. The electorate was asked to choose between (i) Do you want the Danish government's proposal to be put into effect? and (ii) Do you want the Faroe Islands to secede from Denmark? Thorstein Petersen suggested that those who wished Faroe to have dominion status should write "no" against both questions, spoiling the paper.

For the government proposal	5,499
For secession	5,660
Spoilt papers	481
Total	11,640

Regionally, the voting was highly variable. South Streymoy and the Northern Islands were respectively 2 : 1 and $2\frac{1}{2}$: 1 in favour of secession. Suðuroy was 3 : 1 in favour of the government proposal. Sandoy, Vágar and North Streymoy were marginally in favour of secession; Eysturoy was marginally in favour of the government proposal.

D

GENERAL BIBLIOGRAPHY

The following bibliography is selective only. Detailed bibliographies for Faroese studies are to be found in the second and sixth works listed below.

To make an adequate study of the Faroe Islands, it is essential to read Danish, and highly desirable to read Faroese as well. A full bibliography of what is obtainable in English follows in Appendix E, although certain works of special value are listed here also.

GENERAL

Djurhuus, H. A., ed., *Livet paa Færøerne.* Copenhagen 1958.

Dansk-Faerøsk Samfund, *Færøerne I-II.* Copenhagen 1958.

Heinesen, Jens Pauli, ed., *Færøerne i dag.* Tórshavn 1966.

Jacobsen, Jørgen-Frantz, *Færøerne, Natur og Folk.* Tórshavn 1936; second edition with English chapter summaries, Tórshavn 1953; third edition 1970.

Kampp, A. H., *Færøerne, folk og erhverv.* Copenhagen 1950; second edition under the title *Lær Selv Færøerne.* Copenhagen 1967.

Trap, J. P., *Danmark,* 5. udg., bd. 13: *Færøerne.* Copenhagen 1968.

Turistforening for Danmark: *Årbog 1951: Færøerne.* Ringkøbing 1951.

Zetland County Council. *Report on visit to Faroe, May–June 1962.* Lerwick 1963.

EARLY DESCRIPTIONS OF FAROE

Debes, Lucas, *Færoæ & Faeroa reserata.* Copenhagen 1673; recent editions in Copenhagen and Tórshavn 1963. English translation under the title *A Description of the islands and inhabitants of Færoe.* London 1676.

Landt, Jørgen, *Forsøg til en beskrivelse over Færøerne.* Copenhagen 1800; recent edition Tórshavn 1965. English translation under the title G. Landt: *A description of the Feroe Islands.* London 1810.

Svabo, Jens Christian, *Indberetninger fra en reise i Færøe 1781 og 1782.* Copenhagen 1959.

Tarnowius, T., *Færøers beskrifvuelser.* Copenhagen 1950.

ARCHAEOLOGY

Bruun, Daniel, *Fra de færøske bygder.* Copenhagen 1929.

Articles by Sverri Dahl in:

Niclasen, Bjarni, ed.: *The Fifth Viking Congress.* Tórshavn 1968.

Smith, Alan, ed.: *The Fourth Viking Congress.* London 1965.

FÆREYINGA SAGA TRANSLATIONS

Powell, F. York, *The Tale of Thrond of Gate.* London 1896.

Press, Muriel, *The Saga of the Faroe Islanders.* London 1934.

EARLIER HISTORY

Andersen, N., *Færoerne 1600—1709.* Copenhagen 1895; recent edition Tórshavn 1964.

Bruun, Daniel, *Fra de færøske bygder.* Copenhagen 1929.

Evensen, A. C., *Savn til føroyinga søga i 16. øld.* Tørshavn 1908–14.

Jakobsen, Jakob, *Diplomatarium Faeroense.* Copenhagen 1907.

Joensen, Einar, ed.: *Tingbókin 1615–54.* Tórshavn 1955.

    Løgtings- og Vártingsbókin 1655-66. Tórshavn 1958.

    Løgtingsbókin 1666-77. Tórshavn 1961.

    Vártings- og Løgtingsbók 1667-1690. Tórshavn 1969.

Zachariasen, L., *Føroyar sum rættarsamfelag 1535-1655.* Tórshavn 1959–61.

GENERAL AND LATER HISTORY AND POLITICS

Fabricius, Knud ed.: *Det danske Rigsdag 1849-1949*, bind 6, pp. 105–201. Copenhagen 1953.

Jakobsen, Jakob, *Poul Nolsøe, livssøga og irkningar.* Copenhagen 1912; recent edition. Tórshavn 1966.

Mitens, E., *Eg minnist I–V.* Tórshavn 1960–70.

Møller, Asger, *Færoerne – Danmark.* Århus 1968.*

Ølgaard, Anders, ed., *Færinger – frænder.* Copenhagen 1968.

Patursson, Jóannes, *Færøsk Politik.* Copenhagen 1903.*

    Føroya søga. Tórshavn 1939.*

Steining, Jørgen, *Færøerne, fra amt til hjemmestyre.* Copenhagen 1948.

WARTIME IN FAROE

Müller, Eiden, *Fem Aar under Union Jack.* Copenhagen 1945.

Norgate, S., *'Kanska' or the Land of Maybe.* Tórshavn 1943.†

Norønna Forlagið, *Bumbur yvir Føroyar.* Tórshavn 1946.

---

* These works do not attempt objectivity.

† This is an entertaining, though not particularly accurate description of how the islands appeared to the troops during the war.

LAW, LAND TENURE

Bonnevie, Erik, and Edward Mitens, *Færøsk Lovsamling 1559–1931.* Tórshavn 1932.
Jakobsen, Jakob, *Diplomatarium Færoense.* Copenhagen 1907.
Lunddahl, J. A., *Nogle bemærkninger om de færøske landboforhold.* Copenhagen 1851.
Mitens, Edward, *Føroyskt Lógsavn 1687–1953.* Tórshavn 1953.
Petersen, Poul, *Ein føroysk bygd.* Tórshavn 1968.
Tillæg til forslag og betænkninger afgivne af de færøske Landbokommission. Copenhagen 1911.

VILLAGE LIFE

Bruun, Daniel, *Fra de færøske bygder.* Copenhagen 1929.
Rønne, J. Falk. *Færøerne.* Copenhagen 1900.
Williamson, Kenneth, *The Atlantic Islands.* London 1948; second edition London 1970.

ORAL LITERATURE

Dánjalsson á Ryggi, Mikkjal, *Miðvinga søga.* Tórshavn 1940; second edition Tórshavn 1965.
Hammershaimb, V. U., *Færøiske kvæder.* Copenhagen 1851; recent edition Tórshavn 1969.
Færøsk Anthologi. Copenhagen 1891; recent edition Tórshavn 1969.
Jakobsen, Jakob, *Færøske folkesagn og æventyr.* Copenhagen 1898–1901. Recent edition, Tórshavn 1961–4.
Færøsk sagnhistorie. Tórshavn 1904.
Greinir og ritgerðir. Tórshavn 1957.
Króki, Jóannes í, *Sandoyarbók I.* Tórshavn 1968.
Lyngbye, H. C., *Færøiske Qvæder om Sigurd Fofnersbane og hans æt.* Randers 1822.
Matras, C., and N. Djurhuus, *Corpus Carminum Færoensium I–V.* Copenhagen 1951–68.
Smith-Dampier, E. M., tr., *Sigurd the Dragon-Slayer.* Oxford 1934.

MODERN LITERATURE

Matras, Christian, *Føroysk bókmentasøga.* Copenhagen 1935.
Anders Nyborg A-S, *Welcome to the Faroes 1968*, pp. 47–52. Copenhagen 1968.
Ølgaard, Anders, ed., *Faeringer-fraender.* Copenhagen 1968.
The above works are descriptive and critical. For modern literary works see Chapter XII; for Faroese literature in English translation see Appendix E.

COMMERCIAL HISTORY

Degn, Anton, *Oversigt over Fiskeriet og Monopolhandel paa Færøerne*. Tórshavn 1929.
Joensen, J. K., and others: *Føroyar undir frium handli í 100 ár*. Tórshavn 1955.
Pløyen, Christian, *Erindringer fra en Reise til Shetlandsøerne Orkenøerne og Skotland i Sommeren 1839*. Copenhagen 1840; second edition Tórshavn 1966. English translation under the title *Reminiscences of a Voyage to Shetland, Orkney and Scotland in the summer of 1839*. Lerwick 1894; second edition 1896.
Rasch, Aage, *Niels Ryberg*. Århus 1965.

FISHERY

Degn, Anton, *Oversigt over Fiskeriet og Monopolhandel paa Færøerne*. Tórshavn 1929.
Faroe in Figures, published about quarterly from June 1956 by the financial institutions of Faroe.
Nolsøe, Páll J., *Føroya Siglingarsøga 1000–1856*. Tórshavn 1955; second edition Tórshavn 1963.
Føroya Siglingarsøga 1856–1940, 6 volumes. Tórshavn 1962–70.
Patursson, Erlendur, *Fiskiveiði – Fiskimenn 1850–1939*. Tórshavn 1962.
Rasmussen, R., and others, *Føroya Fiskimannafelag 1911–1936*. Tórshavn 1936.

ECONOMIC DEVELOPMENT

Det Rådgivende Udvalg Vedrørende Færøerne: *Den økonomiske udvikling pa Færøerne og investeringsbehovet for Færøerne indtil 1975*. Copenhagen 1969.
Ølgaard, Anders, ed., *Færinger – frænder*. Copenhagen 1968.

E

ENGLISH BIBLIOGRAPHY

BOOKS

Adeane, Jane, *The Early Married Life of Maria Josepha Lady Stanley, with extracts from Sir John Stanley's Præterita,* pp. 55–86. London, 1899. Contains an account of Sir John Stanley's expedition to the Faroe Islands and Iceland in 1789.

Annandale, Nelson, *The Faroes and Iceland.* Oxford 1905. Based on six visits to Faroe between 1896 and 1903. Some close observation of village life.

Anon, *The Northern Adventurers; or An Account of several Methods of taking Birds in the Feroe Islands, and in some other Places.* Intended for Children. London 1827.

Banks, Dr. W. M., *A Narrative of the Voyage of the Argonauts in 1880.* Edinburgh 1881. A privately-printed account of a yacht journey, chiefly to Iceland and Norway, but touching at Faroe.

Borrow, George, *Works* ed. Clement Shorter, Vol. 8, London, 1923, pp. 205–19. A translation of a Faroese ballad.

Blaksley, J., *Travels, trips and trots,* pp. 196–7. London 1903. An account of a brief visit on the way to Iceland.

Brú, Heðin, *The Old Man and his Sons,* tr. J. F. West. New York 1970. A Faroese novel translated by the author of this book.

Burton, Richard F., *Ultima Thule, or a Summer in Iceland,* pp. 297–300. London 1879. Only a few brief and trivial observations, but a fine plate of the cathedral walls at Kirkjubøur.

Chambers, Robert, *Tracings of Iceland and the Faroe Islands.* London and Edinburgh 1856. Based on four days in the Faroe Islands in the summer of 1855. Some interesting observations and rather hasty sociological judgements.

Dasent, G. W., *Jest and Earnest,* Vol. 1, pp. 1–104, London 1873, reprint of article "A Fortnight in Faroe".

Debes, Lucas, *A description of the islands and inhabitants of Foeroe,* tra. J(ohn) S(terpin). London 1676. A classic early account of the islands by a Danish priest who held the living of Tórshavn for many years.

Edinburgh Encyclopaedia: article "Faroe", by Sir George Steuart Mackenzie. Edinburgh 1830. A perceptive, but not always accurate account of the islands, based on a visit in 1812.

English Reports, The, Vol. 165: Ecclesiastical, Admiralty, Probate and Divorce V, pp. 1011 and 1047–51. London 1923. Article: "Thorshaven and its Dependencies". An account of the prize-court action subsequent to the visit of the privateer *Salamine* to Tórshavn in 1808.

Foote, Peter G., *On the Saga of the Faroe Islanders*. London 1965. The text of a lecture delivered 12 November 1964, making a good case for the rejection of the saga as an historical account.

Foote, P. and D. Strømbäck, *Proceedings of the Sixth Viking Congress*, pp. 45–56, London 1971. Article by Sverri Dahl, 'Recent excavations on Viking Age sites in the Faroes'.

Forbes, Charles S., *Iceland, its Volcanoes, Geysers and Glaciers*, pp. 8–21. London 1860. Some sensible observations on Tórshavn and the surrounding country.

Franceschi, Gérard and William Heinesen, *Gandaoyggjarnar /De magiske öer/ The Magic Islands*, Copenhagen 1971. Sixteen pages of English text and nearly a hundred superb full-page photographs.

Galton, Francis, ed., *Vacation Tourists, and Notes of Travel in 1860*, pp. 318–23. London, 1861. A few impressions by a visitor on his way to Iceland.

Gathorne-Hardy, G. M., *A Royal Impostor: King Sverre of Norway*. London and Oslo 1956. A scholarly account of the king educated at Kirkjubøur, setting forward good reasons for believing his claim to be of royal birth to be false.

Graham, M. Helen, *The Adventure of the Faeroe Islands*. London 1930. The impressions of a yachtswoman who visited Faroe briefly in 1929. Republished as part of *Rough Passage*, by Commander R. D. Graham. London 1950.

(Greig, E. H.), *A Narrative of the Cruise of the Yacht Maria among the Feroe Islands in the summer of 1854*. London 1855, reprinted 1856. The author was in Faroe for a week. The party were observant, and got much accurate information also from officials and natives. 11 coloured lithographs, including a fine one of a whale-killing.

Gruisen, Nicholas L. Van, *A Holiday in Iceland*, pp. 12–18, London 1879. One chapter on the Faroe Islands- a few impressions of Tórshavn and Kirkjubøur.

Harris, G. H., *The Faroe Islands*. Birmingham 1927. By a Birmingham clergyman who spent nearly all of July 1923 in the islands, especially the western parts. The scientific observations are good, but the historical and cultural sections are full of gross errors.

Heinesen, William, *Niels Peter*, tr. Ian Noble, London 1939. A translation of a Danish novel by a Faroese author.

Huson, Gordon, *The Faroes in Pictures*. London 1946. Chiefly pictures with brief comments. The information is sometimes inaccurate, the spelling of place-names and other Faroese words often extremely so.

Jacobsen, Jørgen-Frantz, *Barbara*, tr. Estrid Bannister. London 1948. A translation of a Danish novel by a Faroese author.
The Farthest Shore. Copenhagen 1965. A small booklet published by the Danish Foreign Ministry. It contains also an article by Niels Elkær-Hansen, State Commissioner in Faroe 1954–61.
Færøerne, natur og folk, with English summaries of each chapter. Tórshavn 1953. The second edition of a classic description of the islands.

Jákupsstovu, Jákup 1, *Wage determination and working conditions for fishermen in the Faroe Islands.* Tórshavn 1972. Excellent on the fishery; otherwise biassed.

Jensen, A. S. et al., ed., *The Zoology of the Faroes I–III.* Copenhagen 1928–42.

Joensen, J. K., et al., *Føroyar undir frium handli í 100 ár.* Tórshavn 1955. The English summary gives a brief account of Faroese commerce before and after free trade.

Karpeles, Maud, *Folk Songs of Europe,* pp. 8–9. London 1956. The music and a few verses of the *Sjurðurkvæði.*

Kneeland, Samuel, *An American in Iceland,* pp. 38–52. Boston 1876. An account of a brief visit on the way to Iceland.

Landt, G., *A description of the Faroe Islands.* London 1810. A translation of a of a classic description by a Danish priest.

Linklater, Eric, *The Dark of Summer.* London 1956. Contains a fictional description of war-time Faroe.

The Northern Garrisons. London, 1941. A war-time pamphlet containing an account of the Faroe Islands garrison.

Lockwood, W. B., *An Introduction to Modern Faroese.* Copenhagen 1955. A standard work on the Faroese language.

Matras, Christian, and others, *Seyðabrævið,* Tórshavn 1971. Facsimilies, texts and translations of the manuscripts of the law of 1298.

Meginfelag føroyska studenta, *Message from the Faroese students.* Tórshavn 1966.

Mitens, Edward, *Facts about the Faroe Islands.* Copenhagen 1963. A booklet of 36 pages, accurate, and with good illustrations.

Müller, F. H., *Fungi of the Faroes I–II.* Copenhagen 1945–58.

Niclasen, Bjarni, ed., *The Fifth Viking Congress.* Tórshavn 1968. An account of a congress held in Tórshavn in July 1965. Of special interest is Sverri Dahl's paper on Kirkjubøur.

Nicoll, James, *An historical and descriptive account of Iceland, Greenland and the Faroe Islands.* Edinburgh, 1841. A good short account of the islands, though it is doubtful whether the author was writing from first-hand experience. Forms Vol. 28 of the Edinburgh Cabinet Library, and was frequently reprinted.

Norgate, Sydney, *"Kanska", or the Land of Maybe.* Tórshavn 1943 . A serviceman's account of Faroe during the war; colourful, though not entirely accurate.

Ólafsson, Jón, *The Life of the Icelander Jón Ólafsson, Traveller to India.* 2 vols. tr. from the Icelandic by Bertha S. Phillpotts. London 1923 and 1932. A Hakluyt Society publication. The author was a gunner in the Danish navy, and visited Faroe in 1616. The description is in the first volume, pp. 141–6.

Ostenfeld, C. H. and J. Grøntved, *The Flora of Iceland and the Faroes,* pp. 1–28. Copenhagen 1934.

Ostenfeld, C. H., E. Warming, et al., *The Botany of the Faroes, based upon Danish investigations I–III.* Copenhagen 1901–8.

Pløyen, Christian, *Reminiscences of a Voyage to Shetland, Orkney and Scotland, in the Summer of 1839,* tr. Catherine Spence. Lerwick 1894, 2nd ed. 1896. The account of a journey by a celebrated amtmand of Faroe, with many references to conditions in Faroe.

Powell, F. York, tr., *The Tale of Thrond of Gate*. London 1896. A translation of the Saga of the Faroemen, together with a useful introduction and a translation of the Faroese ballad of Sigmund, narrating the same events.

Press, Muriel, tr., *The Saga of the Faroe Islanders*. London 1934. A translation of the saga for the modern general reader.

Prior, R. C. Alexander, *Ancient Danish Ballads*, Vol. 1. London and Edinburgh, 1860, pp. 334–42. A translation of a short Faroese ballad. The general introduction to the book contains some material on Faroese ballad dancing, especially pp. iv–vi.

Rasmussen, R. K., *Gomul føroysk heimaráð*. Tórshavn 1959. A book about folk medicine, in Faroese, but with an English summary.

Russell–Jeaffreson, J., *The Faroe Islands*. London 1898. cheap ed. London 1902. The most laughably inaccurate book in existence on the subject.

Sephton, J. tr., *The Saga of King Sverri of Norway*. London 1899. A readable translation of the saga. The introduction is largely textual.

Small, Alan, ed., *The Fourth Viking Congress*. London 1965. Contains a survey of the archaeological investigations made in Faroe by Sverri Dahl, with diagrams.

Smith–Dampier, E. M., tr., *Sigurd the Dragon-Slayer. A Faroese Ballad Cycle*. Oxford 1934. A translation of the most celebrated of the Faroese ballad cycles.

Smollett, Tobias, *The Present State of All Nations*, Vol. I. London 1768. Contains an account of the Faroe Islands drawn principally from the work of Lucas Debes.

Symington, A. J., *Pen and Pencil Sketches of Faroe and Iceland*. London 1862. Some commonplace observations based on four days in the Islands.

Thomsen, Richard B., *The Tyrants*, tr. by Naomi Walford. London 1955, paperback ed. 1960. A translation of a Danish novel by a Faroese author.

Trollope, Anthony, *How the 'Mastiffs' went to Iceland*, pp. 12–17, London 1878. A few pages of light comment by the well-known novelist, and a pleasant sketch of Tórshavn.

Villiers, M., *The Trade of the Faroe Islands* (Consular Report No. 2984). London 1903.

West, J. F., ed., *The Journals of the Stanley Expedition to the Faroe Islands and Iceland in 1789*. Vol. I: *Introduction and Diary of James Wright*. Tórshavn 1970. The first of three journals describing the expedition of Sir John Stanley's party to Faroe and Iceland.

Williamson, Kenneth, *The Atlantic Islands*. London 1948; 2nd ed. 1970. The author was in Faroe from September 1941 to the end of the war, as a serviceman. His book is extremely good for natural history and folk-life, with excellent accounts of bird-life and intimate details of the communities on Mykines and in Fróðbøur. He preserves a high degree of accuracy, but is not infallible, especially when off his particular interests. The second edition presents an unaltered main text, with an extra chapter on modern Faroe by Einar Kallsberg. This book is the best description of Faroe published in English this century.

Williamson Kenneth, and J. M. Boyd. *A Mosaic of Islands*. pp. 1–28. London 1963. A good deal about bird life, some wartime reminiscences, and records of visits made in 1947 and 1953, including a landing on Stóra Dímun.

Zetland County Council, *Report on Visit to Faroe May–June 1962*. Lerwick, 1963. An excellent all-round view of the Faroe Islands, from the point of view of neighbours anxious to emulate their success.

ARTICLES

Note: This section lists in chronological order the articles of which the author is aware, with the exception of those published in 1900 or after, which deal solely with the natural sciences (e. g. geology or marine biology) and where the connection with the Faroe Islands is one of location only.

Eclectic Review, Vol. 6 pt. 1, May 1810, pp. 450–62. Review of the English translation of Landt's *A Description of the Feroe Islands*.

Quarterly Review, Vol. 4, November 1810, pp. 333–42. Another review (by Robert Southey) of Landt's book.

Transactions of the Royal Society of Edinburgh, Vol. 7, 1815, pp. 213–67. Sir George Steuart Mackenzie, 'An Account of some Geological Facts observed in the Faroe Islands'; and Thomas Allan, 'An Account of the Mineralogy of the Faroe Islands'. Consists largely of scientific observations, but with some description of the country and its inhabitants.

Transactions of the Royal Society of Edinburgh, Vol. 9, 1823, pp. 461–4. Sir Walter Calverley Trevelyan, 'On the Mineralogy of the Faroe Islands'. A purely scientific paper based on observations made in 1821. Reprinted in J. G. Forchhammer, *Rejse til Færøerne, Dagbog*, edited by A. Clément, Copenhagen 1927. Trevelyan wrote other articles on Faroe subjects, for instance on the sheep of Lítla Dímun, but efforts to locate them have proved unavailing.

Penny Magazine, Vol. 1, 31 August 1832, p. 210. Robert Southey, 'The Faroe Islands'. A general article derived from Landt's book.

Chambers's Edinburgh Journal, Vol. 10, 16 September 1848, pp. 180–3. 'Fowling in Faroe and Shetland'. Anonymous article consisting largely of anecdotes.

Contributions to Ornithology, 1850, pp. 106–17. John Wolley, 'Some Observations on the Birds of the Faroe Islands'. An expert's account, based on a five-week visit in 1849.

Chambers's Edinburgh Journal, Vol. 3 new series, 1 September – 3 November 1855, pp. 129–31, 153–5, 164–6, 183–5, 199–201, 217–9, 234–6, 249–51, 260–2, 282–4.

Robert Chambers, 'Tracings of Iceland and the Faroe Islands'. The first four episodes deal with Faroe. The material is the same as in the book of this name.

The North British Review, Vol. 40, May 1864, pp. 287–336. V. Y., *A Fortnight in Faroe, from Unpublished Journals*. Generally gossipy, but of value because of the author's contact with H. C. Müller. By Sir George W. Dasent.

Blackwood's Magazine, Vol. 106. November 1869, pp. 618–30, 701–19. 'The Faroese Saga'. A summary, and a rather uncritical review of the saga.

The Zoologist, Vol. 7, September–November 1872, pp. 3210–25, 3245–57, 3277–94. Captain Henry W. Feilden, 'The Birds of the Faroe Islands'. Largely a list of the birds of Faroe and their occurrence.

Nature, Vol. 7, 12 December 1872, pp. 105–6. R. van Willemoes-Suhm, 'Remarks on the Zoology of the Faroe Islands'. A short but very meaty article.

Transactions of the Chesterfield and Derbyshire Institute of Mining, Civil, and Mechanical Engineers, Vol. 2, 1873–4. pp. 320–36. Arthur H. Stokes, 'Notes on the Coal Seam and Geology of Suderoe.' By an Inspector of Mines, largely on the scientific and technical aspects of Suðuroy coal, but with some comment on the islanders and their coal-winning.

Once a Week, Vol. 30, 1874, pp. 454–7, 476–8, 512–5, 564–7, 577–81, 608–11, 622–6, 656–8. 'A Holiday in the North', On a holiday in Faroe and Iceland in summer 1872. The first three episodes deal with Faroe, principally the Tórshavn and Vestmanna regions.

International Fisheries Exhibition, Edinburgh 1882. H. C. Müller, 'Whale-fishing in the Faroe Islands'. A prize essay, written by one of the most accomplished hunters of all time.

The New Englander, Vol. 41, May 1882, pp. 406–13. W. H. Carpenter, 'The Folk Songs of the Faroe Islands'. A brief account of the state of the language at this date and of the ballad tradition. *Lokka táttur*, a ballad of 96 stanzas, is given in translation.

London Society, Vol. 41. Holiday Number for 1882, pp. 59–63. T. L. W., 'A Day on Shore in the Faroe Islands'. A few superficial observations by a casual visitor.

Transactions of the Royal Society of Edinburgh, Vol. 30, 1883, pp. 217–69 and plates XIII-XV. James Geikie, 'On the Geology of the Faroe Islands'. A comprehensive geological account, including a review of previous work and the results of research in 1879.

Macmillan's Magazine, Vol. 53, December 1885, pp. 121–30. 'A Walk in the Faroes'. Tórshavn to Kirkjubøur, and hospitality at the farmhouse.

The Saturday Review, Vol. 41, 23 January 1886, pp. 117–9. 'The Faroe Lagthing Largely consists of notional early history.

All the Year Round. Vol. 38, new series, 6–13 February 1886. pp. 539–45, 563–7.

'A Faroe Fete Day'. A fictional account of St. Olaf's Day, showing a first-hand knowledge of Faroe and displaying some humour.

Cornhill Magazine, Vol. 6, new series, May 1886, pp. 524–39. 'Some Faroe Notes'. A vivid, impressionistic article for tourists.

The Gentlemen's Magazine, Vol. 264, January–June 1888, pp. 149–63. Charles Edwardes, 'The Faroe Islands'. A journalistic account, principally of Tórshavn.

Chambers's Journal, Vol. 69, 11 June 1892, pp. 378–81. Charles Edwardes, 'St. Olaf's Day in the Faroes'. About the celebrations and the opening of the Løgting.

Belgravia, Vol. 79, 1893, pp. 402–10. Charles Edwardes, 'A Wet Walk in the Faroes'. About a journey on foot from Kollafjørður to Vestmannahavn and then to Saksun. Good descriptions and character sketches.

The Geographical Journal, Vol. 7. January 1896, pp. 1–23. Karl Grossmann, 'The Faeroes'. Based on visits 1892–5. Primarily geological, but with some interesting general observations.

Blackwood's Magazine, Vol. 164, August 1898, pp. 121–30. (Nelson Annandale), 'The Faroes'. An intelligent account, describing Tórshavn and its society, and the traditional economy as seen in Kvívík.

Dublin Review, Vol. 125, October 1899, pp. 385–401. A. Clarke Little, 'Iceland and the Faroe Islands'. An account of a brief stay in the islands.

Good Words, Vol. 42, 1901, pp. 414–8. Elizabeth Taylor, 'A Day in the Faroes'. An account by an American author of a visit to Nólsoy at threshing-time.

Current Literature, Vol. 31, October 1901, pp. 452–4. Elizabeth Taylor, 'A Day in the Faroes'. Probably a reprint of the foregoing article.

Current Literature, Vol. 32, June 1902, pp. 678–9. Elizabeth Taylor, 'Getting a Wife in the Faroe Islands'.

Atlantic Monthly, Vol. 91, February 1903, pp. 248–54. Elizabeth Taylor, 'Absalom's Wreath'. A fictional piece containing much Faroese natural history, especially wild flowers.

Journal of the Anthopological Institute of Great Britain and Ireland, Vol. 33, 1903, pp. 246–58 and plate XXV. Nelson Annandale, 'The Survival of Primitive Implements, Materials and Methods in the Faroes and South Iceland'. A scholarly account of material culture. Fine plates.

Proceedings of the Royal Society of Edinburgh, Vol. 25, No. 1, 1903–5, pp. 2–24. Nelson Annandale, 'The People of the Faroes'. Largely on Faroese physical anthropology, but with a little early history and folk-tale material.

The Scottish Geographical Magazine, Vol. 22, 1906, pp. 62–76, 134–47. James Currie, 'The Færöe Islands'. An excellent account, first of the natural history of Faroe, then of the economy and folk-life of the islanders.

Atlantic Monthly, Vol. 109, February 1912, pp. 278–83. Elizabeth Taylor, 'The Baptizing of the Baby'. Fictional piece including much Faroese baptismal and baby lore.

Atlantic Monthly, Vol. 110, December 1912, pp. 825–32. Elizabeth Taylor, 'The Valley of the Others'. Fictional piece based largely on Faroese superstitions. Like this author's other contributions to the magazine, it is based on the life of the village of Viðareiði.

British Sea Anglers' Society's Quarterly, Vol. 9, 1916, pp. 20–3. Ian Lindsay Stewart, 'Grind a Voe'. An account of a whale-drive.

Badminton Magazine, Vol. 50, June 1918, pp. 582–7. Lady Glover, 'Life in the Faroe Islands'. Little information except on fowling. A few illustrations.

The Atlantic Monthly, Vol. 128, October 1921, pp. 441–51. Elizabeth Taylor, 'Five Years in a Faroe Attic'. Personal experiences of wartime in the Faroe Islands.

Transactions of the Scottish Ecclesiological Society, Vol. 9, part 2, 1929, pp. 136–8. J. Logan Mack, 'Kirkebo: A Church on the Faroes'. A brief original account with a fairly long extract from Landt.

American-Scandinavian Review, Vol. 17, No. 4, April 1929, pp. 206–16. H. G. Olrik, 'The Faroe Islands'. A sound, short account of the scenery, economy, village life and social conditions in Faroe.

National Geographic Magazine, Vol. 58, November 1930, pp. 606–48. Leo Hansen. 'Viking Life in the Storm-Cursed Faroes'. A good general account by an intelligent traveller. Many excellent pictures.

Proceedings of the Society of Antiquaries of Scotland, Vol. 65, 1931, pp. 373–8. P. M. C. Kermode, 'Note on Early Cross-Slabs from the Faeroe Islands'. A factual account of the Skúvoy cross-slabs, with sketches and photographs.

American-Scandinavian Review, Vol. 20, No. 1, February 1932. pp. 86–9. E. M. Smith-Dampier, 'A Faroese Ballad-Dance.' A brief and rather subjective account of Tórshavn and a dance held there.

The Spectator, Vol. 153, 17 August, 1934, p. 236. Hugh MacDiarmid, 'Try the Faroes.' A brief and sympathetic article for prospective tourists.

The Times, 25 October, 1935. 'The Faroese Isolated community'. Journalistic account including a little on the political scene.

The Countryman, Vol. 14, October 1936, pp. 77–90, 106. R. M. Lockley, 'In Search of an Island: 6. Hestö.' A vivid and colourful description of the community on Hestur, written by an ornithologist.

Saga-Book, Vol. 11, 1936, pp. 239–46. N. Smith-Dampier, 'The Song of Roland in the Faroes'. An account of the arrival of the Roland legend in Faroe, with a translation of 26 stanzas of the Faroese ballad.

Blue Peter, January 1937, pp. 8–10. R. M. Lockley, 'The Faeroes Calling!' A brief and superficial article based on a short visit.

The Times, 9 March 1937. 'Faroe Folk at Church'. A short article on church-going, national costume, etc.

Danish Foreign Office Journal, No. 196, May 1937: Faroe Number. Mostly about trade, but articles also on history, crafts and angling.

The Geographical Magazine, Vol. 6, January 1938, pp. 215–24. R. M. Lockley, 'Faeroe Scene'. Good photographs but a rather trivial text.

Country Life, Vol. 87, 18 May 1940, pp. 500–1, R. M. Lockley, 'A Bird-Watcher in the Faroe Islands'. An account for the amateur bird-watcher and photographer.

The Scottish Geographical Magazine, Vol. 57, February 1941, pp. 23–9. Erik Schacke, 'Stepping Stones Across the Atlantic: The Faroes and Iceland'. A topical article by a Danish consul, apparently without any specialised knowledge.

Fanfaroe, March 1942 to December 1943. The Faroe Islands Force Magazine. Main articles of Faroe interest as follows:

No. 1, March 1942, pp. 17–19, Kenneth Williamson, 'Grindaboð'. Very similar to the account in *The Atlantic Islands.*

No. 2, May 1942, pp. 17–19, Kenneth Williamson, 'Chance Encounter'. A brief account of local life and national ideals.

No. 3, November 1942, pp. 7–8, T. King, 'Olavsøkan'. A short and not very accurate account. pp. 15–19, Kenneth Williamson, 'Birdmen of Mykines'. An account of fowling and bird-ringing. pp. 21–2, 26, R. Haynes, 'Grindadráp'. An account by a soldier who took part.

No. 4, July 1943, pp. 14–18, G. I. Jones, 'Faroe Ships and Boats'. A short but excellent article, well illustrated. p. 28, Kenneth Williamson, 'Birds in the Hand'. A list of recoveries of birds previously ringed in Faroe.

No. 5, Christmas 1943, pp. 5–6, F. Scarfe, 'A Frenchman in the Faroes'. An account of the Charcot expedition of 1901. Many inaccuracies, mostly Charcot's. pp. 7, 25, G. A. W.; 'Piscatorial Paradise'. A humorous account of sea-shore fishing. p. 8, Poems translated from the Faroese: "Viðoy" by Christian Matras, and "Summer-Night" by Hans A. Djurhuus. pp. 9–14, Kenneth Williamson, 'The Faroe House'. A good account, including some mention of national foods. pp. 17–20, R. L. Llewellyn Collyer, 'Grindaboð'. Another personal account by a soldier. pp. 21–2, Hans A. Djurhuus: 'Jól'. An article by the Faroese author on Christmas customs.

The Pioneer, started January 1943. Nos. 1–3 published in Faroe, by 30 Group Pioneer Corps. Generally no more than a chatty corps magazine, without any of the literary quality of *Fanfaroe.* Articles worthy of comment as follows:

No. 1, January 1943, None.

No. 2, June 1943, pp. 3–5, P. Wilson, 'The Grindadráp'. pp. 17–22, J. E. Adamson, 'The Faeroes: Facts and Fables'.

No. 3. August 1943, pp. 18–21; J. E. Adamson, 'The Faeroes: Customs and Characteristics of the People'. Part I.

No. 4, December 1943, pp. 18–20, J. E. Adamson, 'The Faeroes: Customs and Characteristics of the People'. Part II. pp. 24–6, "One of Many": 'A trip to Vestmannahavn'. pp. 27–8, 33, Bill and Blondie: 'A Voyage of Discovery'. p. 34, G. C. V. Knowlson, tr.: 'The Faroese National Anthem.' pp. 48–9, Poul Johansen, 'The Church in the Faeroes'. pp. 50–6, E. S., 'We Say Goodbye'.

No. 5, August 1945, pp. 59–65, G. C. W. Shipp, 'Expedition to the Faeroes'.

No. 6, December 1945, pp. 52, G. C. V. Knowlson, tr.: 'The Faroese National Anthem', with a picture of Vágar.

No. 19, Vol. 4, June 1949, pp. 525–37, Sverre Patursson, 'Bird Life at Kirkjubö.'

Of the above articles, the last-named is authoritative and excellent, those by Adamson fairly accurate but colourless. The magazine shows very clearly the warm relationship between the garrison and the civil population.

The Field, Vol. 183, 8 April 1944. Captain Lucien Millen, 'The Faroes: Clouded Mountains of the Ocean.' A sensible, short descriptive article.

The Ibis, Vol. 87, 1945, pp. 249–69. Kenneth Williamson, 'The Economic Importance of Sea-Fowl in the Faeroe Islands'. A full account, including techniques, fowling rights, folk-lore and bibliography.

The Norseman, Vol. 3, No. 1, January–February 1945, pp. 62–72 P. Lucien Millen, 'Sjurdur of the Faroes — portrait and background'. A short story with vivid Faroe background by a former Hiring and Claims Officer of the Faroe Islands Force.

Saga-Book, Vol. 12, December 1945, pp. 255–60. Poems from the Faroese of J. H. O. Djurhuus, translated by Stephen Wilkinson and G. M. Gathorne-Hardy. Sensitive renderings of a few poems.

Antiquity Vol. 20, June 1946, pp. 83–91. Kenneth Williamson, 'Horizontal Water-Mills of the Faeroe Islands'. An authoritative account of the subject, much fuller than the treatment in *The Atlantic Islands*.

Chambers's Journal,Vol. 15, eighth series, September 1946. pp. 478–80. Thomas Henderson, 'Faröe Voyage'. An article about the Shetland fishermen's voyages to Faroe.

Illustrated London News, Vol. 209, 16 November, 1946, p. 549. 'Where Independence from Denmark is in the Balance — The Faroes'. Brief topical comment, and good pictures by Gordon Huson.

Scots Magazine February 1949, pp. 353–7. Alexander Cunningham, 'A Scot in the Faroes.' A short article by a sympathetic and observant visitor.

The Norseman Vol. 7, November–December 1949, pp. 386–402 and two plates. Ian Grimble, 'Faroese Music'. A short account of Faroese music and some general information.

British Medical Journal 4 August, 1951, p. 284. 'Psittacosis in the Faroe Islands'. A brief account of an epidemic of the 1930s.

Saga-Book Vol. 13, part 4, 1952, pp. 349–68. William B. Lockwood, 'The Language and Culture of the Faroe Islands'. An account of the Language, political situation, oral literature, and the need for Faroese philological studies.

Fróðskaparrit, 1952 onwards, annually. Summaries of the Faroese articles in English, and occasional English articles, especially in Volume 13, 1964, on Jakob Jakobsen and his studies.

The Spectator Vol. 191, 24 July, 1953. Moray McLaren, 'The Faraway Islands'. An impressionistic account of a holiday.

Danish Foreign Office Journal No. 12, 1954, pp. 13–18. Niels Elkær-Hansen, 'The Faroe Islands Today.' An excellent short account by a state commissioner. Very good illustrations. Reprinted in *American-Scandinavian Review*, Vol. 43, No. 2, June 1955, pp. 165–71.

The Economist, Vol. 175, 7 May 1955, pp. 479—80. 'Faeroes: Squalls and Heavy Seas'. An account of the Klaksvík affair.

Faroe in Figures, 1956 onwards. Statistical and general information published by the financial institutions of the Faroe Islands, generally quarterly. A first-rate source of information.

English Historical Review, Vol. 71, January 1956, pp. 56–61. G. J. Marens, 'The Norse Emigration to the Faeroe Islands'. A derivative article containing much speculation, but of no historical weight.

The Geographical Magazine, Vol. 28, February 1956, pp. 471–7. Bodo Ulrich, 'Gannet-Hunting in the Faeroes.' Excellent photographs and a brief commentary.

The Norseman, Vol. 14 No. 2, March–April 1956, pp. 89–94. Alfred Joachim Fischer, 'Medieval Nordic Culture on Ice'. On the political, cultural and social situation of the time.

The Norseman, Vol. 14, No. 6, November–December 1956, pp. 391–3. J. F. West, 'The Faroe Islands — our unknown neighbours.' An account of village life. chiefly on Nólsoy.

Manchester Guardian, 27 February, 1958. J. F. West, 'Summer in The Faroes,' An article for the prospective tourist.

The Economist, Vol. 188, 20 September 1958, p. 921. 'Fish and the Faroes:

Islanders Adrift'. A brief article probably written from Danish sources, chiefly concerned with fishery limits, rather inaccurate on Faroese politics.

Manchester Guardian, 22 September, 1958. J. F. West, 'A Faroese Whale-Hunt'. An account of a whale-drive of the previous year.

The Economist, Vol. 190, 28 February, 1959, p. 762. 'Faroe Islands, Six-Mile Limit'. A topical article on fishery limits.

International Folk Music Journal, Vol. 12, January 1960, pp. 82–3. Matts Arnberg, 'Recording Expedition to the Faroe Islands'. An account by an employee of Swedish Radio of a folk music recording expedition in 1959.

World Fishing, November 1960, pp. 33–4. Róland Høgnesen, 'Faroe Wants Half the Faroese Catch for Herself'. On the development of the Faroese fishery, and the need to secure the local grounds.

Acta Philologica Scandinavica, Vol. 25, 1961, pp. 107–24. Ingeslev Simonsen, 'The Kirkjubø Runic Stone'. An analysis of a tricky problem in early Faroese archaeology.

Journal of English and Germanic Philology, Vol. 60, January 1961, pp. 158–60. Haakon Hamre, review of J. C. Svabo's *Indberetninger.* An intelligent, sympathetic and learned review of a monumental source book.

The New Shetlander, No. 56, Spring 1961, pp. 11–13, J. F. West, 'Nationalism and Faroese Prosperity.' An attempt to analyse the success of Faroe compared with Shetland.

The Guardian, 16 May, 1962. (J. F. West), 'Faroese advantages in the war of the fish fillet'. On developments in the Faroese fishing industry.

American-Scandinavian Review, Vol. 51, No. 2, June 1963, p. 182. J. H. O. Djurhuus, "Tova", tr. by Wayne O'Neil. A short poem on a Danish historical theme.

Ethnology, Vol. 2, No. 3, July 1963, pp. 269–75. Otto Blehr, 'Action Groups in a Society with Bilateral Kinship: Case Study from the Faroe Islands'. An anthropological paper on Faroese working groups.

Folk, Vol. 6, 1964, pp. 29–33. Otto Blehr, 'Ecological Change and Organizational Continuity in the Faroe Islands'. An anthropological paper on the dynamics of social change.

Scottish Studies, Vol. 8, 1964, pp. 230–3. Iain A. Crawford, 'The Faroe Islands and the Hebrides: Impressions of a Visit to Faroe in 1964.' The record of an eight-day visit devoted to ethnological and archaeological comparisons.

Scotland's Magazine, Vol. 60, August 1964, pp. 10–13. Tom Weir, 'Voyaging to the Faraways'. A brief account of a visit, spent mainly on Mykines. Good pictures.

Fishing News International, 1964, Kjartan í Jákupsstovu, 'The Fisheries of the Faroes'.

The New Shetlander, No. 74, Autumn 1965, pp. 13–16. Christian Matras, 'Profiles from the Past: No. XXVIII – Jakob Jakobsen'. An account of the Faroese philologist and his rescue of the remains of the Norn language of Shetland.

Scandinavica, Vol. 5, 1966, pp. 71–2. Haakon Hamre, review of the facsimile edition of Lucas Debes, *Færoae* & *Færoa Reserata*. Describes how the book came to be translated in 1676.

American-Scandinavian Review, Vol. 55, January 1967, pp. 392–6. Heðin Brú, 'The White Church,' tr. by Hedin Bronner. A Faroese short story, written by a leading Faroese author.

Welcome to the Faroes, 1967 onwards. An annual tourist brochure containing colour photographs and general articles.

Scandinavian Studies, Vol. 39, February 1967, pp. 52–8. Gösta Franzen, 'Faroese Boat Names'. A short and lively article extending beyond the strict title.

Inter-Nord, Paris, March 1967, pp. 83-97. Aa. H. Kampp, 'The Faroes: Today's Problems.' Learned survey by a leading geographical authority. Many statistical tables.

Institute of British Geographers, Transactions, Vol. 41, June 1967, pp. 159–66. J. R. Coul, 'A Comparison of Demographic trends in the Faroe and Shetland Islands'. An attempt to expound and analyse the contrasting population developments in Faroe and Shetland over the last two centuries, during the transition from subsistence to market economies.

American-Scandinavian Review, Vol. 56, Summer 1958. Heðin Brú, "Emanuel", tr. by Hedin Bronner. A Faroese short story.

Saga-Book, Vol. 17, parts 2–3, 1967–8, pp. 145–55. Alan Small, 'The Distribution of Settlement in Shetland and Faroe in Viking Times.' Correlates historical, archaeological and ecological evidence for population size and pattern in the earliest days of settlement.

American-Scandinavian Review, Vol. 57, No. 4, December 1969, pp. 397–9. "Upsala-Pætur's Christmas", a Faroese folk tale tr. by Hedin Bronner. Translation of one of the folk-tales recorded by Jakob Jakobsen in *Færøske Folkesagn og Æventyr*.

American-Scandinavian Review, Vol. 58, No. 2, Summer 1970, p. 177. Heðin Brú. "Old Halgir", tr. by Hedin Bronner. A character-study of an old shepherd.

Poetry, Vol. 116, Nos. 5–6, August–September 1970, pp. 330–4, Chicago. Faroese poetry in translation.

National Geographic, Vol. 138, No. 3, September 1970. Ernle Bradford and Adam Woolfitt, 'The Faeroes, Isles of Maybe'. Superb colour photographs accompanied by a trivial and inaccurate text.

Department of Geography, University of Durham, Occasional Papers Series, No. 12, 1971.

B. S. John, ed.: "Village Studies from the Faroe Islands". A survey of three contrasting villages on Streymoy.

Danish Journal, Special Edition 1971: "The Faroe Islands". Fifty pages o authoritative articles and excellent photographs.

American-Scandinavian Review, Vol. 59, No. 1, Spring 1971, pp. 55–7. William Heinesen, "The Celestial Journey", translated by Hedin Bronner. A translation of a short story written in Danish by a Faroese novelist.

Saga-Book, Vol, 18, parts 1–2, 1970–1, pp. 19–46. J. F. West, "Land Tenure in a Faroese Village". An account of the village organisation of Nólsoy, by the author of this book.

American-Scandinavian Review, Vol. 59, No. 4, Winter 1971–2, pp. 351-9. Hedin Bronner, "Heðin Brú, Faroese Novelist". An assessment on the author's seventieth birthday.

INDEX

302

310

137